A IS FOR ARSON

A volume in the series
Histories of American Education
Edited by Jonathan Zimmerman and Tracy L. Steffes

A IS FOR ARSON

A History of Vandalism
in American Education

Campbell F. Scribner

CORNELL UNIVERSITY PRESS   **ITHACA AND LONDON**

First published 2023 by Cornell University Press

Library of Congress Cataloging-in-Publication Data

Names: Scribner, Campbell F., 1981– author.
Title: A is for arson : a history of vandalism in American education / Campbell F. Scribner.
Description: Ithaca [New York] : Cornell University Press, 2023. | Series: Histories of American education | Includes bibliographical references and index.
Identifiers: LCCN 2023003101 (print) | LCCN 2023003102 (ebook) | ISBN 9781501770722 (hardcover) | ISBN 9781501770739 (pdf) | ISBN 9781501770746 (epub)
Subjects: LCSH: School vandalism—United States—History. | School vandalism—Political aspects—United States. | School vandalism—Social aspects—United States.
Classification: LCC LB3249 .S39 2023 (print) | LCC LB3249 (ebook) | DDC 371.7/82—dc23/eng/20230201
LC record available at https://lccn.loc.gov/2023003101
LC ebook record available at https://lccn.loc.gov/2023003102

For my parents

Teachers and school administrators are working earnestly and
sincerely each day in an attempt to build constructive attitudes
on the part of young people toward such things as respect for
property . . . but it is exceedingly difficult at times to determine the
reasoning of this type of young person.

Los Angeles Board of Education, 1956

Contents

Acknowledgments

Much of this book was written during the stress of a worldwide pandemic, and it would not have been possible without the support of family, friends, and colleagues.

Most of all, I need to thank my wife, Stephanie, and my mother, Carroll, for their innumerable gifts of time and childcare, as well as taking an interest in the details of the book, which allowed me to talk through many of the arguments. I also need to thank Alvah and Seneca for tolerating my occasionally distracted parenting over the past few years, and for being great kids!

Special thanks to Jonathan Zimmerman, Tracy Steffes, and three anonymous readers for offering patient feedback on the manuscript throughout the review process, and Sarah Grossman and the staff at Cornell University Press for being so supportive and prompt during an expedited production process.

Several colleagues offered thoughtful feedback on preliminary excerpts from the book. Victoria Cain, in particular, gave insightful and sensitive commentary on two separate conference panels, as did fellow panelists Adam Laats and Andrew Grunzke. This project was supported by a generous postdoctoral fellowship from the Spencer Foundation and the National Academy of Education, and in addition to informal interactions at that National Academy of Education conference, the fellowship allowed in-depth discussions with Ansley Erickson and Margaret Nash, who helped improve the early chapters.

Other friends have now been listening to me talk about kids breaking things for years on end, and I have benefited immensely from their questions and comments. All gratitude to Ethan Hutt, Robbie Gross, Frank Honts, Britt Tevis, Christine Lamberson, Nick Kryczka, Kyle Steele, Derek Taira, and Amato Nocera. And at the University of Maryland, in particular, I have appreciated the support of innumerable colleagues, including Barbara Finkelstein, Betty Malen, Claudia Galindo, Sophia Rodriguez, David Blazar, Jing Liu, Lisa Eaker, Sarah McGrew, Alison Jovanovic, and Lena Morreale-Scott. Thanks, as well, to Bill Reese, Adam Nelson, Walter Stern, and John Rudolph for having me out to speak at the University of Wisconsin the day before lockdowns began.

When colleagues discover that you are working on a new project, many also reach out with resources that they have come across in their own work, and these little details can prove immensely helpful along the way. My thanks to Bob Hampel for sharing an anecdote about chair wrecking; to Louis Mercer, for articles on vandalism and police officers in Chicago schools; to Jesse Chanin, for sharing the articles about children vandalizing their New Orleans school; to Michael Glass, for sending along helpful articles about arson on Long Island; and to Aaron Fountain, for sharing information on Latino student strikes.

A number of archivists and research assistants also helped make this book possible. Indispensable archival support came from Laura Wacowicz and the staff of the American Antiquarian Society; Vakil Smallen and the George Washington University Special Collections staff; the staff at the Wisconsin Historical Society; and Carol Smith, the archivist at the Philadelphia Contributorship, for help with eighteenth- and nineteenth-century insurance rates. Research assistance came from Amy Franzen, who photocopied voluminous records at the UCLA archives, as well as a number of graduate students at the University of Maryland, including Camille Fair-Bumbray, Erin Janulis, Justine Lee, Kavitha Kasargod-Staub, and Kayla Bill. Joel Miller went above and beyond in finding resources at the Baltimore City Archives, Neil Dhingra and Chris Hurst provided insightful commentary on early drafts and ideas, and Alisha Butler did a wonderful job generating ARC-GIS maps.

Finally, I would like to acknowledge extensive institutional support from the University of Maryland, including early teaching releases and a competitive Research and Scholarship Award, both of which facilitated the early stages of writing.

A IS FOR ARSON

A FEW WORDS ON SENSELESS DESTRUCTION

I have a confession to make. When I was in fifth grade I brought a box cutter from home and slashed up the back seat of my school bus. I am not really sure why I did it. I was a quiet and bookish kid, I liked the bus driver, and although an apathetic student I did not have any particular hostility toward the school. The act was senseless in a way that I found mystifying even at the time. What on earth could have possessed me? That was what the principal wanted to know as well, although he asked in a tone of exasperation rather than genuine wonder. He was on the edge of retirement and I can only imagine how many cases like mine he had confronted over his career. Broken windows and gouged desks. Ink and whiteout on the walls. Now a butchered bus seat. He sighed as he assigned me a detention and sent me back to class. The wantonness and waste that make individual acts of vandalism so frustrating must become even more incomprehensible over the years. Vandals seem to act on pure impulse, in ways that defy explanation or prevention. Who knows why do they do it?

There is a lot riding on that question. In the United States, vandals destroy over $600 million worth of school property every year, diverting scarce resources for maintenance and repair. Racist and sexist graffiti are pervasive, and there can be links between vandalism and other forms of criminal behavior, such as gang activity. Studies suggest that degraded school facilities make many students feel unsafe and can significantly impede learning.[1] Given these negative associations, there is an understandable expectation that schools should do something about vandalism. But what can they do? It is difficult to respond to a problem without a clear understanding of its source, and property destruction, a phenomenon with complex causes, is usually answered with narrow and ineffective remedies. In 1978, Vernon Allen and David Greenberger wrote that "current theoretical accounts of vandalism could be extensively criticized," and they singled out the scholarship on school vandalism as "acutely embarrassing."[2] Their criticism remains true today. Research on the issue is varied to the point of incoherence. Some characterize vandalism as violence, requiring stricter forms of deterrence and punishment. Others attribute it to problems in the school or society at large, best addressed by antipoverty programs, antiracist pedagogy, beautification projects, or new forms of community governance. Still others interpret vandalism as a developmental pathology, demanding therapeutic intervention. Social scientists pinball between new theories without advancing a comprehensive view of the issue, or narrow their selection of cases in ways that overdetermine its causes. Like the parable of the blind men with the elephant, different modes of inquiry have come to wildly different conclusions, making vandalism not only a practical but a conceptual problem.

Perhaps the confusion is to be expected, for vandals do not speak with a single voice. They are not always children, do not necessarily come from either dominant or marginalized groups, and do not all engage in the same forms of destruction. Vandalism cuts across demographic lines and afflicts every kind of educational institution, from one-room schoolhouses to large urban high schools. There are many reasons to light a fire or scratch a wall, and to describe an act as vandalism can obscure what is in fact an array of behaviors and motivations. Thus, any consideration of why individuals deface schools must draw from a range of academic disciplines—criminology, psychology, even philosophy—while at the same time preserving an element of fundamental uncertainty, an acknowledgment that the sources of destruction will sometimes remain unknowable.

This book sifts through centuries of debris to uncover multiple meanings of school vandalism. By taking a longer view of the issue, it hopes not only to move past the sensationalism of contemporary media reports but to expand the boundaries of existing scholarship, which remains narrow and poorly integrated. It does so in a somewhat unorthodox way. Rather than a single chronological narrative, it offers three parallel accounts of property destruction, communicated in three distinct styles. Each of these accounts invites readers to approach the issue from a different historical perspective. Fuller explanations will appear as the book proceeds, but a quick sketch at the outset should help readers understand how these three parts fit together and how interweaving multiple interpretations of the past may shape our responses to vandalism in the present.

The first account, which unfolds across four chronological chapters, interprets property destruction as an assertion of power. Painted messages, broken windows, and burned-out buildings are often demands for justice by those who lack more articulate means of dissent, not random destruction but a rational and implicitly political bid for recognition. Taking this type of opposition seriously reveals the hidden agendas of schooling and reframes attempts to prevent or punish vandalism as equally political acts. The chapters in part 1 can help readers understand structural changes in the design and administration of schools, implicit assumptions about student misbehavior, and the demands of otherwise unheard children and adults. In drawing attention to unruly forms of resistance, the chapters also raise larger questions about social control and noncompliance in US education.

A second account focuses on schoolchildren in particular and argues that while vandalism is not always political, neither is it wholly destructive. Sometimes property damage communicates needs that are creative, sensitive, and intensely personal, having less to do with negotiations of power than with nascent self-discovery. In these cases, vandalism plays an educational role parallel or even incidental to the official school curriculum. The marks that children leave on their surroundings suggest an emotional fullness that rarely appears in histories of education or childhood: an opportunity to see individuals achieving selfhood in moments of drudgery, wistfulness, or sheer abandon. In short, vandalism offers a glimpse into interior states of being. Part 2 explores these issues through a series of essays, each of which pairs a historical artifact with an emotional impulse to deface it. Ambiguous evidence makes these pieces brief and necessarily speculative, but by incorporating interdisciplinary insights from philosophy and social theory, the essays allow readers to reconsider assumptions about how and what children really learn in school. Indeed, their conjectural approach encourages new perspectives on education in both the past and the present, asking how destructive acts may impart deeper lessons about meaning, belonging, and selfhood.

A final account concedes that some acts of vandalism may be just as senseless as critics claim—what one sociologist describes as "sheer deviltry"—but that senselessness makes them no less significant.[3] While random acts of destruction can be difficult to distinguish from the more purposeful varieties listed above, their ambiguity and irrationality raise important questions about historical interpretation. If an act were entirely impulsive, indeterminate, or wanton, could it be said to be without cause? Would the existence of such an act challenge our understanding of the past as an orderly and intelligible sequence of events? What if there were thousands of such acts? Simply put, to what extent can historical narrative accommodate meaningless absurdity? This book engages these questions not through explicit scholarly argument but aesthetically, particularly in its reliance on anecdotal evidence and its orientation to the sublime. This suggestive, somewhat stylized approach appears sporadically throughout the chapters and essays, but it becomes most explicit in part 3, which presents a short chronicle of school vandalism stripped of chronology or context. This may seem like the most tenuous of the three accounts—hardly history at all—but it is a necessary addition to the earlier parts of the book. By following the causes of vandalism outward (to the systems of power in which schools are enmeshed) and inward (to the soul or subconscious), one begins to grasp tensions between society and the individual. By acknowledging that vandalism sometimes occurs without causes, one can discern all-too-human moments of unruliness and wreckage.

It may be that searching for the meaning of vandalism yields results that authorities would rather not acknowledge, that children only dimly grasp, or that fit awkwardly into existing historical accounts, but these all have important implications for our responses to the phenomenon. Most importantly, surveying the many sources of destruction should temper policy decisions with a degree of humility and forbearance rather than simple condemnation. It should also preserve an element of curiosity or wonder. In the preface to a book of advice from high school students to their teachers, Kathleen Cushman writes, "It's a safe bet that in random high schools all over the United States, some kid has just set the bathroom wastebasket on fire. And deep down, all of us know why."[4] For Cushman, taking property damage seriously demands that we consider the structural sources of student discontent, as well as our own emotional experiences of schooling. These are both important sources of knowledge, but they remain incomplete. So varied are the sources of deviant behavior, and so different the contexts in which it plays out, that any study of vandalism should begin by admitting that we can never fully explain why people wreck schools in the first place. Even when we look "deep down," destruction remains something of a mystery. There are feelings that are hard to put into words, and fires that are hard to put out.

Part I

VANDALISM AS
POLITICAL RESISTANCE

Authorities often describe vandalism as a wanton act, making it seem both purposeful and purposeless, the result of conscious decisions but lacking clear objectives or a coherent message. That contradiction performs several functions. First, it ascribes culpability to perpetrators without establishing their intellectual or moral capacity for wrongdoing. Doing so violates basic principles of justice and is especially problematic when applied to children, whose criminal immunity has given way in recent decades to punitive disciplinary policies and children's reclassification as adult offenders.[1] Wantonness also prioritizes property over human well-being, suggesting that destruction originates within a deranged individual rather than as a response to unacceptable conditions, and that monetary costs are more important than understanding, rehabilitating, or truly correcting the culprit. Because wantonness is incomprehensible, it seems to preclude forgiveness or the basic educational notion that wrongdoers should learn from their mistakes. Finally, it strengthens established sources of authority by implying that resistance to them is inherently irrational. Freighted with unspoken assumptions about vandals' depravity, wantonness forecloses investigation into the actual sources of their behavior, ignoring injustice and inviting overly harsh responses.[2]

There are good reasons to reject this characterization, to interpret destructive acts as meaningful signifiers and perpetrators as rational agents, even if they sometimes seem mistaken in their choice of targets. Doing so draws attention to the hidden structures against which vandalism is directed, forcing one to examine the built environment of schooling, the systems of governance, administration, and instruction in which damage plays out, and the theories of childhood and criminality that ascribe meaning to it. These are shifting categories, and none of them are neutral. Schools necessarily impose forms of control on both children and communities, and property destruction has been a means for many groups to express their dissatisfaction with the powers that be. Thus, vandalism orients us to the inescapably political dimensions of schooling and the latent power of its subjects, who express their opinions in everyday acts of disobedience.

Unmasking the connections between property destruction and power relations has long been a pillar of Marxist scholarship. Beginning in the 1970s, historians such as E. P. Thompson and Eric Hobsbawm introduced readers to an eclectic group of squatters, bandits, and saboteurs from the eighteenth and nineteenth centuries. They reinterpreted these outlaws, previously dismissed as misfits or opponents of progress, as critics of the industrial order, and acts of wreckage as a form of political protest. Inarticulate ruffians found new voice in their struggle against capital and the state, becoming sources of inspiration and popular resistance in the present.[3] More recently, historians such as Robin D. G. Kelley have emphasized the "daily, unorganized, evasive, [and] seemingly spontaneous actions" of African Americans and others in resisting racist indignities. Far from acquiescence or petty criminality, for these scholars acts of mischief and noncompliance derive from a broader political consciousness.[4]

Similar arguments have appeared in educational literature as "resistance theory," which portrays the oppositional acts of working-class children as a struggle against systems of cultural and economic stratification.[5] Resistance theorists see misbehavior not as a personal failing but as a way to defy injustice, ascribing meaning to otherwise incomprehensible forms of student protest.[6] Defiance implies a degree of personal agency, which ostensibly differentiates resistance theory from more mechanical accounts of cultural reproduction. Rather than observing a strict correspondence between economic forces and institutions such as schools—reducing students to passive victims of the capitalist system—resistance theorists envision children exercising power to some effect. As one writer remarks, "We do a disservice by turning 'hooligans' into a pure reflex of capitalism, their degree of viciousness depending upon current wage restrictions and the level of unemployment. . . . The nice bright-eyed working class kid in acting out his frustration is affirming life, affirming the possibility of influencing his environment, in no matter what blind way."[7] Thus, misbehavior offers both an opportunity for structural critique and a space for individual agency.

The image of blind striving, however, also speaks to an unresolved relationship between agency and self-awareness at the heart of resistance theory. In rejecting accusations of wantonness, resistance theorists ascribe to children not only power but intentionality and some degree of political consciousness. Noncompliance may be an entirely reasonable reaction to schools that routinely fail working-class and minority students, but the question remains whether the children themselves are aware of those reasons, and on this point resistance theorists offer a somewhat equivocal account. For example, reviewing Paul Willis's *Learning to Labor* (1978), the field's foundational text, Ken McGrew finds some passages in which resistance is merely reflexive, others in which it emerges from working-class culture, and still others in which delinquent boys "self-consciously" oppose authority to forge their own counterculture. Each of these explanations, he observes, emphasizes individual agency more than cultural-reproduction models do, but by stressing conscious forms of resistance they may overdetermine the rationality of destructive acts.[8]

Even more problematic, from a historical perspective, is that many types of people damaged schools. While some groups of students may be especially prone to noncompliance, the fact is that most children resent the strictures of compulsory schooling and occasionally seek escape. Complicating the matter further is the fact that property damage has never been limited to children. When one adds innumerable attacks by parents, vigilantes, thieves, the mentally ill, and teachers themselves, motivations become even less clear. Resistance certainly developed along lines of economic class, as theorists claim, but also along lines of age, race, religion, region, and nationality, in ways that could cloud the distinction between oppressors and the oppressed. When Americans destroyed school property, they enacted any number of identities, "resisting" racial segregation and racial integration, anti-Catholic bias and Catholicism, bourgeois or merely adult social norms. Sometimes their actions were sincere, sometimes they were ironic, and sometimes, for inscrutable reasons, individuals posed as outside antagonists to target their own communities. None of this is to deny the utility of a resistance framework in particular cases. It is merely to say, first, that schools represent multiple forms of established power, so that opposition springs from indeterminate and overlapping sources, and second, that vandalism may be too low a threshold to distinguish explicitly political resistance from more general forms of misbehavior. Although property destruction is a helpful reminder of political struggles in general, in particular cases its targets can be difficult to decipher.

A second critical tradition, drawn from the work of Michel Foucault, offers a broader explanation of what vandals were resisting and how destruction could forge both self-consciousness and class consciousness. With the rise of public education in the nineteenth century came new forms of social power, built around increased state supervision, a shift from moral to medical understandings of deviant behavior, and a greater gentility in the control of students. Foucault doubted that any of these changes were as progressive as proponents claimed.[9] In his studies of prisons and madness, particularly, he argued that modernity replaced state violence with a ruthless process of institutionalization, norming, and internal discipline, using a discourse of moral uplift and medical diagnosis to elicit conformity and curtail freedom.[10] Historians of education have used Foucault's theories to explain both the systemization of schooling and its intersection with other institutions: describing the educative purposes of prisons and the military, for instance, while illuminating the penal aspects of schools. From this perspective, it is unsurprising that some scholars have focused on reformatories as archetypes of, rather than exceptions to, modern education writ large. The logic of surveillance, discipline, and governmentality seems endemic to both.[11]

Historians of education have been less explicit about the positive side of the Foucauldian project, which argues that any assertion of social control presupposes the exercise of freedom. "At the very heart of the power relationship, and constantly provoking it, are the recalcitrance of the will and the intransigence of freedom," Foucault wrote, identifying "an 'agonism' . . . which is at the same time reciprocal incitation and struggle."[12] The struggle against authority, particularly visible in schools, produces parallel spaces outside the gaze of normative power and forges selfhood in opposition to imposed forms of subjectification. In both respects, anarchic struggle, according to Foucault, "constitutes a frontier for the relationship of power," a point from which social reproduction emanates but where it also remains precariously unsettled. Just as education produces normative senses of the self, it inevitably produces pockets of unruliness. And as we shall see, almost every innovation in the control of vandalism has provoked new forms of resistance.[13]

Foucault's approach is particularly helpful in capturing the perspectives of the people moving through public institutions. Consider Philippe Artières's Foucauldian analysis of nineteenth-century tattoos, which on one hand were "the autobiography of the poor," commemorating voyages, jail stints, and past lovers, and on the other became a means of identification by doctors and the police, whose records rendered ink-stained skin legible to the state and, later, to historians.[14] Property destruction, too, reveals plaintive expressions of humanity in institutions that increasingly sought to routinize and constrain behavior. Illicit markings on school buildings not only call into question the imposition of normative power but give a sense of the personalities that it attempted to efface, another way to hear the voiceless not only as a class but as individuals. Surreptitious acts of wreckage, graffiti tags, and anonymous messages on bathroom walls all generated a type of Foucauldian space, which was dependent on (and therefore an assertion of) the very forms of privacy and community that institutions tried to stifle. These artifacts are especially important to the history of education and childhood because children leave few documents of any kind and are rarely accorded the status of full historical agents with the power to reject or modify the social systems in which they live. Approaching vandalism as a form of resistance accords them a measure of respect.[15]

Drawing from both Marxist and Foucauldian perspectives, the following chapters examine destructive acts and authorities' responses to them as an ongoing negotiation of power, unfolding across a range of periods and settings. Each explains how vandalism reflected an era's broader educational trends before offering a specific contribution to our understanding of education in the past.

The first chapter, "Populism and Property Destruction," discusses rioting in the early United States, outlining the ways in which the era's democratic culture sanctioned wreckage and arson in defense of customary rights. Children damaged schools to protest harsh treatment or overwork, while adults did so to resist taxation, spite political rivals, or reassert commitments to Protestantism and white supremacy. The prevalence of these acts troubled proponents of public education, who saw vandalism as a harbinger of social strife and vowed to address it through improved teaching, centralized administration, modern infrastructure, and stronger legal sanctions, although their efforts proved ineffective. The chapter culminates with the construction of African American schools in the decade after the Civil War and the violent wave of repression that left hundreds of them in ashes. Although many historians have described particular incidents of school burning during the Reconstruction era, this marks the first attempt to quantify attacks and to understand the bureaucratic and political shortcomings that prevented a fuller accounting.

Chapter 2, "Modern Education and Its Discontents," examines the consolidation of school governance at the turn of the twentieth century and the spasms of local resistance that it incited. School systems modernized their facilities during this period, but it was hardly a smooth process. Large segments of the population believed that centralized education was not in their interest and took their grievances out on newly constructed schools. Indeed, most of the era's educational changes—from compulsory attendance and high school construction to early attempts at racial integration—were met with rocks, torches, and bombs from parents and taxpayers. Students, too, engaged in widespread vandalism, taking advantage of new technologies and hidden spaces in modern buildings, and rejecting increasingly restrictive institutions such as reformatories. The chapter concludes with a brief history of school fire insurance, a decentralized means of imposing order and improving safety. Again, this reform yielded mixed results. While insurance promised to rationalize risk, questions about its price, purpose, and means of provision delayed implementation for decades, weakening its impact and foreshadowing the difficulties that would confront later antivandalism policies.

Chapter 3, "Diagnosing Delinquency," discusses rising high school enrollments between the 1930s and the 1950s, which brought an attendant rise in property damage and a nationwide panic over juvenile delinquency. Of particular importance during this period were issues of legal liability. When children damaged a classroom, who was supposed to pay for it? Parents? Taxpayers? Insurance companies? State courts equivocated on these questions, underscoring the difficulty of assigning blame for children's misbehavior, as well as the struggle to absorb the costs of catastrophic destruction. It was during this period that educators developed new perspectives on the causes of vandalism and new disciplinary responses. Although the mid-twentieth century witnessed the broadest intellectual engagement with vandalism and produced many of the sociological and psychological theories that frame scholarly analysis today, none of these approaches explained its origins sufficiently to control its effects.

The final chapter, "Vandalism and the Security State," extends earlier discussions of racial violence, property insurance, and social science research and explains how, during the 1970s, they combined to form a new, punitive paradigm in public education. The chapter examines vandalism as a form of racist intimidation during the civil rights movement and a harbinger of social disorder following school desegregation. With a detailed study of the Los Angeles public schools, it also demonstrates how vandalism became a stand-in for racial animus and antitax sentiment, pushing municipal, state, and federal authorities to criminalize students and reallocate funds for police and school security. Although these changes disproportionately affected urban schools, suburban districts also suffered from property damage during this period and were forced to incorporate similar security measures by their insurers. All of these changes were underwritten by social science research, which shocked voters with the first comprehensive estimates of the costs of vandalism and simultaneously suggested that its causes could be found in the school environment rather than in individual psychosis. Taken up by state and federal policymakers, these findings tightened the nexus between schools and the criminal justice system, both through the "school-to-prison pipeline" and through increasingly restrictive forms of school architecture.

Several themes emerge from these chapters. The first is the evolving relationship between vandalism and political conflict. Schools were attacked by majoritarian populists and by various minority groups who felt that they lacked a voice in the public sphere. These blunt messages of breakage recur throughout the book, but they became less frequent by the mid-twentieth century. One reason is that, with the rise of compulsory attendance, property destruction shifted from an undertaking for all ages to one associated primarily with children, which minimized its political overtones. Another was the rise of new forms of social control, with regulators, courts, and corporations increasingly able to measure and respond to acts of destruction. These institutions greatly expanded their capacity to shape school policy, but they still relied on social science to direct their efforts. As sociological theories struggled to identify the precise causes of vandalism, they produced responses that were increasingly punitive but still largely ineffective. Thus, the story across the four chapters is one of depoliticization and criminalization, but at the same time one of ongoing ambiguity and futility.

POPULISM AND PROPERTY DESTRUCTION, 1790–1890

As public property, school buildings are inevitably caught up in political conflict. Their maintenance depends on local taxation. Access to their classrooms requires a recognition of civil rights. Their very existence depends on a negotiated consensus. Damage to schools, then, is often a political act, a response to perceived violations of the social compact. Destructive protest has appeared throughout US history and will recur throughout this book. What has changed since the nineteenth century is the public's interpretation of its legitimacy, and more broadly the role of populism in the politics of education.

Populist vigilantism played a significant role in American life from the colonial period to the early twentieth century. Mobs took it upon themselves to impose community norms, white supremacy, and Protestant respectability when authorities would not.[1] Reenacting practices from early modern Europe, crowds ushered vagrants and undesirables out of town with raucous celebrations, playing "rough music" on pots and pans and carrying them on a rail. They beat or lynched minority group members, especially African Americans, for challenging their economic or political subordination. They demolished brothels and saloons for flouting moral codes. They tore down fences to prevent the enclosure of common land and wrecked factory equipment to protest working conditions. They attacked or defended ethnic neighborhoods by setting on others' religious processions and houses of worship. They harassed tax collectors and bank agents, from the Boston Tea Party and Shay's Rebellion to the agricultural riots of the 1930s. Public violence constituted a long-standing tradition of demonstrative community action. In each of these cases, rioting gave voice to a self-identified public who felt that they had too long suffered in silence. "In a luminescent moment," writes the historian Paul Gilje, "amid the shouting roar of the crowd, the 'inarticulate' became articulate."[2]

This violence was rooted in particular notions of justice, but in some ways its fundamental character remained ambiguous. For example, was vigilantism democratic in any positive sense of the word, or was it merely an eruption of latent violence and personal vendettas? Critics complained that mobs violated the United States' founding ideals. Disregarding the rule of law in the name of public will was perhaps understandable in a monarchical system but became both anarchic and redundant in a representative democracy. Why would the people need to protest government action or inaction when they already controlled the government through the franchise? Moreover, critics asked, if mobs truly had numbers and right on their side, why did so many of their actions occur furtively, in the dark of night?[3] Other commentators were more forgiving, noting that public administrations of justice created a sort of sublime citizenship, in which individuals subsumed themselves to the whole and reaffirmed their place in the body politic, regenerating the frontier spirit of action and self-reliance. According to this view, violence was regrettable but necessary to sustain the nation's revolutionary ethos.[4] A related question was whether such violence was irrational. On one hand, mobs rarely engaged in random attacks: they targeted specific property or persons in response to particular transgressions. On the other hand, as Gilje observes, "there is always a certain element of the irrational in any given tumult. Rioting was not a daily routine. . . . Emotions and passions surfaced; people got carried away with what they were doing."[5] The same uncertainties will color our investigation of school vandalism. Students, parents, and teachers damaged schools in ways that could be both criminal and restorative, calculated and irrational, sometimes all at once. While vandalism was a ritualistic act meant to reaffirm community norms, Americans divided on whether it deserved the condemnation of law or the deference of custom.

This chapter discusses school property destruction from the late eighteenth to the late nineteenth century, examining its role in classroom dynamics and local politics, its impact on ethnic and religious minorities, and its value to common school supporters, for whom damage to local schoolhouses became an impetus for large-scale reform. The chapter introduces these subjects in part to foreground shortcomings of the era's populist politics. Readers should abandon any illusions of quaint villages or orderly classrooms. Americans regularly ransacked their schools. Worse, they often did so to reaffirm existing inequalities. Populist claims of mutual obligation and common dignity were underwritten with dubious assumptions about who constituted "the people" to begin with, and high-minded rhetoric often concealed selfish motives. Yet this chapter also presents the era's naked aggression as a counterpoint to the centralized and increasingly abstract governance of schools in the century to follow, which reduced vandalism to a symptom of poor administration or individual maladjustment rather than a self-consciously political act rooted in group interests. If destructive impulses of the past were not as virtuous as perpetrators claimed, they were still an assertion of rights that demanded to be taken seriously. Schools today come in for their share of damage, but its significance has been muted, derogated, or lost. Our understanding of vandalism is diminished without recourse to the traditions and explicitly political rhetoric of the past. Thus, while it would be naive to take populist claims at face value and undesirable to recreate the social context of nineteenth-century education, a fair consideration of school vandalism in that period nevertheless offers a valuable perspective on educational politics in our own.

The Populist Roots of School Vandalism

Most nineteenth-century schools were modest, one-room buildings staffed by itinerant male teachers and attended by students between the ages of three and twenty. They were community spaces, sites of public exhibitions, dances, and town meetings. Hundreds of thousands would appear by the end of the century, sustaining a vital and intensely local vision of self-improvement and civic participation. Yet they also reflected the economic priorities of an agrarian society. School boards were dominated by farmers who leased the land and donated materials for the buildings, and expenditures depended on their willingness to pay taxes. Most boards had low conceptions of educational adequacy, and schools suffered from deferred maintenance and neglect. Structures were made of logs, sod, clapboard, or brick, with drafty and smoky interiors, low ceilings, and dingy, unpainted walls. "Any kind of building that would keep out the rain in summer [and] the snow in winter," noted one commentator, "was good enough for a schoolhouse."[6] Another recommended that prospective teachers tour the school building with board members before accepting a job. "Possibly, there will be some expression of surprise at the state of affairs," he mused. "Broken window panes, rickety desks, demolished benches, fragments of a chair, [these] are the promising prospect for the 'new teacher' to commence school with."[7]

Financial constraints not only kept damaged infrastructure in service but compounded the problem with underqualified teachers and overcrowded classrooms. Confined to uncomfortable seats and forced to memorize arcane lessons, bored students would deface any surface close at hand. Names appeared on desktops, charcoal images on the ceiling, initials on exterior walls, and smutty drawings in the outhouse.[8] Eli Rapp, who grew up in the 1820s, recalled classroom walls that were scarred from "every possessor of a jack-knife [laboring] over them with much idle hacking and carving." A European visitor had a similar impression of the American schoolhouse, which he described as "a miserable hovel," "a dark, gloomy, and ill-ventilated room [with] benches to sit upon . . . which could not but excite in the minds of school-boys the desire to wreak their vengeance in the form of every degree of injury which a knife can inflict."[9]

An authoritarian atmosphere of surveillance and whipping set up an ongoing battle of wills between teachers and students, which the latter saw in expressly political terms. Excessive punishment was liable to spark revolt, and both sides could damage the school building to assert their rights.[10] A common ploy was for pupils to break into the building before hours and blockade the door so that the teacher could not enter. In a typical incident, a group of West Virginia students became restless when their teacher denied them a holiday. That night, seeking to reestablish his authority, the teacher pried open a top-story window and obstructed the flue with old building materials, meaning to lock the students in

FIGURE 1.1. Nineteenth-century students frequently damaged the schools to "bar out" the teacher, who could also damage the building to gain admission. *Southern Life in Southern Literature*, 1917.

the classroom and gag them with smoke. The children discovered the plan and the next morning barricaded the door before the teacher arrived, refusing to let him in until he pardoned them. The teacher tried to break the door down but was driven away.[11] Another "barred out" teacher tried to break a hole in the wall with a fence post to gain admission to his school, though he, too, was repulsed.[12] A third group of students defended their position by thrusting an iron poker through a crevice near the door, accidentally killing the teacher outside.[13] It is noteworthy that in each of these examples, school buildings were in disrepair even before altercations began, and their integrity was hardly a concern for either side in the heat of battle.

Children's destructive power was not confined to carving benches and barring doors. They also smashed windows, toppled outhouses, and tore down fences around the schoolyard, allowing sheep and cattle to wander onto the grounds and do further damage.[14] Some returned at night to set fire to the school, either to revenge themselves on cruel teachers or to secure an early vacation. It is hard to say how prevalent such acts were during the nineteenth century, but there were dozens of cases in which children were credibly accused of arson, and it stands to reason that they were responsible for some of the hundreds of unsolved incidents that occurred in towns from Washington to Maine.[15]

By the end of the century, newspapers had reduced children's school burning to a cliché, with fictional stories about students plotting fires and a whole genre of corny jokes, such as,

> MAMMA: Johnny, do you know what tomorrow is?
> JOHNNY: Yes, mamma; my birthday.
> MAMMA: And what would you like for the occasion?
> JOHNNY: I'd like to see our schoolhouse burn down.[16]

Children themselves referenced destruction in public addresses and poems, playfully but usually with a larger point in sight. For example, a girl from Louisiana pointed out that the same "great men" who touted education's moral effects were the ones responsible for the strife of the Civil War. Why should students put any stock in their claims? Decrying such hypocrisy, she wrote,

> I wish I was the President
> Of these United States,
> I'd veto all the schools
> And burn the books and slates.

Such references were stylized, of course, but they speak both to the pervasiveness of property attacks and to students' awareness of their political significance.[17]

FIGURE 1.2.   Nineteenth-century students would often carve or paint their names into the sides of school buildings. Delaware County, Ohio. Author's collection.

Indeed, it could be difficult to distinguish childish pranks from the politically motivated acts of adults. Local voters also burned or pulled down buildings in the middle of the night, whether to protest unpopular decisions by the school board or to threaten individual members. In Texas, a group of men burned the Rose Hill school and left a note for one of the trustees, according to a newspaper account, "warning him to leave the country, and that he would be burned next."[18] In Washington, a minister's purchase of the local schoolhouse touched off a rivalry between local church groups, one of which warned "that it would retain control of affairs, even if it had to resort to fire." The building was a charred ruin soon thereafter.[19] It can be hard to discern the issues underlying these disputes. Most newspapers limited themselves to vague references about "bad feeling in the neighborhood."[20] Antitax sentiment was a common cause, but the fundamental questions were less about total spending than about the entitlements that one's taxes secured—a deeper politics of recognition and public virtue. For example, did elected boards represent all community members, or only the wealthiest? Did they accord children equal access and fair treatment? Were particular students, teachers, and community groups worthy to use public facilities? These questions repeatedly appeared around a handful of administrative decisions.

The first point of contention was teacher selection. When tight-fisted board members chose cruel or ineffective candidates in order to save money, parents expressed their displeasure by stoning or burning the school.[21] Sometimes teachers themselves lit fires after being passed over for jobs or slandered by local residents.[22] Another sensitive subject was the placement of the schoolhouse, which would determine the distance that children would have to walk each day. After a vote failed to relocate a school in Blooming Grove, Wisconsin, one of the board's opponents walked over to the building and kicked down the door.[23] Voters sometimes resolved school placement by harnessing a team of horses and hauling whole school buildings away during the night. A one-room school in Lawrence, Kansas, moved back and forth several times as neighbors squabbled.[24] Another building, in Madison County, Virginia, was constructed on a wheeled frame so it could be hauled to a trustee's home each night, where an armed guard slept inside to deter incendiaries.[25] A final source of disputes was access to the building after hours. As the historian Paul Theobald observes, "school board members were charged with the protection of school property. Sometimes this was construed to mean denying certain groups the convenience of meeting in the local schoolhouse," especially those of unorthodox religious or political beliefs.[26] Dissenting groups protested their exclusion by occupying or vandalizing the space. For example, in 1867, a school board in western Pennsylvania arranged for the arrest of John Morrow, a popular doctor and former teacher, for conducting an unsanctioned sing-along with youth in the school building. The reason for the board's objection remains obscure but seems to reflect partisan rivalries. As the constable escorted Morrow to court, his supporters returned to the school and removed "all the furniture, doors, windows, shutters, stove and everything belonging to the house and piled them on the public road."[27] These actions reflect the blunt realities of small-town politics, in which conflicts about majority rule, minority rights, and public virtue inevitably aligned with personal resentments, blurring distinctions between justice and lawlessness. Whether or not authorities prosecuted a particular incident of vandalism, when community sympathies shielded the culprits they had little choice but to accept it.

Property Damage and the Origins of Common Schooling

School reformers saw all of this damage, from desktop graffiti to breaking and entering, as a harbinger of broader social dysfunction. Many argued that unkempt surroundings disposed children to criminality, citing contemporary work in environmental psychology.[28] Henry Barnard claimed that cramped classrooms coarsened children's souls, evident in the walls "cut and marked with all sorts of images, some of which would make heathens blush."[29] Josiah Holbrook argued that exposure to classroom graffiti turned students into "thieves, midnight assassins, and incendiaries."[30] A writer in Michigan likewise complained of "indecent, profane, and libidinous marks . . . spread out in broad characters on the walls," as well as "a much greater number in small character, upon the tables and seats of the students . . . constantly before the eyes of those who happen to occupy them." What lessons were these smutty scrawls teaching children, and what kind of adults would they produce?[31]

Vandalism not only portended social strife in the future; it was an indictment of present political arrangements. That such markings could linger for years, in full view of the religious congregations and town councils that met in the schoolhouse, seemed evidence of voters' apathy and the inadequacy of local institutions to safeguard public morals.[32] Fears of crime and discord were a driving force in the expansion of public education during the nineteenth century. Rather than allowing local farmers to determine educational quality, common-school supporters called for a professional teaching corps, centralized school administration, increased funding, and more commodious buildings, in which, as Thomas H. Burrowes put it in 1856, "the noblest feelings of the human heart might be trained . . . instead of the ruthless disposition to destroy."[33] Just as run-down classrooms could corrupt children, reformers believed that "neatness in the furnishing induces or begets habits of neatness in the pupils," that aesthetic improvements would "strike at the root of the destructive propensity of our boys, and implant in its stead a love of the beautiful."[34] Curbing vandalism would instill principles of self-control, they believed, and from them self-government, replacing the cycle of destruction with one of civic virtue. But voters first had to accept a broader conception of the public good and be willing to outlay tax revenues.

Reformers hoped to convince them that spending on school buildings would be offset by savings on prisons, police, and maintenance. It was with this logic that Burrowes warned school boards not to skimp on school furniture. "That which is cheap and common will be apt to receive rough usage," he wrote. Simple pine desks would be "so cut with knives, furrowed with slate pencils, and discolored with ink" that a district would have to clean them annually and replace them every five years, whereas "furniture of a neat and ornamental description is not often purposely abused or injured." Selecting higher-quality furnishings was a cost savings not merely for the school but for all of society. "The constant contemplation of agreeable and appropriate objects," Burrows continued, "cannot but have a powerful tendency towards the formation of a correct taste. . . . Besides, no one will deny that the habit of destructiveness should be controlled, and those of preservation and care implanted and encouraged in childhood. If fully impressed then, they will rarely disappear in after life."[35]

Common-school proponents also sought public support through stricter enforcement of school rules. Since taxpayers were unlikely to invest in classroom infrastructure only to see it defaced, Horace Mann, secretary of the Massachusetts Board of Education, urged teachers and parents "to preserve buildings from injuries, such as cutting the tables, loosening and splitting the seats, [or] breaking the doors and windows." "Schoolhouses will be more readily built and repaired," he wrote, "when instructors shall use more exertions to save them from the folly and indiscretion of children."[36] School boards increasingly published codes of conduct that forbade property destruction. One ordered students not "to cut, scratch, chalk, or otherwise disfigure, injure, or defile, any portion of the building," "to use a knife, except on the conditions prescribed," or "to meddle with ink unnecessarily." Others outlawed "obscene pictures or representations" on the furniture, and declared liable any student who should "injure any school property, whether fences, gates, trees or shrubs, or any building or any part thereof; or break any window glass, or injure or destroy any instrument, apparatus or furniture belonging to the school."[37]

These prohibitions suggest not only the types and scope of student misbehavior but the rising formalism of school governance. By the second half of the nineteenth century, not only local school boards but state legislatures began to codify penalties for school property damage. Several states passed laws holding parents liable for their children's actions, although these remained poorly enforced and (as later chapters will discuss) were of questionable legality. Rule violations also became a means for state courts to regulate due process in schools, expanding the power of administrators and elected boards at the expense of family sovereignty and student rights. A commonly cited example came from Vermont, in 1859, where the Supreme Court ruled that schoolmasters had the right to administer corporal punishment for "acts done to injure or deface the schoolroom," as well as for "writings and pictures placed so as to suggest evil and corrupt language, images, and thoughts to the youth." "Such power," the court warned, "is essential to the preservation of order, decency, decorum, and good government in schools."[38] Likewise, in 1888, the Illinois Supreme Court upheld the suspension of a boy who refused to inform on a classmate who had painted obscene messages on the side of the schoolhouse, arguing that public order and the school's standing *in loco parentis* outweighed his claims of privacy.[39] Similar decisions elsewhere strengthened the legal standing of school boards and sustained a coercive disciplinary apparatus that would not be significantly revised until the 1970s. Thus, as we will see in subsequent chapters, diffuse forms of noncompliance by children and local communities became the basis for increasingly centralized state authority.[40]

Vandalism, Nativism, and White Supremacy

In addition to improving classroom aesthetics, reformers had faith that public education would defuse social tensions. Damage to schools in the nineteenth century was often a byproduct of broader political, ethnic, and religious violence, and a means to intimidate minority groups. These actions sometimes derived from bigoted positions of principle, as when an entire town took up torches and stoned a Native American school after learning that one of its students was marrying a white woman.[41] At other times, public prejudice excused simple hooliganism, as when a band of teenagers broke all the windows of a Jewish school in San Francisco.[42] Most confrontations were a mix of the two, with assertions of public virtue devolving into demonstrations of brute force and tribalism.

Reformers hoped that daily intercourse and a unifying curriculum in the common schools would end these demonstrations by fostering mutual respect between groups. Unfortunately, because schools remained implicitly white, Protestant spaces, increased attendance could as easily incite further acts of violence. Debates over the use of the King James Bible, for instance, led to street fights between Protestant nativists and Catholic immigrants, with Protestant mobs burning Catholic schools in Massachusetts in the 1830s, Philadelphia in the 1840s, and elsewhere through the end of the century, and Catholics breaking into public schools to wreck furniture and burn Bibles.[43]

Race was even more fraught than religion, with attacks on African American schools by far the most common example of property destruction. There were dozens of incidents in the North in the decades before the Civil War and over a thousand in the South in the decades after. These attacks underscore the virulence of white supremacy in American society, but they also speak to contemporary uncertainties about racial diversity in a democracy.

While many of the Founders assumed that slavery would end of its own accord, it became clear almost immediately after the American Revolution that this was not the case. In the South, slavery revived with westward expansion and the emergence of an international cotton market. Securing the unpaid labor of millions of human beings required an absolute prohibition on literacy, both to maintain the fiction of enslaved people's intellectual inferiority and to limit the flow of information that could enable escape or rebellion. Thus, Southern planters banned formal instruction for the enslaved, and rejected provisions for public education writ large. Their efforts resulted in almost universal illiteracy among enslaved people and depressingly high rates among Southern freedmen, white and Black. As a result, while slavery perpetuated shocking forms of violence and ignorance, it had comparatively little effect on school property: enslaved people persisted in many forms of surreptitious education in the decades before the Civil War, but in most of the South there were simply too few African American school buildings to destroy.[44]

Meanwhile, in the North, emancipation confronted the public with a different set of questions. If it was clear by the 1820s that African Americans should not be slaves, most Northern whites were equally convinced that they could never be citizens, whether because they doubted their moral and intellectual capacity or because they believed that prevailing prejudice would forever prevent assimilation. Whichever the case, the assumption was that the United States would remain a white republic. To the extent that white Northerners favored African American education at all, it was in the context of strict segregation and the understanding that former slaves would return to Africa. As Hilary Moss points out, this program of uplift and expulsion was tenuous from the beginning. Many abolitionists questioned its endorsement of racially homogenous citizenship, while working-class whites objected to any educational opportunity that might attract more Black residents to their communities.[45] The latter group framed their opposition in terms of majority rights. On the island of Nantucket, for instance, opponents warned that educating Black children meant "that fundamental principle of democracy, 'the greatest good of the greatest number,' is overborne by the few." School officials, they argued, "had no right to gratify the wish of a small portion of [African American] citizens for a social amalgamation offensive to the rest."[46]

Again, this sort of populist rhetoric became justification for pervasive violence. White mobs regularly set on African American schools, breaking windows in Baltimore, "gutting" a building in Boston, and burning several during the New York City draft riots.[47] In Washington, DC, a gang swept through the city and damaged the buildings and furniture of every African American school they found. They particularly targeted Union Seminary and its principal, John F. Cook, an outspoken civil rights advocate, who narrowly escaped with his life.[48] Violence also broke out in small towns, where integrated schools attracted freedmen and their families. After the Noyes Academy in Canaan, New Hampshire, began admitting Black students, residents pulled the structure off its foundations.[49] When Prudence Crandall did the same at her girls' school in Waterbury, Connecticut, townspeople fouled her well, broke windows, and overturned furniture.[50] Similar cases occurred throughout the region and persisted well into the second half of the nineteenth century, when the issue of Black citizenship was ostensibly resolved and racial uplift (if not integration) had become a pillar of educational reform.[51]

Surveying the Destruction of African American Schools in the South

Racist violence assumed new dimensions following the Civil War, when it aligned with sectional divisions and became a topic of national political interest. The greatest outbreak of violence against African American schools occurred in the

FIGURE 1.3. In 1866, at least six African American schools were burned during riots in Memphis, Tennessee. *Harper's Weekly*, May 26, 1866.

postwar South, where new schools, often built with support from the Bureau of Refugees, Freedmen, and Abandoned Lands (or the Freedmen's Bureau), became a means for freed people to assert political and social equality, and consequently became a target for those who opposed their advancement. Hostile white Southerners would frequently harass teachers and students and burn or vandalize school buildings, one of many types of violence during Reconstruction. These acts were widely known; they were publicized not only by government reports but through oral traditions, the African American press, missionary organizations, Republican newspapers, and Thomas Nast's political cartoons. All of these sources established school burning as an iconic image of the postwar era, an emotionally laden symbol of repression and perseverance.[52]

Unfortunately, the lack of specific reports made it difficult to grasp the extent of damage, both at the time and in the present.[53] Drawing from a diffuse source base, historians have described the destruction of African American schoolhouses anecdotally or in highly local contexts. There has been no survey of the number or location of schools destroyed, the causes of their destruction, or the costs incurred by African American communities, and we have very little sense of the scale of the phenomenon.[54]

The remainder of this chapter undertakes two tasks. First, it hazards an estimate of the number of African American schools destroyed in the South between 1864 and 1876, based on archival evidence from the Freedmen's Bureau, the published findings of a congressional committee investigating the Ku Klux Klan, and an extensive survey of historical newspapers and secondary sources.[55] The final tally is necessarily an underestimate, but it nevertheless provides a starting point for historical judgment and further research, and offers a stark reminder of the hardships that vigilante violence imposed on African American communities in their quest for education. This evidence, like much of the scholarship on African American education since the 1980s, parallels arguments first introduced in W. E. B. DuBois's *Black Reconstruction in America* (1935): among them, the centrality of educational reform to the Reconstruction project; the initiative of African American communities in building, funding, and staffing their own schools; and their role in lobbying for statewide systems of public education.[56]

The second task is to explore the occlusion of historical evidence that might have provided an even more comprehensive account—that is, to identify the sources of our ignorance. In the period between 1864 and 1876, many factors contributed to an atmosphere of ambiguity and deniability in which criminal acts went unpunished, among them the surreptitious nature and diverse motivations of property destruction, changes to newspaper reporting, political divisions, and a federal bureaucracy ill equipped to process large amounts of information. Although federal documents provide somber and sometimes stirring witness to the desperation of the postwar South, they are also beset by silence, euphemism, and elision. Even when the Freedmen's Bureau could document incidents of school burning, their significance was colored by the ideological biases of the bureau's commanders in Washington, DC, and of its agents in the field.

Taken together, these issues speak not merely to the violence and discrimination that denied equal educational opportunity, but to the potent forms of political and historical obfuscation that accompanied it. In this regard, school burning extends recent ontological questions about Reconstruction as a whole to its educational aspects in particular: for instance, how power relations have influenced perceptions of truth for historians and their subjects, how emotions such as fear or hatred appear in the archives, and how one reckons with uncertainty or absence in the historical record.[57] While a survey of the destruction of African American schools in one sense represents a strictly physical accounting—of the dire consequences when wooden structures met oil and matches—in another it broaches questions of historical interpretation, exploring the destruction of evidence through poor planning, wishful thinking, self-deception, apathy, and cynicism, as well as arson.

The resources and infrastructure necessary to sustain Reconstruction were vast. The Freedmen's Bureau devoted millions of dollars to the construction of schools and the organization of public education systems, a demand of African American voters and a central piece of the Republican political platform. By the time it ceased educational operations in 1870, the bureau supported 2,677 primary schools, 74 high schools or normal schools, and 61 industrial schools, serving almost 160,000 students in all. Hundreds of other schools opened under private auspices, sometimes in loose coordination with the bureau, and these gradually secured public funding. Indeed, as historians have documented, it was the demands of African Americans that impelled Southern states to honor their commitment to public education for all children.[58]

It is important to note, however, that the expansion of educational infrastructure was uneven: many counties lacked schools through the mid-1870s, and only a fraction of African American children ever attended a Freedmen's Bureau school. Some areas lacked enough African American students to sustain racially segregated schools, the only feasible option in most communities, and some were too poor to generate support from African American parents, who bore the brunt of the cost. Even where the will existed, many white property owners refused to lease land or buildings to freedmen, or would withdraw leases under community pressure. Finally, as Ronald Butchart has documented, thousands of teachers—both white and Black, Northern and Southern, male and female—were threatened, whipped, or killed for their work with African American students. Building and teacher shortages remained the primary impediment to African American education, far more extensive than physical destruction, and attacks on schools were less frequent than other forms of violence against freedmen and their families.[59]

That being said, for white southerners, destroying a school building remained a signal act of rebellion. Schools—like churches, in which they were often housed—stood as physical manifestations of both African American and federal political power.[60] In addition to providing the literacy and numeracy with which freedmen could defend their interests, they were often used as meeting sites for the Republican Party, Black Leagues, and Northern benevolent organizations, providing a space for an emerging civil society.[61] Their destruction drew support from political opportunists and paramilitary organizations, both of which hoped to blunt Republican power and regain "home rule," as well as a broader swath of Southern society, for whom ritualistic acts of destruction reaffirmed white supremacy and traditional social arrangements.[62]

Attacking schools imposed monetary and psychic costs on the most vulnerable segment of Southern society. Although most of the structures destroyed were small, valued between $400 and $1,000, African American communities financed at least half of their construction, a significant outlay of capital to go up in flames, especially since few of the buildings carried insurance. Normal schools, industrial institutes, and colleges valued as high as $200,000 were also destroyed, and in increasing numbers as they expanded operations. One gets a sense of the attacks' psychic costs from Emma Caughey, principal of the Emerson Institute, in Mobile, Alabama. After an arsonist burned her school, she wrote, "Emerson Institute is lying in ruins. For the second time in her history she is smoldering in ashes, and we are mourning for the destruction of our little church, made dear by so many sacred and hallowed associations, and our beautiful school building in which so many happy hours of toil have been spent and labors of love performed. . . . The enemy approaches again and applies the torch—this time with marvelous success." Whatever the persistence of her enemies, Caughey proved more determined still, moving the school to a church basement and reopening it in 1882.[63] The Emerson Institute could stand in for innumerable acts of African American persistence and resistance in the face of violent intimidation. When they could, Black communities organized armed patrols to protect their schools. When they could not, they rebuilt, sometimes two or three times in succession.[64]

Unfortunately, their antagonists could prove just as determined, promising, "If they should rebuild the schoolhouse it will be burned again," and frequently following through on that threat.[65] While African American education was contentious in Mobile, there were other counties where schools suffered total destruction. A man riding through Madison County, Alabama, passed "the ruins of probably a half dozen colored school-houses that have been burned" and not rebuilt.[66] In Chatham County, North Carolina, witnesses "heard tell constantly of the burning of school-houses and meeting-houses."[67] In Winston, Mississippi, a correspondent wrote, "There was [an order] to put down every free school, and I do not believe there is a single free school in that county; the information is that they are all closed."[68] In East Texas, several African American teachers testified that burned churches left them to teach in the open air.[69] Moreover, acts of arson and vandalism could have cascading effects. "In consequence of several school-houses having been burned," wrote the Freedmen's Bureau agent in Greenville, Alabama, "all the colored schools have been discontinued except one."[70] In Walton, Georgia; York, South Carolina; and many other counties, credible threats of property destruction shut down African American education entirely.[71]

A survey of federal documents and historical newspapers reveals at least 631 attacks on African American schools between 1864 and 1876. Taken as a fraction of the schools operating by the end of that period—or by the 1880 census, in states that did not distinguish "colored" schools in their annual reports—that means that at least one school in twenty was significantly damaged or destroyed. These incidents did not conform to particular geographic or demographic boundaries. They occurred in rural counties from Texas to Virginia, with the highest levels of damage in Mississippi, Alabama, and Tennessee. Fires also erupted in urban areas such as New Orleans, Memphis, and Dallas, where the destruction of buildings reflected more complex geographies of racial self-assertion and oppression, foreshadowing the contentious color lines that would later make cities hotbeds of lynching.[72] Most Southern counties suffered no documented destruction of schools, but the 264 counties in which recorded incidents occurred suggest that property violence was endemic elsewhere as well. Moreover, there are reasons to believe that the current tally is a significant underestimate, and not only because many fires had unknown origins. If one looks at figure 1.4, there seem to be areas (such as southeastern Georgia) with suspiciously few incidents, and others (such as Northwest Louisiana) in which notoriously high levels of racial violence seemed to yield comparatively little damage to school buildings. There also exist several reports of statewide destruction that, because they do not specify particular locations, are omitted from the total. For example, a state superintendent recounted seventeen schools burned in Tennessee in 1866, sixty-one in 1867, and forty in 1869. Documents reveal slightly more (twenty-two) for 1866, but only seventeen for 1867 and eight for 1869. Similar disparities in other states suggest that the actual number of schools destroyed could be 50 percent higher than this map suggests, with perhaps one thousand buildings ruined, and hundreds of thousands of dollars lost.[73]

Why don't we have a clearer picture of the damage, even in hindsight? There are three broad reasons: the Freedmen's Bureau's limited ability to collect data, the politicization of schooling, and the diverse causes of destruction, both intentional and unintentional. Together, these factors created an atmosphere of uncertainty that allowed attacks on African American schools to go untallied and largely unchecked. Disorganized reporting rendered documentation useless as a form of institutional knowledge and facilitated its abstraction into partisan political discourse.

Historians have subjected the Freedmen's Bureau to multiple rounds of condemnation and rehabilitation. For much of the twentieth century, those sympathetic to the Southern cause maligned the agency as corrupt and incompetent, making little mention of its role in educational reform.[74] Since the 1970s, scholars have pivoted to its pioneering role in promoting a federal civil rights agenda and valiantly (if tragically) confronting resurgent violence in the South.[75] While it is important to acknowledge the difficult circumstances under which bureau agents labored, one should not overstate the efficacy of their educational administration. "On paper," notes the historian Richard White, "[the bureau] was powerful, with a sweeping mandate and the legal means to enforce it. On the ground, it was understaffed, underfinanced, and incapable of achieving its goals."[76] Even sympathetic scholars have described the bureau's records as a

TABLE 1.1.   African American schools damaged or destroyed, 1864–76

	SCHOOLS DESTROYED	OPERATING (1876)	PERCENTAGE (1876)	OPERATING (1880)	PERCENTAGE (1880)
Alabama	81	1415	5.7%	—	—
Arkansas	9	—	—	601	1.5%
District of Columbia	3	—	—	115	2.6%
Delaware	2	—	—	50	4.0%
Florida	5	—	—	301	1.7%
Georgia	33	1075	3.1%	—	—
Kentucky	32	532	6.0%	—	—
Louisiana	52	—	—	1479	10.9%
Maryland	12	340	3.5%	—	—
Missouri	5	338	1.5%	—	—
Mississippi	158	—	—	2147	7.4%
North Carolina	31	1371	2.3%	—	—
South Carolina	47	—	—	1205	3.9%
Tennessee	76	827	9.2%	—	—
Texas	55	—	—	1507	3.6%
Virginia	29	1181	2.5%	—	—
West Virginia	1	—	—	122	0.8%
TOTAL	631		4.2%		5.1%

Note: A dash indicates that no data were available.

Sources: Data were compiled from multiple sources, including Freedmen's Bureau Records, the Joint Select Committee, newspaper searches, and secondary literature. See note 55.

"morass," and note that despite soliciting numerous reports and surveys, the central office had no way to aggregate or act on much of the information that it received.[77] Moreover, while the bureau posed open-ended questions about the state of local schools and white sentiment toward African American education, it never asked about destruction directly. Whether or how to report attacks fell to the discretion of individual agents, leading to significant discrepancies between government records and popular accounts in the same states and over the same years. J. W. Alvord, the bureau's superintendent of education, often referenced property violence in his published reports, but in impressionistic rather than systematic ways. While it hardly follows that a dedicated survey question would have altered bureau policies, it remains true that actionable information depended on predesigned pathways for collection and processing. Without them, the relevant reports remained diffuse.

Another cause of the bureau's ineffectiveness was its lack of manpower and inability to operate in hostile territory. Met with direct affronts to its authority—such as racist rioters in Memphis, who burned at least half a dozen schools—the bureau invested resources to rebuild and protect school buildings.[78] But the situation was much different in rural areas, where agents could not even venture into the countryside to see the schools, and knew of their erection or destruction

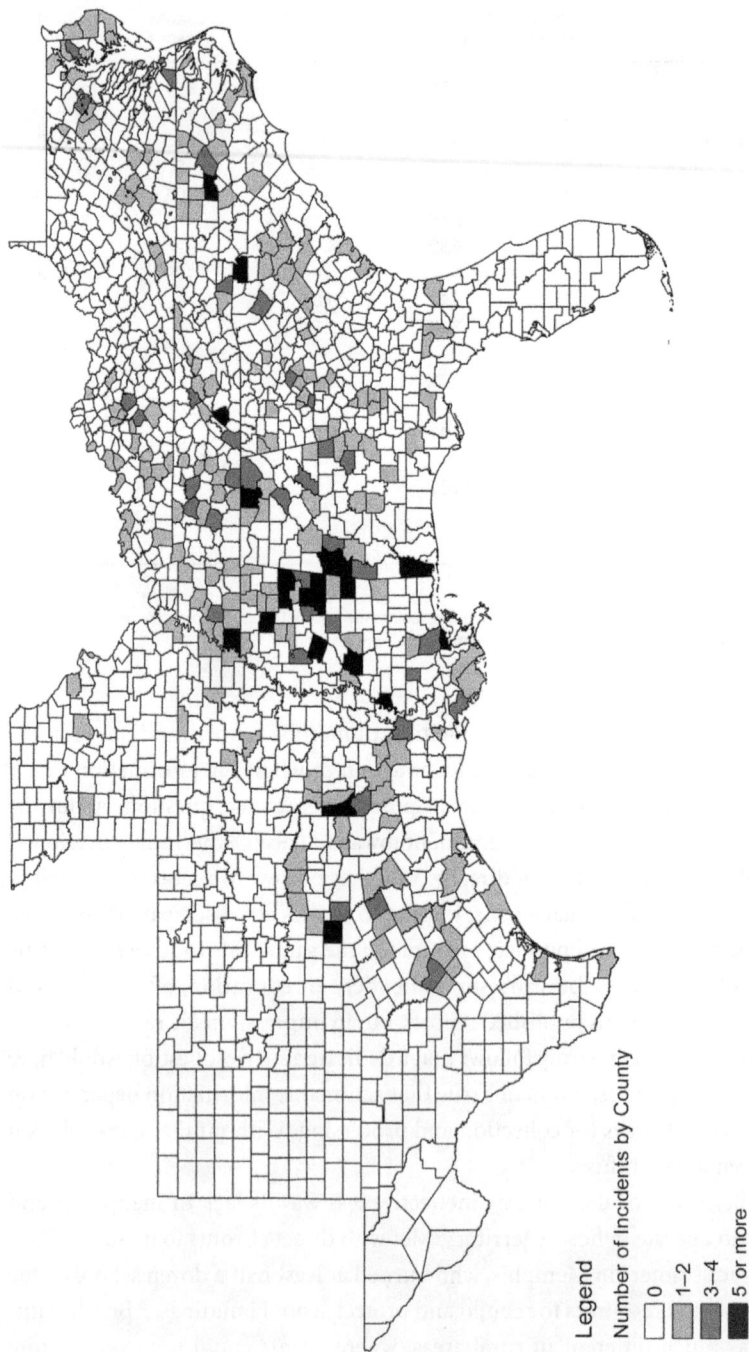

FIGURE 1.4. African American schools damaged or destroyed, 1864–76. Data were compiled from multiple sources, including Freedmen's Bureau Records, the Joint Select Committee, newspaper searches, and secondary literature. See note 55.

Legend

Number of Incidents by County

0
1–2
3–4
5 or more

largely by hearsay.[79] In North Carolina, one bureau agent complained that he had no idea how many freedmen's schools operated in his district: they "disappear so rapidly," he wrote, as to make accurate reporting of their numbers "quite impossible."[80] In Alabama, agents admitted being confined to their camp, which meant that "little information [could be] obtained respecting schools." "Under the present state of affairs," one wrote, "I do not consider it safe to visit the remote localities in this country, where these outrages have been committed, to investigate the circumstances of the murders and arson, and therefore base my report upon the most reliable information received in my office."[81] Elsewhere, agents had to abandon their posts "in consequence of violence towards others & threats against [themselves]."[82]

Without a systematic means of quantifying violence, the bureau's local, regional, and state offices could put very different interpretations on the information they received. Many remained optimistic about race relations through the late 1860s, despite setbacks. References to "occasional local disturbances" were common, but always with promises such as, "With a little prudence, patience and courage [they] would soon disappear."[83] An agent in Louisville, Kentucky, saw school vandalism as a test of the bureau's resolve. "When in the early part of the month I rented in this city a building for a freedmen's school," he wrote, "hostility then took the form of open violence. The building itself was attacked, the glass broken, the door beaten down, and it was found necessary for a time to place a guard over it. When it became evident that the Bureau was determined to open and protect the school, these violent demonstrations ceased, and the school is now in successful operation."[84] Another, writing from Columbus, Mississippi, remained "convinced that all prejudice against the education of freedpeople will soon disappear," even as he reported the destruction of a large school.[85] In the space of a single letter, the agent in Eufala, Alabama, praised "a greater revelation in public opinion than the most sanguine imaginations could have anticipated"—noting that "schools are demanded now in almost every neighborhood, while a year ago in many places in this district it would not have been safe to . . . establish them"—before acknowledging ongoing reports of "the burning of School-houses occupied by the colod people [sic]."[86] These mixed messages, combined with vague or inconclusive data and the lack of any statistical attention to property violence, made it difficult to form a full picture of the bureau's educational accomplishments and reverses.

By 1868, the bureau's political support was running short and superiors began to ask agents when they thought they could withdraw. Yet, regarding the consequences of withdrawal, too, the bureau suffered from conflicting reports. The superintendent of education in Louisiana warned, "If the military power should be withdrawn, and the State once more resume all her functions, our schools would cease to exist, and the whole moral and political influence of the people [would] be brought to bear against them." The state's military commander disagreed. "The white population of the South feels the power of these schools," he wrote, and the "assent, if not the favor, of the better men is being gradually obtained."[87] On the whole, local agents were not sanguine about the future of their schools. Another Louisianan promised, "It could be impossible to establish any schools in several parishes . . . except [that] they were guarded by U.S. troops."[88] The agent in Paris, Texas, found hatred so strong that, without military protection, the freedmen's school "would not live a single hour."[89] Another Texan questioned the wisdom of investing in school buildings at all, since they were "easily and often destroyed and the investment lost."[90] After the Freedmen's Bureau withdrew, it became even more difficult to ascertain the state of affairs across the region, though some statewide reports bore out agents' concerns. Most Southern states expressed direct opposition and only grudgingly adopted the systems of public funding and oversight demanded for readmission to the Union.[91] Although state departments of education assumed responsibility for their schools by the end of the 1870s, and published the same sort of surveys that one found in Northern states—tallying the numbers of schools, teachers, and students—these official documents proved no more sensitive to acts of destruction than the Freedmen's Bureau's had been.

Another, related source of obfuscation was partisan politics, which could excuse or call into question the perpetration of terrorist acts. The federal government relied on two primary sources of information about violence against schools: the Freedmen's Bureau reports referenced above, and a congressional inquiry into the Ku Klux Klan, which toured Southern states collecting testimony and published its findings in 1872. As the historian Elaine Parsons has explained, there were concerted attempts by Democrats, liberal Republicans, and even some within the Grant administration to undermine the credibility of both of these sources.[92] In a typical example, when a Republican senator read an "official list" of crimes attributed to the Ku Klux Klan in Kentucky, a Democratic colleague asked what list he meant. Stating that it was a Freedmen's Bureau report, "he was met with what the *Tribune* described as 'derisive laughter' from the Democratic side." Democrats "explained that [they] did not recognize the Freedmen's Bureau as an authority."[93] As Klan attacks became a rallying issue for Republicans, they became equally valuable for Democrats seeking to discredit the Reconstruction project. Many Democrats denied the very existence of the Klan, or dismissed reports of its violence as Republican exaggerations, to the point that, according to Parsons, "the very act of calling a violent act a Ku-Klux attack cast doubt upon its legitimacy."[94] Thus, individuals within the government not only chose how to document or interpret evidence of Southern violence but actively undermined attempts to gather information in the first place. Even before they were collected, partisan interests transformed the facts of school burning into politically charged abstractions.

Democratic politicians in particular exploited the value of misinformation in educational politics.[95] A common strategy was to pounce on small inaccuracies in reporting while advancing larger inaccuracies of their own. When a witness referenced a school burning in York County, South Carolina, for instance, Democratic congressmen pointed out that the incident had in fact taken place in Fairfield County. "If such a crime has been committed anywhere in [York] county," they added, "we have failed to obtain the slightest evidence of the fact." Actually, by the committee's own tally, at least twelve such crimes had occurred.[96] Likewise, a public official from Kershaw County, South Carolina, denied that there had been any "systematic hostility . . . [against] common-school education for the negroes." Upon subsequent questioning, however, he admitted that he had authorized a report citing rampant violence and arson in the area.[97] When asked if he had heard of "the burning of any churches and school-houses of colored people," an Alabama man "[could not] specify the burning of any church on either side," an answer that simultaneously diminished and deflected the question.[98]

Part of the political battle involved establishing school burners as a "type" in the public imagination. For opponents of the Freedmen's Bureau, attributing crimes to the Klan segregated members of the Klan from mainstream politics, normalizing and moderating practically all other state and local actors. Thus, witnesses could assert that anyone who burned a school could not be a local resident or "an honest man," attributing arson to lower-class misfits and outside agitators rather than Southern society writ large.[99] To be sure, Southern whites varied in their tolerance for freedmen's schools, and roving bands of toughs did cross state and county lines to commit acts of violence.[100] Yet there were also many examples of plantation owners offering their land for schools only to discover that their "neighbors, respectable men . . . [had] burned the school-house." Investigators likewise discovered that the "incendiarism practiced by ignorant, deluded and bad men [had been] suggested in many instances and encouraged by a class of . . . more responsible [men]," undermining the distinction between types of culprits.[101]

Apologists further deflected scrutiny by parsing arsonists' motives. James Gross, a resident of Unionville, South Carolina, assured federal investigators that outrages against school buildings were "all political, directed against voting" rather than against education.[102] Elsewhere, as well, hostile Southerners claimed that schools were destroyed to inhibit voting and intimidate Republicans, noting that they "were burned before the election, in the fall of 1870," as if political motives absolved the criminals.[103] Other witnesses told Congress that school violence did not represent opposition to education per se, but to "extravagant" expenditures on furniture and teacher salaries.[104] In Louisville, Mississippi, local whites reasoned that if they "could get shut of the school-house, they would get shut of taxes."[105] These remarks correspond to a broader trend of racializing tax expenditures, which became justification not merely for neglecting but for destroying African American schools.[106] By parsing motives and narrowing 'real' school burning to acts of hatred or an intrinsic hostility to education, Southerners legitimized other forms of the phenomenon, establishing a distinction without a difference and providing political cover for perpetrators.

The same sort of partisanship and misinformation played out even more starkly in white newspapers of the time. As early as 1866, Republican papers used school burning as shorthand for all forms of Southern disloyalty, omitting reference to specific incidents in favor of blanket statements. In a typical example, the *National Republican* wrote, "If banishing Unionists, shooting ex-Federal soldiers, hanging freedmen, and burning freedmen's school-houses mean 'tranquility,' then, indeed, [Kentucky] is in a remarkably tranquil condition."[107] Another referred to Louisiana Democrats as "negro-hating, school-house burning, fire-eating Bourbonists, who never outgrow prejudice."[108] By the same logic, however, school burnings became fodder for letter writers on the other side. One complained that "the New York *Tribune* would have the country believe that the constant occupation of the Southern people is to murder freedmen and burn their school-houses."[109] Another grumbled that "the *Chronicle* proceeds to indulge the usual twaddle . . . and to repeat the stale slanders concerning 'Ku Klux outrages' and 'schoolhouse burnings' by [Southerners]—which have been accepted as Gospel truths by their political enemies in the North."[110] "Here we have seen the laws of states and their whole people denounced as being steeped in injustice," noted a third writer, "because some hoodlum set fire to a negro school-house or for some such circumstance for which the officers of the law were not responsible."[111] In each of these cases, accounts of school destruction were rejected outright because of perceived partisan bias in the reporting. Even when reliable information appeared, readers were apt to dismiss its importance.

Democratic editors also echoed the era's sarcastic editorial tone to deflect the significance of school burnings. In Jackson, Tennessee, one wondered whether the military would station a Gatling gun at the site of a school that had been blown over by a tornado, noting that "under the civil rights bill, negro school-houses have no right to fall down."[112] There were also accusations of reverse racism. "There have been six schoolhouses burned since the public schools were established in this country," observed a writer in Memphis, "and every one of them were schools for white pupils. In every instance it is supposed to have been the act of incendiaries, and yet no white man has accused a negro of doing it. Suppose negro schoolhouses had been burned?"[113] This resentful tone became commonplace. Writers routinely ridiculed opponents of school burning as biased and overly sensitive. It is notable that critics fixated on the causes of property destruction rather than its effects, and on the tenor of reporting rather than its substance. In the process, they ascribed a subtle and undeserved legitimacy to criminal acts, establishing a moral equivalency between biased commentary and the reality of smoldering buildings.

Unfortunately, these critics also had a point. If the public split over the question of responsibility for school destruction, it was because there was plenty of blame to go around and rarely much certainty. Arson is an inherently ambiguous crime, and its anonymous nature has long made it a weapon of subordinate peoples, which both freedmen and white redemptionists (by their own lights) were.[114] Thus, newspaper reports attributed many acts of incendiarism to African Americans, as responses to corresponding acts of white terrorism.[115] In several cases, a town's Black and white schools burned down in quick succession, apparently in reprisal attacks.[116] A white mob lynched three freedmen in Tuscumbia, Alabama, under suspicion of burning an academy for white women.[117] In Bennettsville, South Carolina, African Americans allegedly burned two boys' academies "because the white people had held Democratic meetings there," usually the charge against freedmen's schools and Republicans. When a local newspaper declared that "incendiarism, rapine and murder, is the ruling spirit of the party now in power," it referred not to the Ku Klux Klan but to African Americans and their Republican allies.[118] After someone broke into a white church in Edgecombe County, North Carolina, and scrawled vulgar graffiti around the building, the press blamed "a party of black fiends who go to one of the freedmen's schools in the vicinity."[119] Meanwhile, in Moore County, a story circulated that a gang of Black men had been burning local barns and "were meeting in the [freedmen's] school to burn more" when they were discovered by a gang of white men—who, coincidentally, had come to burn down the school.[120] The neat parallelisms of these stories strain belief, and one can imagine them either as flimsy justifications for racist violence or as projections of white guilt. On the other hand, they (or others like them) could well be true, examples of revenge or self-defense in a society on the brink of a race war.[121] The uncertainty surrounding these cases is inherent in any community with significant asymmetries of power. Whose story could one trust, and on what basis?

That question created an evidentiary problem that white Southern apologists accentuated whenever possible. By advancing alternate theories about school burnings, they strewed pebbles of plausibility across the road to justice. Missouri senator Francis Blair Jr., was a master at generating uncertainty for political gain, and emerged as the enabler for hostile witnesses in congressional hearings on the Ku Klux Klan. For instance, Blair encouraged a Mississippi lawyer to talk about two white men acquitted of burning African American schoolhouses. After exonerating his clients, the lawyer offered a vague counternarrative. "We have had white boys," he said, "who, as in old time, want to quit school, and would burn the school-houses," implying that Black students had perhaps done the same to theirs.[122] Other witnesses, too, fingered students as the likeliest culprits, such as the "colored boy, who had been dismissed from school by the teacher" and allegedly returned to torch the building.[123] They may have been right. White students burned down hundreds of schools during the nineteenth century, as any casual newspaper reader would have known, and there were certainly cases of African American students engaging in the same behavior. Whether this was the cause of any particular fire, who could say? In another instance, a witness blamed the teacher himself. "Some of his own neighbors suspected him," he said. "One of them published a card to the effect that Avery burned his school-house to keep from teaching school; and if he could make it appear that other parties did it, he would get his pay anyhow." Under cross-examination, the witness acknowledged that this was perhaps not a "better theory" than the Klan, but he still aired it.[124] There were more credible accusations as well. When the congressmen investigated two schools attacked in South Carolina, "it was generally said that the K.K. burned them; that was common report," but subsequent testimony revealed a "rivalry between factions of two male teachers who had solicited the occupancy of the building from the school trustees."[125] At least eight other incidents of arson were rumored to have been intraracial, usually the product of denominational squabbles between African American churches, as were several more in subsequent decades.[126]

Senator Blair promoted other theories as well. He sometimes asked whether vagrants could have broken into schools and caused the fires. One witness tartly replied, "I reckon an idea of that kind never occurred to anybody but you."[127] When he asked an official from Cleveland County, North Carolina, if there was any doubt about local schools being purposely burned, the man snorted, "No, sir, of course not!"[128] But Blair was savvy about public opinion. Accidental or unexplained fires were even more frequent than arson, and presumably more believable than the massive criminal conspiracy that Republicans were suggesting. Given the sheer number of schools destroyed, it seemed likely that some were the product of mischievous children or faulty flues, and if enough people accepted that premise, it could weaken the crackdown on Southern violence writ large. Whether or not one was convinced by these speculations—indeed, how one interpreted *any* of the evidence of school destruction—was of course a subjective judgment, and for opponents of federal intervention that was exactly the point. A well-placed exception could outweigh a mountain of contrary evidence, calling into doubt the political commitments necessary to sustain educational Reconstruction. Whether or not an acknowledgment of destruction could have altered the political landscape, it is instructive to see how power and truth bore recursively on each other at all levels of decision-making, and to see how individuals advanced or contested claims about the information that did come to light.

The destruction of African American schools presents something of a paradox for historians: a widely recognized event that remains clouded by obscurity. This is not because it was suppressed, exactly, but because its particulars were often overlooked by federal agents or sensationalized by politicians and the mainstream press. School burning's political significance and the outlets through which it was publicized made the phenomenon a matter of partisan contention before it could be fully documented as simple fact. While the African American press doggedly reported violence against Black schools and the Freedmen's Bureau recorded hundreds of incidents that would otherwise have gone unreported, a combination of selective documentation, local violence, political obstruction, and underlying uncertainty made a full accounting impossible. Without specific knowledge of its extent, contemporaries could treat the destruction of schools as common knowledge or dismiss it as hearsay, depending on their own biases.

The same selective vision that affected the government's response during the 1870s continues to inform our understanding today. Faced with evidence that is at once abundant, disparate, and incomplete, historians have used anecdotal examples of school burning to extrapolate broader lessons about white Southerners' resistance to African American citizenship, exposing violence and repression that were too long ignored; but at the same time they have struggled to convey its scale in detail. Quantitative evidence conveys the geographic extent and numeric scale of white Southern resistance, extending the lessons of existing case studies and drawing attention to states and localities where attacks were particularly prevalent. It also offers a degree of recognition to many incidents that would otherwise go unexamined. Most of these incidents appear only fleetingly—"the colored School House at Springfield in this county was burned by unknown parties Several weeks ago"—with no backstory or particular context.[129] A diligent historian could perhaps uncover the details underlying each case, but would soon meet diminishing returns. There were too many attacks, and they were too similar, to document each one. If they are unlikely to be told, these stories can at least be counted.

Although the legacy of slavery, the belated growth of public education, and an armed occupation and insurgency were conditions unique to the South, in many ways the burning of freedmen's schools was merely an amplification of national trends. Southern arsonists were little different from racist attackers in the North during the same period, and while African Americans suffered disproportionately in both regions, their plight was not categorically different from that of Catholics, Native Americans, or others. In each case, minority groups' attempts to educate their children met with spasms of violence, an aggressive reminder of the populist commitment to white supremacy and majority rights. Even rudimentary education could challenge the economic and political privileges of white freeholders. Meanwhile, to sanction minority education, whether in separate or integrated institutions, was to acknowledge the possibility of a racially and ideologically diverse citizenry. All of these concerns, bolstered by individual pettiness, cynicism, mistrust, and cruelty, sustained a repressive apparatus of property destruction in local educational politics.

As the common school model expanded, however, destroying schools as a political statement became less frequent. Communities brokered compromises around religious instruction, while racial subordination and resistance became a matter of structural maneuvering instead of overt violence.[130] With larger districts, increased regulation, and state subsidies, systemization promised greater resources overall while ensuring that educational advantages would continue to accrue to dominant groups. By the end of the century, the question at hand was no longer whether African American students would receive *any* public education, but the (inequitable) terms under which they would attend schools and the (vocational) ends to which their education would be put.[131] Sporadic outbreaks of property damage continued, but as physical destruction became unnecessary for the maintenance of majority rights, its perpetrators struggled to claim the mantle of public virtue. Future attacks on schools would be portrayed merely as depredations of the misguided, the criminal, or the insane.

2

MODERN EDUCATION AND ITS
DISCONTENTS, 1890–1930

Frank Koma said that he lit the fires to measure time and bring good weather. Asked to explain, he reached for a scrap of paper, on which he drew a circle and wrote "World." Inside the circle he put nearby villages. Everything else he labeled "Sky." Gesturing with his finger, he told his questioners, "Between sky and earth is the weather. Every three years must make fire to make weather good." Apparently the weather had not improved, though twelve schoolhouses had been reduced to ashes.

Koma was arrested in western Pennsylvania in the winter of 1920, accused of arson attacks that caused over $5 million in damage and baffled the police for weeks. During the month of November, fires broke out in lumberyards, churches, and garages, but most frequently in small schoolhouses along the Monongahela River. The police had been following Koma for some time and were unsettled by what they found. The Polish laborer lived alone in an unfurnished garret. His wife had left him some months before, and he subsisted on spare cuts of meat from the butcher shop. He never appeared during the day, but would emerge at dark to take long bike rides through the countryside, following unpaved roads illuminated by the demonic flicker of coke ovens. Investigators described the man as "demented," citing his claim that voices and dreams commanded him to light the fires, which he believed would "purify the air."[1]

Koma was not the first suspect in the case and he would not be the last. A divisive strike had racked the steel industry the previous year and tensions remained high throughout the region. Authorities originally blamed the school fires on labor organizers, reasoning that "education in the public schools is a

37

most effective antidote for Bolshevism" and thus that burning schools might suppress free enterprise and incite radicalism.[2] They made a few cursory arrests of union leaders, but the attacks continued. After Frank Koma, the police arrested a boy, Albert Smith, who also claimed responsibility. "I am insane," Smith assured them. "I get pains in the back of my head and I just don't know why I did it. . . . The pains in my head told me I should." Unfortunately, while Koma and Smith were in custody another school burned down on the outskirts of Pittsburgh. Two more ignited a week later. The situation was getting out of hand. It was unclear whether these fires were the work of a disturbed individual, copycats, or an organized gang, but it was obvious that the police were powerless to stop them. Angry residents grumbled that unless there was a swift resolution, they would have to "adopt [their] own measures in dealing with the arson ring."[3] In January 1921, the police arrested their final suspect, John Shroka, another Polish immigrant, who had sent threatening letters to school authorities. Officers alleged that Shroka chiseled crosses in the stone of school buildings, perhaps an esoteric protest against anti-Catholic bias, perhaps the symptoms of another psychotic. At any rate, they threw him in jail as well.[4]

In hindsight, these arrests look like clumsy efforts to scapegoat radicals, foreigners, and the mentally ill for social unrest, akin to the Sacco and Vanzetti trial that took place later that year. Even at the time, however, some observers recognized deeper forces at work, battles over educational policy and parents' rights. Child labor laws had recently pushed immigrant youth out of the workplace and into school, often over their parents' objections. "Foreigners at work in the mills and mines here are up in arms against the strict enforcement of the anti-truancy law," noted a Pittsburgh reporter. "At a time when boys from fourteen to sixteen have been able to earn as much as $5 to $7 a day . . . foreigners might have taken it into their heads to try to burn down all the schools in order to benefit financially from the earnings of their children." Legislation intended to improve the quality and duration of children's education faced widespread hostility among the immigrant population, and it is possible that there were actually dozens of culprits in the school fires, a popular outbreak of incendiarism giving voice to working-class frustrations.[5] Whatever its source, the arson campaign eventually died down and the area returned to a more customary rate of school burning, for more customary reasons. A few years later, a pair of local ten-year-olds doused their school with gasoline and set it ablaze. "The school term was too long," they complained, "and the weather too nice to go to school."[6]

The destruction of schools in western Pennsylvania, as well as hundreds of other cases around the country, offers new insight into the Progressive Era, a tumultuous period in which the line between political resistance, juvenile antics, and outright insanity was not always clear. Given the repeated acts of destruction that cost thousands of dollars and sometimes lives, it was perhaps natural to interpret school fires as a symptom of mental illness. During the 1890s, developments in the forensic detection of arson went hand in hand with new psychological theories of pyromania, part of a hardening pseudoscience that claimed that criminality was inborn rather than environmental and was most prevalent among the poor, immigrants, and people of color.[7] The language of mental illness predominated even in cases that seemed to call for older conceptions of evil. In 1908, for example, an unidentified perpetrator twice tried to burn down San Francisco's Mission High School while classes were in session, going so far as to arrange accelerants in the basement and to shut off the school's water supply. In Wilkes-Barre, Pennsylvania, a package filled with dynamite and steel slugs detonated on the steps of West Pittston High School. In Bath, Michigan, a disgruntled farmer detonated a time bomb under the local elementary school and killed thirty-eight children. These were not "boyish pranks," to be sure, but neither were they spontaneous outbursts of madness.[8] By obscuring proximate causes, accusations of insanity stripped the moral and political significance from acts of destruction, ascribing an air of inevitability to changes in school governance and making populist resistance to them seem misguided. Destroying a building may have sent a message to local school boards during the nineteenth century, ran the thinking, but perpetrators *had* to be crazy if they thought that it would stop the growth of school systems in the twentieth.

To some extent, that line of thinking was correct. By the end of the Progressive Era, populist attacks on schools began to wane and procedural maneuvers overtook collective violence in school politics, a byproduct of the state's newfound ability to monopolize force and manage social unrest.[9] It was during this period that centralized governance checked (what opponents perceived as) local political corruption, that architectural improvements made schools safer and healthier, and that insurance began to curb the costs of school fires. Yet these changes were neither inevitable nor as effective as reformers implied. Cities and towns were accommodating unprecedented numbers of students, vastly expanding and integrating the institutions tasked with their well-being, updating architecture and equipment, reallocating political power, and outlaying a lot of money in the process. Reactionary forces failed to stop these changes, but they continued to benefit from the deference to local control and family rights that prevailed during the nineteenth century. It was in defense of these traditions that almost every educational reform of the Progressive Era found its counterpart in acts of calculated destruction. The argument of this chapter, then, is that even in the face of rapidly changing norms, property violence remained the means for adults and children to assert their interests in school politics, a process that would continue into the 1950s. Politics provided tinder for school fires, which became visible representations of a smoldering society.

Social Change, School Reform, and Grassroots Resistance

During the Progressive Era, public education became the means to cope with all sorts of social changes, a decentralized but influential institution through which various organizations sought to implement their particular visions of morality, citizenship, economics, and public health. Most of these campaigns were couched in the language of child welfare and good governance, in pointed contrast to what middle-class reformers perceived as the unseemly corruption of the era's political culture. The hope was that a modern curriculum and professional administration—embodied in up-to-date school buildings—would do away with the social strife of the nineteenth century, improving educational outcomes for children and the operation of US society as a whole. As we shall see, however, schools remained trapped in political conflict, and vandalism remained a common recourse for opponents of reform.

One of the most dramatic changes confronting schools was the new wave of foreign and domestic migration. Arrivals from Southern and Eastern Europe reached their peak between 1870 and 1920, when millions of newcomers disembarked on American shores and up to 15 percent of the nation was foreign born.[10] Assimilating these immigrants and their children prompted an emphasis on Americanization and displays of civic pride in the schools, such as the newly composed Pledge of Allegiance and the celebration of the "cultural gifts" that each nationality brought with it.[11] Nevertheless, religious and ethnic rivalries remained a point of discord, and property damage was a popular way to remind outsiders of their tenuous social status. Anti-Catholic sentiment led to sporadic attacks on parish schools, while the Protestant bent of the public schools continued to stoke acts of Catholic vandalism.[12] A wave of xenophobia following World War I led to the defacement or destruction of several German-language schools, as well as those serving children of Japanese, Jewish, and Mexican descent.[13]

Property damage came from the other direction as well. The distance between school administrators and ethnic communities fueled a general suspicion of the school's intentions toward immigrant children, which often sparked riots. Without an active hand in school operations—and finding their cultures denigrated by some teachers and textbooks—immigrant parents were understandably leery about their children's safety in the classroom.[14] On multiple occasions, crowds of Italian mothers descended on schools in New York and Chicago, breaking down doors, fences, and windows to retrieve their children after hearing rumors that the Mafia planned to dynamite the buildings.[15] Similar rumors agitated parents from other ethnic enclaves. In 1907, a number of Jewish students in New York City had enlarged adenoids, a condition that doctors falsely associated with mental retardation. In the name of public health, one principal set up an operating theater in his school and proposed to remove the growths without parental consent. Parents besieged the school for days, knocking down doors because they thought their children's throats were being cut.[16] School leaders portrayed these as incidents of mass hysteria, but they are better interpreted as a bid for parents' rights in the face of new regimes of expertise and professional administration.

Domestic migration caused new strains as well, as African Americans fled racist violence in the South and pursued opportunities in the Northeast and Midwest. The decades between the 1890s and the 1910s are often described as the nadir of US race relations, with a rash of lynchings, "race riots" (a euphemism for violence against Black communities), and somewhere between three and ten African American school burnings every year. Many of the latter incidents resulted from the so-called "Exoduster" migration, in which Black farmers moved into states like Missouri, Arkansas, and Oklahoma, as well as into new settlements in southern Florida.[17] In these areas, the expansion of African American schooling remained very much a contested issue. Drawing from older traditions of populist violence, there was a presumption that burning down schools might inhibit the arrival of Black families into previously white towns.[18] The grisly violence of race hatred could affect white schools, too, albeit indirectly. In one case, a Missouri lynch mob chained a man to the roof of the building where he had allegedly raped a teacher and burned the structure down.[19] Another white school, in Oklahoma, was dynamited, injuring dozens of attendees, when a group of African American students used the space to stage a concert.[20]

The race question took on new dimensions in Northern states, which had adopted ostensibly nondiscriminatory procedures for public education during the latter half of the nineteenth century.[21] While in practice African American students remained segregated in underfunded and overcrowded schools, machine politics and ward-based school boards allowed Black communities a degree of patronage similar to that of other ethnic groups, with some influence over policy and an allotment of teaching and janitorial jobs.[22] Administrative reforms tested these arrangements with increasingly centralized systems of governance, including consolidated school boards and professional oversight of pupil placement and teacher hiring and promotion. Citywide school boards were less responsive to Black political demands, and new teaching qualifications allowed districts to selectively and systematically deny employment to African American teachers.

All of this inhibited the development of a Black professional class and hurt the quality of education for Black students.[23]

Whether parents would accept these shifts was unclear, and some used property damage to defend their interests. For example, when Sheffield, Massachusetts, opened a segregated school for Black pupils in 1903, there was resigned acceptance. When the school board subsequently replaced the school's African American teacher with a white woman, however, it not only stigmatized the students but denied the community a modicum of self-determination. Angry parents immediately sent their children back to the town's integrated school. When ordered to stop, they burned the segregated school down, leaving integration as the only option. Similar incidents occurred in towns and cities across the North.[24]

If new administrative arrangements at times seemed to perpetuate a high-handed racism, they also had the potential for color-blind application, opening professional opportunities for Black educators and a means for civil rights activists to push for student integration. It was the very prospect of professional rather than political decision-making that worried Northern whites, who insisted on strict racial boundaries despite the lack of legal segregation. Threats to the color line frequently sparked racist violence, which not only hurt children but damaged school buildings.[25] To take one example, when a Chicago school brought in an African American teacher in 1920, white students stormed out of the classroom to pelt the building with mud and rocks.[26] The toll of racial strife in Northern and Southern schools will be discussed in greater detail in subsequent chapters, but it is important to underscore here that centralized administration did not resolve racial tensions, and that when districts failed to uphold structural inequalities, white residents often resorted to violence against persons and property.

Changes to school governance angered taxpayers as well as parents and students. Across the country, local tax revenues for education rose from just over $100 million a year in 1890 to $1.7 billion by 1930, while state subsidies increased from $27 million to over $353 million during the same period. These funds fueled a massive expansion of educational infrastructure.[27] In rural areas, the closure of one-room schoolhouses and the construction of consolidated schools was especially divisive. As late as 1915, over two hundred thousand single-teacher schools remained in operation. When these were not burning down over the usual disputes about corporal punishment, teacher selection, political representation, and school location, they faced the threat of forced closure by the state.[28] Legislatures worried about high rates of illiteracy and malnutrition in rural areas and, hoping to impose systems of school administration that had worked in cities, began punishing districts that lacked adequate tax bases or amenities such as indoor plumbing, while increasing subsidies for those that operated larger, age-graded schools.[29] These inducements confronted rural communities with hard choices. There were heated debates about whether to remodel old schools or to build new ones, and residents frequently questioned the cost of it all. Proponents of consolidation promised that state aid and economies of scale would lower the tax burden for property owners, but that was often not the case.[30] Bad feelings led dozens of new schools to burn down in the wake of district consolidation.[31] In Algona, Iowa, in 1915, the building touted as the state's "model rural consolidated school" was found smoldering a week after its construction, its emergency water supply drained ahead of time.[32] "Spiteful persons" placed seven sticks of dynamite beneath a consolidated school in Middletown, New York, though they did not explode.[33] Meanwhile, the deadly bombing in Bath, Michigan, came after the foreclosure of the perpetrator's farm, which he blamed on the construction of the consolidated elementary school and an attendant tax hike.[34]

High school construction stoked similar resentments, in rural areas and in cities. Between 1890 and 1930, an average of one new high school appeared every day in the United States.[35] Enrollment rates increased by a factor of ten over the same period, and graduation rates shot up from 3.5 percent to 29 percent, prompting weighty discussions about the institution's clientele and purpose.[36] Here, too, issues of cost overlapped with questions of access and local control. Secondary education remained out of reach for most American children and seemed of little use to those pursuing manual labor, yet high schools were far more expensive to build and maintain than elementary schools, leading to objections on egalitarian grounds. Explosives became one way to express those objections. In April 1896, dynamite tore through the high school in Saginaw, Michigan, following a dispute over the local millage rate.[37] An even larger charge destroyed a high school in Mayfield, Ohio, in 1922.[38] Authorities in Coytesville, New Jersey, found dynamite placed under a building whose construction had been the subject of "considerable agitation" in the community—one of several cases in which undetonated explosives were found in walls or basements—while, as usual, a slew of suspicious fires broke out across the country.[39]

Vandalism as Childhood Resentment and Resistance

Damage to elementary and high schools was the result not only of antitax sentiment but of newly enforced attendance laws. Between 1890 and 1930, the average school term increased by thirty-seven days a year, and the daily attendance rate jumped from 64 percent to 83 percent of enrolled children.[40] As we saw with the arson campaign in Pittsburgh that opened this chapter, efforts to end child labor

FIGURE 2.1. In 1927, a disgruntled farmer dynamited the consolidated elementary school in Bath, Michigan, killing thirty-eight children. Courtesy of the *Lansing State Journal*, USA TODAY Network.

were unpopular with immigrant and working-class parents, who stood to lose income, and frequently led to vigilante violence against school buildings.[41] By keeping children in school longer, compulsory attendance also created a class of adolescents who were potentially more destructive than younger children had been, as well as a peer culture that encouraged reckless behavior and pranks.[42]

It would be a mistake, however, to attribute acts of arson solely to exuberant immaturity. In an era of public demonstrations and partisan rancor, children also engaged in property destruction as a form of political protest. For example, following the presidential inauguration of 1897, a high school in Paterson, New Jersey, hung placards with the names "McKinley and Hobart" to honor Garret Hobart, the vice president and a Paterson native. That weekend, students broke into the building and ransacked its classrooms. Over the presidential placards, they scrawled, "We are Bryan men," referring to William Jennings Bryan, the Democratic candidate popular with immigrant, working-class, and anti-Prohibition voters.[43] In 1914, New York City switched some of its schools to the Gary system, a method of more efficiently utilizing school facilities for work and study, which critics associated with industrialism and (damningly) with German influence. Angry boys on the Upper East Side smashed over one hundred windows at their school rather than submit to such regimentation and marched to Central Park for a rally with socialist agitators. The window breaking brought out a negotiator from the central administration. "His advice was greeted with hoots and derisive cries," noted a reporter, and "the boys renewed their efforts to destroy the school property." When the police began to make arrests, a schoolwide strike broke out, with students carrying banners reading, "Down with the Gary System!" and "Can the Kaiser!" Some made signs for Morris Hillquit, the Socialist Party's candidate for mayor.[44] Meanwhile, in Elmsford, New York, students reacted to the dismissal of a popular principal with tactics they "had picked up from the labor and suffrage demonstrations": they besieged a board of education meeting, smashing windows and doors, before marching to the school, breaking the door down, and ringing the bell to call off classes.[45] Five boys demolished a high school in Medford, Oregon, in support of several teachers who had been fired.[46] Other students rioted when forced to sing patriotic songs, and wrecked cafeterias whose food they considered unsanitary or unappetizing.[47] In each of these examples, we see students using vandalism as an open and self-consciously political form of protest, responding to issues that ranged from local to national importance.

Some children used more clandestine forms of property destruction to assert their rights. While the first decades of the twentieth century are often associated with child-centered teaching, it was also an era in which schools became increasingly coercive—and at times totalizing—educational environments.

Authorities subjected children to harsh discipline and, if they stayed away or refused to submit, could ensnare them in a dragnet of social workers, truancy officers, children's courts, and juvenile detention halls. For children used to work or the freedom of the streets, these measures called for active resistance.[48] Students often lit fires to revenge themselves on strict teachers. In California, a boy swore to "get even" after being whipped by a teacher, leading him to burn not only his own school but two others to boot.[49] In New Jersey, vandals splintered walls, desks, and the school organ with an axe to send a message to an overly harsh principal.[50] Students also exacted revenge for academic failures. One boy incinerated student records when he was not promoted to the next grade level.[51] Dozens of others burned buildings down after failing exams, growing "displeased with their grades," or being expelled.[52] Whatever their particular reasons, they were dogged in these attempts. In 1916, children in Oregon burned down their school and, told to meet in a local church, burned that down as well.[53] A boy in Massachusetts destroyed his schoolhouse twice over a period of four years because "he did not like school," and it was not uncommon for children to light three, four, or five blazes before being caught.[54]

Student resistance became more frequent and was interpreted in the most explicitly pathological terms as the surroundings became more restrictive. Male and female inmates set dozens of serious fires in penal institutions from the 1860s, when the first reformatories appeared, to the 1920s, when almost every state operated a system of juvenile corrections.[55] These flare-ups have informed a particular strand of critical scholarship, which interprets prisons as archetypes for the disciplinary power of the school system writ large, and incendiarism as a signal of racial, gender, or working-class resistance.[56] In *The Irony of Early School Reform* (1968), for example, Michael Katz uses a fire at the Westborough, Massachusetts, industrial school to critique the punitive aspects of state welfare agencies, which could incarcerate children until they reached adulthood for crimes as vague as "stubbornness."[57] In *Bad Girls at Samarcand* (2016), Karin Zipf likewise cites fire as a protest against the inhumane treatment of female inmates in a North Carolina institution. In both cases, children quite reasonably concluded that arson charges would get them transferred to the comparative comfort of adult prisons. "I thought that if I set it on fire they would send me out," one of the North Carolina girls confessed. "I was tired of that place." Unfortunately, the overseers at Samarcand made their own use of the fires, which, according to Zipf, allowed them "to jettison Victorian models of reform and to formulate new eugenics-based classification policies." Casting the female arsonists as mentally unstable, the school directors nominated them as the first candidates in the state for forced sterilization, an outcome the girls had not bargained for. Here again, madness became a slippery and cynically useful criterion for the expansion of government power over children's bodies.[58]

The same dynamics played out at American Indian schools, which were growing rapidly at the turn of the century. Fires occasionally broke out at reservation schools but were especially prevalent at the more remote boarding schools, where arson was a regular occurrence. Long overlooked by historians, the latter institutions have recently attracted attention for their use of surveillance, punishment, and manual labor to strip native students of their culture and prepare them for participation in a market economy.[59] This "civilizing" process was implicit in the education of other minority groups and in some ways in public education writ large, but the terms were especially harsh for Indian students, who were forbidden to speak their native languages, subjected to military standards of dress and grooming, and denied contact with their families. Native children engaged in passive forms of resistance, such as running away, as well as more direct forms of sabotage. Students set fires at the Flandreau Indian School, in South Dakota; the Albuquerque Indian School, in New Mexico; the Creek missionary schools, in Oklahoma; the Friends Indian Asylum at Steamburg; and the federal boarding school at Carlisle, Pennsylvania.[60] The Winnebago Reservation, in Nebraska, suffered four school fires in three months before authorities caught the culprit.[61] Lizzie Cardich, a fifteen-year-old Menominee girl facing life in prison for burning down the reservation school outside Shawano, Wisconsin, wrote a personal appeal to President Theodore Roosevelt, whom she had met during a visit to the area. He commuted her sentence.[62]

One problem with all this wrecking was its asymmetrical nature. What were schools supposed to do when any sullen ten-year-old could inflict thousands of dollars of damage with items he brought from home? And worse, what if those items were of unprecedented destructive power? Wastebasket fires were one thing, but by the turn of the century, children had access to kerosene and other refined fuels, as well as to dynamite, which had become a standard tool in demolition.[63] One can imagine the sickening realization of a family in New Mexico when their dog ran into the living room with a stick of dynamite in his mouth. A quick investigation discovered that schoolchildren had stolen a large quantity of explosives from a local warehouse. Their plan, they confessed, was "to blow up all the school houses in the city so they would not have to go to school any more."[64] A number of similar plots were foiled before they came off.[65] During the demobilization after World War I, boys in Brooklyn secured surplus gunpowder, which they packed in jars and exploded in their classroom.[66] A gang in Pennsylvania stole dynamite from a quarry and partially demolished their elementary school, complaining that "vacation [had] not been long enough." As technological advances concentrated explosive force, it was unclear what anyone could do to stop such incidents.[67]

Also troubling was children's seemingly casual capacity for anarchy. It was not just the brutal conditions of reform schools that impelled students to arson, nor was it only the buildings that Upton Sinclair described as "dark, unsanitary fire-traps" that suffered its effects.[68] Even the modern classrooms that reformers thought would inhibit school vandalism often fell victim to it. Indeed, the very amenities that common-school advocates had extolled as preventives—the spatial manifestations of order, professionalism, hygiene, and student interest—could prompt new forms of destruction. Age-graded classrooms encouraged specialized instruction and established teachers' authority by breaking sight lines within the school, but just as teachers closed hallway doors on the prying eyes of the principal, they created isolated environments for misbehavior.[69] To take one example, reformers recommended adding coatrooms to classrooms so that students could hang up their personal effects, clearing the aisles of clutter. They cautioned that these rooms should "not open into corridors but only into the classroom," giving "the teacher full control of classroom and wardrobe at all times." Apparently such control was lacking, as coatrooms became the most frequent site of fire setting.[70] Modern ventilation systems were more hygienic than the stuffy and drafty schools of years before, but students regularly filled air shafts with scrap paper and dropped in matches.[71] Faulty flues gave way to more efficient gas furnaces, which were usually housed in the basement next to flammable rags and the cans of oil and turpentine with which janitors lacquered the floors.[72] Curricular changes gave children access to stoves, lab apparatus, chemical compounds, gas jets, athletic equipment, industrial machinery, and canisters of flammable film. These were the schools of tomorrow. What could possibly go wrong?[73]

Fire Insurance and the Protection of Public Property

We should pause a moment to note that vandals were not responsible for all catastrophic losses of school property. Careless construction, human error, overcrowding, and poor zoning were the sources of many conflagrations, and together with intentional acts of wreckage they were regularly denounced by progressive school reformers.[74] Whether these incidents were accidental or intentional, their cost led to a search for solutions, especially the possibility of private insurance to safeguard public property.[75]

Historians often use insurance as a stand-in for broader political and economic changes during the early twentieth century, arguing that commodified risk was a prerequisite for modern capitalism and that, in more subtle ways, it restructured social and political arrangements.[76] On the positive side, Deborah Stone argues that shared liability constituted a form of "moral opportunity." "To participate in a risk-pooling scheme is to agree to tax yourself not only for your own benefit should you incur a loss," she observes, "but also for the benefit of others who might suffer from loss when you do not." Thus, insurance built civic capacity by expanding the "number and kinds of events that we consider adverse and worthy of collective responsibility," drawing individuals out of isolation to subsidize their neighbors' undertakings.[77] On the other hand, critical scholars point out that those individuals were drawn into a surreptitious disciplinary system, operating beneath or behind public authority, that routinized social life and circumscribed nonnormative behavior. Actuarial techniques replaced punishment or moral sanction with subtler forms of coercion (such as penalties for "unhealthy" lifestyles), encouraged individuals to bear their own surveillance, reorganized social relations along lines of predictability, and ultimately left private interests to determine acceptable levels of risk and the makeup of protected classes. While these are valid criticisms, one should not overstate the industry's disciplinary power. For even as insurance shifted social control from elected politicians to corporations and administrative agencies, basic regulatory questions remained contentious and unavoidably political.[78]

The relationship between private insurers and public oversight comes to the fore when applied to institutions like schools. In her book on state educational policy, Tracy Steffes argues that the immense scale of school reform during the Progressive Era was possible precisely because it occurred through decentralized and largely voluntary channels. Rather than imposing oversight from above, successful reforms secured support from local school boards and private interests before any attempt was made at statewide enforcement.[79] Insurance spread along similar lines, providing a voluntary, quasi-private means of handling property damage while at the same time encouraging rational management of school finances and laying the groundwork for subsequent safety regulations. Like other aspects of school reform, it developed at similar times and in similar ways across the country, popularized by the same network of professional conferences and journals. Without much state oversight, however, school property insurance also remained hobbled by market imperfections and public apathy, and its benefits took much longer to realize than reformers hoped.

Until the turn of the twentieth century, the market for public property insurance remained too small to attract serious attention from school boards, state governments, or scholars, and although the number and value of school buildings dramatically increased financial liability, difficult decisions remained unresolved.[80] For example, how likely were fires, and how much insurance was appropriate? Should school boards purchase policies from corporations, or simply hold some money in reserve and rely on taxpayers to raise funds in cases of emergency? Should they incorporate expensive but potentially cost- and life-saving technologies when building or renovating schools? Most importantly, should these decisions be made ad hoc by local officials, dictated by prices on the private market, or settled through state regulation? All of these questions touched on the issues of efficiency and rationalization that defined the Progressive Era, but, unlike other reforms, they did not yield a clear resolution until decades later, leaving the efficacy of public insurance, and the best methods for its provision, somewhat ambiguous.

Risk assessment was fairly simple during the nineteenth century. Schools were rated by the same criteria as factories or warehouses, usually based on the materials of their construction, their type of roof, and whether there were hazardous goods stored on the premises. Most insurance companies remained undercapitalized and unable to cover major losses, and most school boards carried little to no insurance. During the early 1900s, private insurers made several changes to expand the market. First, they encouraged higher amounts of coverage through coinsurance clauses. Whereas school boards had previously insured buildings for only a fraction of their value—forcing insurers to absorb small claims while leaving school boards responsible for catastrophic events—coinsurance offered discounts for higher levels of coverage and split the risk for lower amounts with the policyholder, making small claims less remunerative. Insurers also introduced schedule ratings, in which buildings received credits and penalties based on access to hydrants, fire department protection, and other safety features. This development met some resistance within the industry, as it moved away from the mathematical surety of actuarial tables, but it lessened scrutiny from state regulators, who viewed actuarial data as a form of rate fixing and demanded greater transparency in pricing.[81] Schedule ratings also allowed industrial associations such as the National Board of Fire Underwriters (NBFU, founded in 1886) and the National Fire Protection Association (NFPA, founded in 1896) to forge new relationships with policyholders, who were encouraged to upgrade their structures, and with state and municipal governments, whom they lobbied to improve safety infrastructure and building codes. To heighten public awareness, the NBFU and NFPA began to publicize fire statistics, including pamphlets about school fires, and in 1911 they inaugurated National Fire Prevention Day, which was observed in schools nationwide.[82] By all accounts, these changes induced more school boards to carry private insurance and to do so at higher amounts, allowing insurers to achieve economies of scale as larger pools of policyholders spread risk more evenly. They also lowered insurers' exposure at the expense of taxpayers.[83]

FIGURE 2.2.   School fires were frequent and deadly during the early twentieth century, and resulted in campaigns for safety features and fire insurance. *School Board Journal*, December 1907.

Nevertheless, adoption remained inconsistent, an annoyance for those hoping to standardize school administration. By the turn of the century, the *American School Board Journal* ran a regular column called "Recent Schoolhouse Fires" to encourage better insurance management among its members.[84] The hundreds of incidents described in these columns speak to rising building costs around the country: from an average of $500 to $2,000 in the late nineteenth century, a 1920 survey found that almost half of school fires yielded damages between $10,000 and $100,000 and another 20 percent between $100,000 and $1,000,000. They also revealed a roller coaster of coverage, ranging from unprotected buildings to those insured above their actual value.[85] Given the rising costs of school construction and the increasingly scientific management of both education and insurance, what accounted for such a haphazard distribution?

Why school boards went without insurance was no mystery. Taxes were unpopular and risk seemed remote, making insurance an extravagance, especially for elected officials who would likely be out of office by the time tragedy struck. Causes of overinsurance were more varied and perhaps less obvious. One was that districts purchased policies in standard, five-year terms but often lacked the foresight to add them or allow them to lapse strategically, causing budgets to vary widely year to year and creating redundancies in coverage.[86] Also, perhaps unsurprisingly, as insurance payments siphoned public funds into the private sector, conflicts of interest arose between school boards and agents. Board members frequently took positions in the insurance industry after leaving office and sold coverage back to their colleagues. More brazenly, some wrote policies while serving on the school board themselves, an illegal practice that took a while to expose and correct.[87] States had to crack down on other questionable practices as well, such as boards borrowing money against inflated insurance policies or using payouts for purposes other than repairing schools, the sort of "moral hazards" common to immature markets. Many districts veered toward under- or overinsurance because of a lack of public scrutiny and poor industry standards.[88]

Another reason for uneven coverage was the shifting relationship between insurance premiums and safety measures in schools. Reformers had hoped that these factors would be mutually reinforcing. Insurance companies had an interest in fire prevention, and if they lowered rates for schools with fire escapes, wired-glass windows, or cinder-block walls, reformers assumed, price signals would impel districts to upgrade their buildings accordingly. Unfortunately, such improvements could still be costly, and while several studies proved that they did lower losses, that was not always a winning political argument.[89] Some districts faced pressure to build several cheap schools rather than fewer safe ones, or to wait and add safety features only when building new structures. Without a legal mandate to carry insurance, they could always drop their coverage rather than pay rising rates.[90] Nor did rates necessarily reflect buildings' actual risk. Even districts that upgraded found that "loose methods" of assessment did not pass along savings, an oversight that systematically favored the insurance industry.[91] In most cases, insurance companies needed to maintain loss ratios below 50 percent—that is, they had to pay out less than half the money they collected in premiums in order to stay profitable. As fireproofing technologies spread, loss ratios plummeted and profits rose.[92] It was not uncommon for a given school district to find that it had only $2,000 in losses over a decade, while it paid approximately $30,000 in premiums, a paltry 6.7 percent return on investment.[93] Statewide findings were less dramatic—average returns in New York and

Pennsylvania between 1925 and 1935 were both about 36 percent—and of course there was no objective measure of how profitable insurance should be in the first place, but improved safety measures did not lower premiums enough to satisfy the public. Many school boards began to question why safer structures needed insurance at all.[94]

Corrections to overcoverage and rate inflation began to appear during the 1910s and 1920s, when urban districts assumed more of their own liability, taking out smaller policies or moving entirely to self-insurance. In theory, cities could spread risk evenly between their buildings and simply absorb losses as operating expenses. Again, however, there was no consensus on how big a district had to be to do so or on how much private coverage was appropriate, and these judgments were determined as much by politics as by the mandates of mathematics or the market.[95] In 1913, Buffalo, New York, allowed insurance to decrease to only a quarter of its buildings' total value, which experts claimed was far too low and merely pandered to taxpayers. The costly incineration of a high school the following year seemed to bear out their concerns.[96] On the other hand, Des Moines, Iowa, required a concerted political campaign to drop its private coverage, despite ample evidence of waste. Suspicious of their colleagues' cozy relationship with insurance agents, a few board members hired their own appraiser to recalculate credits for safety features, publicized the district's low return on its annual premiums, and proposed a self-insurance plan that would save $5,000 a year, which eventually passed.[97] Omaha, Nebraska, kept its private fire insurance but shifted from a "general blanket form" to a more refined model, in which it assessed each building individually and capped the amount awarded to any one company. Actions like these were school districts' first attempts to bring the insurance industry to heel.[98]

The buildings least likely to carry adequate insurance were rural schoolhouses. With wooden construction and no access to municipal fire hydrants, these structures regularly fell into the high-risk pool, with costs at or above ten mills—that is, premiums of at least $1.00 and as high as $3.50 for every $100 of coverage. Most of these structures were worth only a few thousand dollars to begin with, so costs were low in absolute terms, but they were enough to dissuade board members from taking out policies, which, in turn, gave companies little incentive to lower rates, even as industry watchdogs put their profits at nearly 80 percent. "Insurance companies have failed to adjust their rates in relation to losses," observers complained, but unlike urban areas, rural districts were too small to self-insure. Instead, as with power utilities, telephone service, and many other industries, the development of rural school insurance seemed to require state intervention.[99] In 1903, Wisconsin became the first state to allow rural school boards to form mutual insurance companies, in which members pooled their cash reserves and split their losses. Based on the model of cooperative farm insurance, these companies had to meet certain minimum requirements—in this case, twenty-five districts participating and at least $250,000 in insured assets—after which they could be recognized by the state insurance commissioner.[100] But there were some legal questions about the arrangement. Several states argued that the cooperative loss structure made the financial liabilities of individual districts less clear and, without fixed premiums, structured the policy like an indeterminate loan, which violated public accounting laws. Other states, particularly in the Midwest, approved the model and succeeded in driving down overhead costs.[101]

Protection for rural schoolhouses also became the impetus for the first state-issued insurance policies. "If insurance companies will not initiate a study of their losses on public schools with a view to reduction of rates," wrote one critic, "the question arises, 'Shall the state take over the insurance on public school property?'"[102] The answer was yes, but slowly and incompletely. Wisconsin was also the first state to create a public insurance fund, which it opened to school districts in 1913. With rates half as high as those offered on the private market, one would think that state insurance was a natural choice for rural (and perhaps all) public schools. Yet similar initiatives failed to pass other state legislatures. By 1930, only North Dakota and South Carolina provided comparable insurance pools, and South Carolina alone required participation.[103] Many Wisconsin school boards exercised their right to refuse coverage, and as late as 1966 the state insured fewer than half of its 572 school districts. Rural schools remained an acute problem and in some ways symbolized larger challenges facing school insurance: their unprofitability confounded the private market, while their parsimony and insistence on local control weakened public provisions. Without requiring insurance coverage, neither model could work.[104]

Local intransigence also slowed the development of fireproof building standards. Because insurance premiums alone were unable to ensure safety measures in schools, advocates turned to government regulation. In 1913, the NFPA released its first Safety Code, a regularly revised template for state and municipal governments to craft fire safety legislation.[105] Until then, there had been little action at the state level: only Ohio, Connecticut, and Massachusetts had laws requiring up-to-date fireproofing in schools, and only sixteen states exercised any meaningful oversight of building plans. In the words of one critic, twenty-two others had "no laws or regulations whatever to prevent school buildings being built as crematories."[106] There was some hope that if cities adopted stringent fire codes and imposed them on their schools, fireproof construction would gradually extend to rural districts, as had so many other school reforms. Yet here, too, the decentralized model hit a snag, for cities and states differed in their handling of the issue.[107]

Fire codes raised unexpected questions about the state's ability to regulate public health and safety. Municipal governments and school boards were both "creatures of the state," subordinate to legislatures, but what was their relationship to each other? Were schools bound by city ordinances, or as state property were they exempt? State courts were unsure how to answer these questions. Some found that cities *could* regulate school safety measures, reasoning that public health was the reigning principle.[108] Others took a less pragmatic, more formal position, arguing that "the State will not be presumed to have waived its right to regulate its own property, by ceding to the city the right generally to pass ordinances of a police nature," and that any upgrade of school construction required statewide legislation.[109]

This legal ambiguity slowed the adoption of fire prevention, which proceeded fitfully and usually responded to particularly devastating events. In 1908, a fire in Collinwood, Ohio—perhaps started by girls playing with matches—killed 167 students and teachers and led to a flurry of new regulations regarding fire escapes and evacuation drills.[110] A gas explosion in a Texas schoolhouse in 1937 killed almost 300 people and changed regulations for the installation and management of fuel systems. Finally, in 1958, a fire struck Our Lady of the Angels, a Catholic school in Chicago, killing 92. A ten-year-old boy confessed to starting the blaze, though he later recanted his testimony.[111] The latter catastrophe revealed that Chicago's schools still operated under an outdated fire code and were not subject to regular inspections, and quickly led to legislation and safety upgrades around the country. Our Lady of the Angels became the last school fire to claim more than ten lives, but it underscores that as late as 1960, fire prevention remained ad hoc and subject to political inertia. In its aftermath, the State of Illinois immediately passed a revised version of the NFPA's Safety Code but, perversely, it exempted the City of Chicago and did not enforce compliance by parochial schools. Thus, the campaign to ensure the safety and structural integrity of schools, begun in the 1890s, featured an exceptionally long and incomplete epilogue.[112]

Reforms at the turn of the twentieth century profoundly reshaped American schooling. By the 1920s, all states could boast bona fide systems of public education, with increased tax subsidies, consolidated school boards, state and county superintendents, and increasingly stringent administrative requirements. Teachers were better trained, and with the enforcement of truancy laws, students remained in school longer. Urban schools began to offer wider curricular programs, with opportunities for manual training, home economics, and physical education, as well as a range of medical and social services. Although these changes incited a backlash from farmers, immigrants, taxpayers, and schoolchildren themselves, frequently taking the form of vandalism or arson, the ideological coherence of reform, coupled with concessions to localism and public sentiment, blunted potential resistance. A coalition of "schoolmen," grassroots reformers, and business interests successfully equated the new regime with progress and its opponents with backwardness and irrationality. Vandalism had never been fully sanctioned, of course, but as systemization subordinated violence to smoother, structural forms of opportunity and inequality, destruction lost whatever legitimacy it once had. Burning a school evolved from an expression of the people's will to a mere spasm of extremism, madness, or delinquency.

The same groups promoting the rationalization of school governance also worked to mitigate the effects of property damage. Administrators and school board associations cooperated with the insurance industry to promote safe construction and to limit liability through shared risk. These initiatives, too, required deference to local policymakers and took longer than expected, but by the middle of the twentieth century their combined effects yielded results: state and municipal fire codes made schools significantly safer.

During the 1920s, insurers began to quantify and categorize the destruction of school buildings. Between forty and ninety fires were reported each year between 1925 and 1935, with annual losses ranging from $5 to $10 million. Analysis from multiple surveys—encompassing over two thousand incidents—found only 7.8 percent of fires to be intentional, although primitive investigative techniques had difficulty distinguishing between accidents and arson, and without a central clearinghouse it is likely that hundreds of cases went unreported.[113] Whether or not these studies represent a reliable baseline, they soon identified an unsettling trend. As the incidence of fatal fires was decreasing across the country, the rates of arson seemed to be rising precipitously. Between the 1940s and the mid-1950s, there were about three thousand school fires a year, with 12.6 percent attributed to arson. Between 1957 and 1964, that number jumped to 32.5 percent. By the early 1970s, there were upward of twenty thousand fires a year, causing at least $100 million worth of damage, and 76 percent were set intentionally. Some of this growth in absolute numbers is attributable to increased enrollment and improved reporting, and the higher percentages may reflect the concurrent decline of accidental fires. Yet these statistics clearly contradicted the idea that modernization would diminish destruction in schools. To the contrary, it seems merely to have shifted the demographics of the perpetrators, from a motley collection of malcontents to a more discrete class of juvenile delinquents, confined to the classroom and eager to wreak havoc.[114]

The next two chapters will examine the rising tide of adolescent rebellion as contemporaries understood it. Although their appraisals were often ahistorical, built on memories of compliant children and wholesome communities, which we have seen to be baseless, the challenges they confronted were real and required original solutions. As a result, many of the psychological diagnoses, disciplinary techniques, and governmental structures that emerged during the Progressive Era dramatically evolved or expanded during the mid-twentieth century. The norms of schooling shifted, but property destruction remained depressingly constant.

DIAGNOSING DELINQUENCY, 1930–60

The middle decades of the twentieth century mark an important turning point in the history of school property destruction. The economic depression that gripped the United States between the 1920s and the 1940s dried up the market for child labor, pushing more young people into school and keeping them there for longer periods of time. Delayed entry into the workforce established adolescence as a distinct stage of childhood, a period in which legitimacy in the eyes of one's peers became separate from (and often oppositional to) the approval of adults. For their part, parents, teachers, and taxpayers were mystified and increasingly alarmed by the behavior of schoolchildren. It was during this era that school vandalism became associated exclusively with youth, and when it seemed to become a national rather than a strictly local problem.[1] The result was new categories through which to understand misbehavior and new institutions through which to respond. Economic crisis prompted expansion at all levels of government, with local, state, and federal programs for youth employment and recreation on one hand, and on the other a disciplinary apparatus of welfare agencies, psychiatric clinics, and juvenile courts and detention. These institutions were already dogged by many forms of racial and economic inequality, but in contrast to later decades, antivandalism policies remained largely preventive and rehabilitative rather than punitive, speaking to the era's uniquely liberal faith in education and professionalism.

This chapter describes the inadequacy of those policies, which failed to curb school vandalism, and the shallowness of that faith. The problem was not only that liberal politicians sought to address destructive behavior without radically altering social arrangements (a common critique), but that the theoretical accounts available to them did much the same thing. Rather than interpret vandalism either as a function of unequal political and economic structures or as a normal aspect of child development, sociologists and psychologists described it as a disorder in an otherwise sound system, a pathology to be isolated, diagnosed, and treated. The underlying assumption was that vandalism was a unitary problem, susceptible to targeted intervention, when in fact scholars from different fields were often perceiving fundamentally different phenomena. The following sections outline common approaches to prevention and restitution during the mid-twentieth century, which they contextualize within broader theories of juvenile delinquency. While it is difficult to establish causal connections between theory and practice—to prove that policymakers were unable to control vandalism simply because experts were unable to define it, or to imagine a counterfactual in which a different research paradigm yielded radically different policies—the chapter argues that both were limited by the same ideological assumptions, a liberal worldview whose failure would shape educational policy for decades to come.

Preventive and Rehabilitative Responses to Vandalism

It is difficult to overstate the effects of the Great Depression on US education.[2] As the economic downturn decimated local tax bases, districts struggled to pay teachers and made do with outdated buildings and deferred maintenance, which in many areas persisted into the 1970s.[3] Fears of encroachment prevented the federal government from funding local districts directly, although policymakers managed to distribute resources through other channels. For instance, the Works Progress Administration, the New Deal's largest public-works program, renovated school buildings and built athletic fields, auditoriums, and classrooms that districts would otherwise have been unable to afford. By 1943, the agency had constructed more than 5,900 schools, put additions on another 2,170, and renovated or modernized 31,000 more.[4] The National Youth Administration, which provided employment and educational opportunities to teenagers, also undertook beautification projects.[5] The federal government intended these programs to ward off radicalization by keeping young people busy. It also intended them to be temporary. As World War II put Americans back to work, sending men overseas and drawing women into wartime industries, employment programs were disbanded and many adolescents were left unsupervised.

At the same time, child labor laws increased high school enrollment and graduation rates. Whereas only 29 percent of students graduated from high school at the onset of the Depression, it was 52 percent by 1940 and 65 percent by 1960.[6] The historian William Graebner points out that suddenly "high schools were overflowing with all kinds of youths—black, the working class, second-generation immigrants—who had in the past gone directly from grade school to the workplace. Instead, they were now in the schools, rubbing shoulders, exchanging notes, and sharing their lives and subcultures with the white middle class that had always been there."[7] Much of the panic around juvenile delinquency during this period stemmed from racism and class prejudice in these newly diverse schools, but there were also reasons to believe that wartime disruptions sparked an actual increase in criminality. Juvenile court referrals jumped between 1941 and 1954, as did the number of teenagers convicted of auto theft, robbery, sex crimes, murder, and gang violence.[8]

As far as school vandalism went, the new crime wave looked much like its predecessors. Children often resorted to wreckage to assert their interests. They destroyed property to get revenge on teachers or parents, to erase academic records, to escape punishment for tardiness, to burglarize the building, or simply to alleviate boredom.[9] The types of destruction, too, were largely variations on earlier, nineteenth-century pranks: stolen school bells, desecrated flagpoles, wrecked bathrooms, wastebasket fires, dynamite explosions, chairs with the screws removed, and buildings adorned with painted messages and subversive banners.[10] There were some elements of change. For example, Halloween mischief became a national pandemic between the 1920s and the 1950s, with thousands of cases of serious destruction and injury.[11] Increased access to firearms also allowed children to shoot at school buildings, occasionally hitting classmates.[12] And although an earlier generation of students had smuggled blasting caps into the classroom, by the 1940s there was an emerging explosives market that specifically targeted teenagers with spending money. Black powder charges such as torpedoes and ashcans were joined by spherical firecrackers previously called globe salutes and now renamed "cherry bombs." Comic books and films portrayed these munitions as harmless fun; in fact, they contained as much as ten times the gunpowder as standard firecrackers and caused serious injuries and property damage before they were banned by the federal Child Safety Act of 1966.[13]

It is hard to say to what extent these antics represented a departure from previous decades, when fewer children were in school and reporting was more haphazard, but the public grew increasingly concerned about delinquency in general and school vandalism in particular. The federal government kept Americans alert to the delinquency problem—the Federal Bureau of Investigation and the Children's Bureau publicized statistics, and Senator Estes Kefauver convened congressional hearings—but it was not until the early 1960s that Congress disbursed grants-in-aid for local agencies to control youth crime. In the meantime, the response fell to individual states and localities.[14]

More than anything, it was the disjuncture between national attention and local policies that made the era's responses to vandalism so unsatisfying. Civic leaders portrayed vandalism as a threat to national security and a matter of almost metaphysical importance. Nihilistic youths were symptomatic of a broader crisis of modernity, they claimed. Mass media had penetrated the family and weakened the individual. Under the shadow of genocide, propaganda, and nuclear annihilation, the very substance of human nature seemed under attack. Just as the specter of totalitarianism demanded a renewed commitment to the "American way," it also required the "containment" of any forces that might threaten normalcy, whether international Communism, civil rights activism, homosexuality, or juvenile delinquency, all of which seemed to form a creeping tide of subversion.[15] Having stoked these fears, however, policymakers offered little reassurance besides the provision of more social services.[16] As the historian James Gilbert points out, commentators presented "a frightening picture of the status of America's youth caused principally by delinquency," but at the same time they proposed nothing but "easy—and vague—solutions," initiated not by federal agencies but by helping professions such as social work, public health, and teaching.[17]

To combat property destruction in schools, educators called for stronger community partnerships and a commitment to "democratic education"—in short, more of what they were already doing.[18] Curricular units urging respect for property appeared in social studies, language arts, mathematics, and art classes, as well as in all-school assemblies and community meetings.[19] In keeping with the topical, project-based methods of the progressive education movement, students investigated the causes of vandalism, interviewed janitors and administrators about cleanup, discussed how to maintain school facilities, surveyed their peers, graphed their findings, wrote articles for school newspapers, and signed antivandalism pledges.[20] Some districts created "vandalism accounts," which set aside money to repair property damage but disbursed remaining funds to the student council, giving students an incentive to maintain the building.[21] Educators ascribed to these interventions almost limitless potential, writing glowingly about the prophylactic effects of morning announcements, guidance counselors, vocational courses, and playgrounds.[22] Newspapers and professional journals frequently cited cases of hardcore vandals transformed into well-adjusted citizens after a single counseling session.[23] And, as they had for a century, teachers continued to assert a close relationship between children's surroundings and their behavior, arguing that "a dull, uninteresting room or building invites marking and marring much more than does a clean, attractive, well lighted building."[24]

Confronted with rowdiness and destruction, schools proposed a cheerful dose of cooperation and gentle redirection.

Restitution and Parental Liability

When positive forms of engagement failed, authorities tried to reestablish order through symbolic acts of responsibility, usually by compelling vandals to clean up or pay for the damage they caused. Restitution for minor damages had been a common practice since the nineteenth century, when boards of education scrupulously tallied the fines recouped from students, and newspapers reported settlements as small as ninety-five cents.[25] During the early twentieth century much of this enforcement shifted to juvenile courts, which could impose community service and repayment as part of a child's sentencing. By the 1950s, however, there was a growing sense that juvenile justice was too bureaucratic to be effective, and that children were often unable to reimburse the costs of their destruction.[26]

Many districts began handling the issue more directly, demanding that parents pay for the damage.[27] Doing so raised both legal and practical questions. Common law did not hold parents liable unless children acted directly at their behest, and authorities initially questioned whether they could sue families for the destruction of school property when the children were under the school's supervision.[28] During the 1950s, however, state courts began to rule in favor of districts on a statutory basis, implicating parents in their children's misbehavior and encouraging states to pass or strengthen parental liability laws.[29] In an early case, the General Insurance Company sued the parents of an eleven-year-old who had set fire to the curtains in his school auditorium, hoping to use North Carolina's new liability statute to recover some of the $3,000 that the company had paid the district. The courts upheld the legislation as a legitimate use of the state's police power, resulting in similar rulings elsewhere.[30]

Trying to squeeze money from parents exposed other legal questions as well. Consider the case of the South Dakota student who broke into his school, poured a sack of cement across the hallway, and flooded the building. The law protecting school property (like many written during the nineteenth century) indicated that parents would be liable for damage "on the complaint of the teacher." Did damage that occurred after school hours fall under the teacher's purview? The state supreme court ruled that it did not and that the parents would not have to pay, prompting many other states to review and update their statutory language.[31] Another question was whether parents could use their own insurance policies to cover the cost of vandalism, or whether (as one of "the insured") a child's intentional destruction invalidated their coverage. The California Supreme Court ruled that it did not. Reasoning that the inclusion of underage family members was meant to broaden rather than restrict coverage, the court ordered private insurance companies to assume the costs of school destruction.[32] By far the most disputed issue was the purpose and extent of parental liability. Could state law force parents to pay for potentially unlimited damage to public property? In 1959, a New Jersey district demanded almost half a million dollars from the parents of a middle-school arsonist. The parents claimed that the fine violated their due process rights, imputing responsibility for behavior that was outside their knowledge or control. The court disagreed, arguing that the state was permitted to establish guidelines for the operation of its schools and that parents implicitly accepted liability when they enrolled their children. It was unfair to shift vandalism costs from parents to taxpayers, the judges wrote, and parents unwilling to assume responsibility for their children's actions were advised to send them to private school instead.[33] The same court, however, later reversed course, noting that most parents could not afford private schools and that exorbitant fines based on nothing more than the parent-child relationship posed an unconstitutional burden. Instead, the judges recommended limited liability, intended as a penalty rather than full compensation for children's damage.[34]

But even limited liability proved legally suspect and politically ineffective. For fines to work, vandals had to be caught, parents had to have the means to pay, and penalties had to motivate them to monitor or threaten their children.[35] These were all shaky propositions. Fines could not be so onerous as to spark public backlash or simple noncompliance, and skeptics pointed out that whether it was $100 or $500, the allotted amount was "simply absurd . . . in view of cases in which thousands of dollars in damage was inflicted by youngsters."[36] Later studies found that parent restitution in urban districts offset less than 2 percent of total costs.[37] More than anything, liability laws seemed to underscore the profound asymmetry between children's capacity for destruction and adults' willingness to pay for it.[38]

It is important to point out that while liberal responses to vandalism were largely ineffective, that did not make them either neutral or benign. As numerous scholars have documented—and as we will explore further in chapter 4—ostensibly humane systems of juvenile justice were riddled with racial and class bias from the beginning, and authorities frequently detained and punished children unfairly. As midcentury high schools accommodated children who earlier might have dropped out, they systematically shunted students from marginalized groups into special classes, separate schools, or juvenile detention.[39] Nevertheless, it is noteworthy that when confronted with acts of lawlessness, both principals and politicians still tended to speak in a language of rehabilitation rather than punishment. Typical was the case of three boys who, in 1945, destroyed twenty-one classrooms in a New York City school. Asked for comment, the city's police commissioner grew thoughtful. "Once a boy or girl puts a foot on the bottom step leading to the police line-up," he said, "we have failed. That path leads almost inevitably to the penitentiary." Mayor Fiorello La Guardia agreed. "Given the opportunity under proper family surroundings and guidance," he promised, teenage vandals would not have to go to jail; no one was "beyond salvation."[40] National surveys found that while some principals favored "less coddling, stricter penalties [and] greater police protection" in their schools, the vast majority thought that "positive programs of character development" would suffice to end delinquency.[41]

Comments like these reflected a faith not merely in professionalism but in the disciplinary knowledge that underwrote professional expertise. To understand the era's response to school destruction, one must trace contemporary developments in the social sciences. What did policymakers see as the causes of vandalism, and how could understanding these causes lead to its prevention? The following sections will describe two broad explanations for destructive behavior, both of which informed disciplinary policies between the 1930s and the 1960s. One was sociological, focused on the interplay of space, demography, and group dynamics. The other was psychological, focused on children's internal conflicts and emotional development. Readers should not draw too sharp a distinction between these approaches: they often overlapped, and both struggled to effect real change, as contradictory evidence and loose terminology undermined the validity of their claims. Yet, taken together, they provided the intellectual foundation for the era's responses to school vandalism.

Sociological Theories of Destruction

During the first decades of the twentieth century, scholars interested in juvenile delinquency moved away from ascriptions of innate depravity or a physiological propensity for crime.[42] Applying techniques developed at the University of Chicago, many began to examine the relationship between space and social structures, producing the first ecological accounts of delinquency.[43] The foundational text in this area was Frederic Thrasher's *The Gang: A Study of 1,313 Gangs in Chicago* (1927).[44] Thrasher argued that neighborhoods followed predictable patterns of growth and decline, and that delinquent behavior resulted from processes of dislocation or disorganization in transitional zones.[45] According to Thrasher's reading, "purely residential and well-organized suburbs of the better type such as Oak Park and Evanston, are practically gangless, for the activities of the children are well provided for in family, school, church, and other established institutions." Youth crime was concentrated in urban neighborhoods, he argued, where migration, poverty, and anonymity undercut traditional sources of authority. In such contexts, youth gangs represented a "blind groping for order" amid a society in flux.[46] Critics have since noted the faulty assumptions underlying these claims. Like many of his contemporaries, Thrasher equated "order" with social homogeneity and "dislocation" with various forms of diversity, leading him to pathologize immigrant groups, disapprove of racial integration, and lament the eclipse of small-town institutions such as churches and schools. As we shall see in chapter 4, the same sort of structural explanations—with the same judgmental overtones—would shape policy discussions of vandalism for the remainder of the twentieth century.[47]

In the short term, however, and at the level of individual districts, Thrasher's greatest impact came not from his broad theoretical conclusions but from his street-level ethnographies. Interviewing hundreds of boys, Thrasher found that most gangs emerged from neighborhood play groups that had "integrated through conflict"; that is, they developed self-consciousness and organization by fighting rivals for territory or access to public amenities, and progressed from youthful pranks to vandalism and more serious offenses.[48]

Thrasher suggested two ways to interrupt this process. The first was to provide playgrounds and wholesome recreation, which would satisfy boys' need for excitement and prevent their energies from being misdirected.[49] Policymakers took up this proposal with gusto, probably because it was already familiar. Playground associations had been campaigning for recreational programs since the turn of the century, and a superficial reading of Thrasher implied that criminality was merely a lack of structure. As the historian William Graebner writes, there was an assumption that "delinquent behavior occurred almost inadvertently," as a result of "overabundant leisure." By this logic, children vandalized schools not for legitimate or even intentional reasons but simply because there was nothing else to do.[50] In his history of New York City gangs, Eric Schneider argues that public officials believed that "gangs were unstructured, informal groups that demanded and received little loyalty from their members," that gang violence was "senseless, random, unorganized, [or] committed by psychopaths," and that more after-school programming would mitigate the problem.[51] This argument became the basis for "drift" theories of crime, in which young people fell in and out of illicit activity largely by happenstance.[52]

A second method of controlling gangs, Thrasher argued, was to co-opt their organizational structure. The greatest danger was to suppress rather than redirect boys' need for agency and self-determination. Thrasher offered several examples of school administrators appointing gang members as leaders of athletic teams or student clubs, and cautioned against punishing them. One

Chicago principal took a conciliatory approach to a local gang, which responded well, transformed itself into a debating society, and became the core of the school's student government.[53] Yet reconciliation, too, could prove ineffective, especially when school administrators assumed that gangs' latent political functions could simply be redirected to support existing practices. Students often had other ideas. In New York City, for instance, an organization called the Boys Brotherhood Republic, formed to curb "unruly or rowdy" behavior by teaching students the importance of self-government, learned its lesson a little too well, presenting the school board with a detailed report that blamed delinquency not on students but on disrespectful and abusive teachers.[54] Elsewhere, recalcitrant gangs simply refused to cooperate, informing principals that they intended to run the school themselves and would not be so easily tamed. Unless schools were prepared to share real power with student groups, they were unlikely to win their allegiance.[55]

Perhaps the most interesting of Thrasher's conclusions, which received little attention from either sociologists or school leaders, was his Romantic account of delinquency, which foregrounded imagination as the source of misbehavior. Thrasher devoted an entire chapter to the influence of radio, cinema, and comic books on children, describing them not as harmful influences—as Frederic Wertham famously would, in Seduction of the Innocent (1954)[56]—but as sources of adventure and excitement that adult authority could not match. Families, churches, and schools continued to function, Thrasher wrote, but they "failed to speak in meaningful ways to these youth." As modernity produced a vibrant fantasy world, it created a crisis of meaning in day-to-day life. Gangs not only provided order and belonging but transformed the city into an object of "genuine fascination."[57] Thus, according to Thrasher, vandalism could never be entirely solved by the organization of kickball leagues or guidance programs: destruction was an eruption of emotional fullness, an almost existential expression of joy or anger. Property destruction could result from high spirits, it could be revenge against adults who stifled the child's autonomy, or it could result from "a general soreness at the world."[58] Jane Addams made a similar point in The Spirit of Youth and the City Streets (1909), in which she ascribed childhood criminality to feelings of unrequited longing, "gaiety," "enthusiasm," and "delight."[59] While the emotional attraction of destruction would remain a subtext in the scholarly literature on vandalism, these deep-seated sources of delinquency tended to overmatch the small-bore reforms preferred by school administrators, which seemed pat and inauthentic by comparison, and they were largely overlooked by subsequent generations of researchers, who were more interested in Thrasher's thoughts on social organization.

By the 1930s, Thrasher's work had laid the foundation for "social process" theories of crime, which looked to social settings as conduits for delinquency and argued that criminal actions were learned in peer groups.[60] By tracking the frequency, intensity, and duration of children's contact with criminal environments, researchers speculated, one could gauge their propensity for destruction. Interpreting delinquency as an ecological phenomenon rather than a product of individual pathology, they argued that a child's "reference group"—beginning with the family and extending to street gangs—was the best place to find the causes of vandalism.[61] Unfortunately, while these studies claimed to elucidate subcultures of crime, the background conditions that they described, such as the influence of growing up in a "broken home" or "slum," were usually little more than proxies for socioeconomic class, which in turn was far less predictive than they claimed.[62] The same theories suggested that schools should leverage positive social bonds—for instance, by hiring community members as teachers and aides. (As one contemporary quipped, "A kid isn't going to throw a rock through a window of the school where his mother works.")[63] Yet these initiatives, too, remained piecemeal and never seriously challenged the era's movement toward professionalization and bureaucratic organization.[64]

Perhaps the most popular explanation of delinquency during the 1950s was Robert Merton's "strain" theory. Merton argued that societies sanction certain forms of economic success and are structured for their attainment. Only when individuals lack access to these structures do they turn to illegal means of acquisition (such as theft) or expressions of disaffection (such as vandalism).[65] Applied to schoolchildren, strain theory suggested that either lower- and working-class students would find themselves thwarted by a lack of middle-class jobs and "lose support for society's structure and norms," or schools would increase opportunities for social mobility and delinquency would disappear.[66] Merton assumed that the United States was a fundamentally sound society in an age of unprecedented prosperity, and thus could expand and equalize wealth. The same beliefs underwrote the Elementary and Secondary Education Act (1965) and other Great Society programs during the 1960s. Unfortunately, an emphasis on rational decision-making and material gain—questionable explanations even for adult crime—proved especially ill-suited to underage criminals, who often acted in less calculated ways.[67]

By the late 1950s, these shortcomings prompted a turn to countercultural theories of delinquency, which focused less on socioeconomic factors than on the subjective feelings through which children defined themselves.[68] Albert Cohen's pathbreaking book, *Delinquent Boys: The Culture of the Gang* (1955), urged sociologists to interpret property destruction as a way for working-class students to set themselves against mainstream society. As proof of membership in their peer group, Cohen argued, boys needed to flout middle-class norms, especially respect for property. Vandalism was "right precisely *because* it [was] wrong by the norms of the larger culture."[69] Talcott Parsons likewise argued that, as modern societies prolonged childhood and attenuated ties between boys and their fathers, adolescents were turning to peer culture for meaning and belonging.[70] From this perspective, delinquency took the place of traditional puberty rites, in which acts of daring proved one's masculinity. It also extended Thrasher's earlier notions of social dislocation. Whereas premodern societies controlled crime through inhibitive customs, in the United States the loss of adult role models, together with what John Martin called "a mélange of changing people, customs, and morals," undermined any attempt to stigmatize lawbreaking or assimilate youth into constructive adulthood.[71]

Unfortunately, even as notions of social disorganization, economic opportunity, and countercultures gained traction, huge explanatory gaps remained. The era's criminologists tended to apply narrowly empirical methods to diffuse phenomena with poorly defined premises. For all of these reasons, contemporaries admitted that "research on the vandal has been largely unproductive [and] few consistent patterns have emerged."[72] Basic research into the identity of vandals, begun in the 1920s, remained unresolved into the 1970s. There were, to be sure, general correlations between vandalism and academic achievement, truancy, suspension, and alienation, but researchers could not specify which of these variables were most influential.[73] Nor could they decide whether most of the crime in schools could be attributed to "emotionally disturbed young people," whether vandalism correlated with learning disabilities, or to what degree socioeconomic class and home environments were actually determinative.[74] Some studies presented the vandal as a "lower-class minority male," but others were quick to point out that vandalism was rampant in middle-class suburbs, was overwhelmingly committed by white students, and was perhaps as likely to be perpetrated by girls as it was by boys.[75] Various researchers concluded that vandalism resulted from either affluence or material want, or from too much, not enough, or inconsistent punishment in the classroom; that it most likely occurred before school hours, during free periods, after school, or at night; and that it was especially prevalent during the winter, spring, summer, and fall.[76] Finally, and not for the last time, they concluded that a significant amount of destruction appeared to occur "without reason."[77] What were schools supposed to do with these findings?

Ambiguous or contradictory research suggests several shortcomings in the response to vandalism during the mid-twentieth century. First, it reveals a gap between policymakers' claims to scientific authority and the reality of

FIGURE 3.1. During the 1950s, psychologists struggled to identify the specific motivations for student misbehavior. Blanche McDonald, *Successful Classroom Control* (Dubuque, IA: W. C. Brown, 1959).

decentralized education systems in the United States, which suffered from inconsistent methods of reporting and few means to track longitudinal or comparative data. It also speaks to the faulty assumption that there was, as the contemporary critics Matt Long and Roger Hopkins Burke put it, "one singular truth or rationale behind the act of vandalism," which could be isolated and remedied. As other critics have observed, property destruction could result from any number of sources, and, "in the theoretical murk surrounding school vandalism," establishing a correlation between a particular variable and vandalistic acts rarely supported causal inference.[78] Finally, it is important to point out that the era's empirical approach tended to accept existing racial and socioeconomic inequalities at face value and to reinscribe them as objective facts, presenting demographic factors themselves as causes of school vandalism rather than situating both within a broader field of inquiry.[79]

Psychological Theories of Destruction

Just as sociologists worked to position vandalism within social systems, psychologists placed it in a sequence of individual growth. Studies of psychopathology in children grew significantly during the late nineteenth century and were closely related to the professionalization of teaching and school administration. Just as schools became sites of vaccination, nutrition, and other forms of public health, reformers sought to improve the "mental hygiene" of their students. By the 1910s, many school districts had opened psychiatric clinics for children who exhibited abnormal behavior and hired school psychologists and guidance counselors to manage an emerging system of intelligence testing, ability grouping, and special education classes. This entire apparatus depended on therapeutic assumptions: namely, that child development was a medical or scientific matter, that educators had relevant expertise in the diagnosis of psychological disorders, and that schools could best incorporate children into healthy social relationships.[80]

Yet mental hygiene lost much of its scientific rigor as it migrated from the clinic to the classroom, where it infused the rhetoric of child welfare with an underlying commitment to discipline and efficiency. Therapeutic approaches tended to impose normative assumptions about gender and sexuality, racial characteristics, interaction with peers, and obedience to authority. In the process, they not only punished but pathologized noncompliant students. They also positioned the school as a corrective to an almost inherently dysfunctional home environment, castigating parents as overly or insufficiently affectionate, "undemocratic" in their exercise of authority, and less qualified in childrearing than teachers or social workers.[81]

These trends predated Sigmund Freud's visit to the United States in 1909, but they explain the spread of Freudian psychology in educational circles over the subsequent decades, evident in ubiquitous references to sexual drives, family taboos, and the effects of repression on personality development. By the end of the 1920s, it was common for school counselors to complain that traditional methods of classroom management did not deal with the "underlying emotional causes" of misbehavior, and for child psychologists to align treatment with "deeper, instinctive drives."[82] Descriptions of "unconscious motivations" in college textbooks increased tenfold between 1930 and 1955, while scholarly articles on childhood psychosis grew at a similar rate.[83] Descriptions of vandals began to shift as well, as older categories of "feebleminded" or "dull" children were overlaid with a new attention to family dynamics. In a typical case from the 1950s, an academically successful teenager was brought to children's court for making a mess in his high school library. While the cause seemed straightforward—he threw books and dumped bottles of ink on the desk of a librarian he disliked—the court's psychiatric clinic diagnosed him with "schizoid personality," noting that he was "clandestinely hostile toward his parents and his brother" and likely to develop "phobic, obsessive, or paranoid symptoms," for which it recommended psychotherapy.[84]

Freudian interpretations of vandalism grew as a flood of psychoanalysts fled fascism in Europe. August Aichhorn, Ernst Simmel, Fritz Wittels, Fritz Redl, and Bruno Bettelheim all arrived in the United States during the 1930s and 1940s, and all published influential articles on delinquency and vandalism. Bettelheim suggested that playing with paint or smearing dirt represented anal preoccupations.[85] Simmel attributed arson attempts to a "repressed infantile masturbatory impulse."[86] Aichhorn thought that teenagers broke windows and furniture to release an "impotent rage and hostility against authority," and argued that such behavior should be allowed to proceed in clinical settings as a way to air repressed feelings.[87]

Aichhorn's conflation of vandalism and aggression is significant. Freud's early focus on the "pleasure principle" suggested that tolerant, antiauthoritarian school settings could prevent psychological neuroses, and in some contexts Freudian approaches were used to challenge negative perceptions of school vandalism. For instance, "art therapy" positioned free-associational scribbling and clay sculpture as opportunities to work through psychic tensions.[88] Art therapists wrote that by "getting dirty, 'wasting' materials, [and] engaging in primitive childish pleasures," disturbed individuals could break through taboos, express "forbidden wishes and impulses," and master "painful and frightening experiences." These approaches repositioned vandalism as communicative rather than purely destructive, a signal of vulnerability rather than depravity.[89] Art therapy techniques were practiced with several groups of traumatized children during the 1940s, most famously with captives of the Terezín concentration camp and Holocaust refugees in the United States, as well as with students at the Wiltwyck School for emotionally disturbed boys, in New York.[90] But art therapy remained well outside the mainstream. By the 1940s, most psychologists were interpreting property destruction through Freud's later concept of the "death instinct," which paired the sex drive with deep-seated aggression. Freud hypothesized the death instinct to explain repetition, self-inflicted pain, and "innate destructive urges" in children's play, of which vandalism seemed an obvious manifestation. He also argued that restraining aggression was necessary to protect civilization and guide individuals toward the "reality principle," an emphasis on control rather than liberation, which accorded well with the Cold War rhetoric of maturity and containment.[91]

Freudian subtexts frequently appeared in media portrayals of school vandalism. Most explicit were the informational films shown in middle and high school classrooms. *Boredom at Work* (1961) features a white, middle-class boy in the suburbs who cannot get his father to play with him and begins to lose interest in school. In a working-class neighborhood, another white boy shoots craps "to escape the monotony of slum life" and begins to develop "a deep hatred of authority." The film suggests that malaise will lead both boys to delinquent behavior, yet it ascribes their discontent less to their present circumstances than to developmental struggles in infancy. "When he was a baby, [the middle-class boy] acted spontaneously," notes the narrator, but diapers, bottles, and sleep training led him to develop a stutter and a resentment of adults.[92] Another film, *Why Vandalism?* (1955), written by Bruno Bettelheim, ascribes destructive behavior to a child's "inner motivations" and "hidden personality," which the film attributes, variously, to a slovenly home environment, a lack of parental affection, latent sexual frustration, and existential angst. "[The vandal] has become an outsider," warns the film, "made so by complex circumstances that he himself cannot fully control or understand. . . . Inside he is eaten away with resentment and a desperate urge to get even." All it takes is an unlocked window for the boy and his friends to unleash their rage on an empty classroom. The film concludes with a judge admonishing the boys: "You alone are responsible for the shocking, appalling waste you caused. But we know today there is more to it than that. You parents must share the responsibility. . . . By denying the love, security, and sense of belonging that is important to every living being, you have hurt [the boys] as surely as if you had denied them food. Perhaps our doctors, our social workers, and others on our staff can help you overcome the fear and hate which has brought you before this court."[93] An episode of the television show *I Led Three Lives* (1953) features a Communist agent encouraging local children to vandalize their school. After foiling the plot, the show's protagonist drafts a letter to parents: "Most parents know that junior—especially before he could talk—was the most ruthless tyrant that ever breathed. He reached for everything he saw and screamed lustily if he didn't get it. He [was] a natural little vandal in the making." But, he writes, "with education and guidance and care, our little vandal becomes a useful citizen—a credit to his community—the backbone of the country."[94] All of these portrayals suggest that, because destructive behavior originates in psychological neurosis, it can be resolved through therapeutic intervention.

Freudian accounts of vandalism began to wane by the 1970s, mirroring a broader cultural decline. By that time several weaknesses had become apparent. First was the common criticism that psychoanalysis was imprecise and unfalsifiable. When applied to vandalism, it seemed to blur lines between normal phases of development and the onset of adult neuroses. The adult psychopath may have been a "perennial child" who exhibited impulsivity and self-centeredness, but school authorities were too quick to equate all childish

FIGURE 3.2.   Many informational films attributed vandalism to Freudian neuroses and recommended psychotherapy for perpetrators. *Why Vandalism?*, 1955.

behavior with maladjustment, taking property destruction as a self-evident sign of mental illness.[95] As Anna Freud later conceded, child psychologists "tried to spot from surface manifestations . . . specific unconscious impulses, incestuous or sadomasochistic fantasies, castration anxieties, [and] death wishes" that they could not actually substantiate.[96] Guessing games were hardly surprising, given the many types of vandalistic behavior that children exhibited and their equally diverse causes. At this degree of abstraction, psychology offered little guidance to educators, who tended to apply it selectively and in support of existing practices. Thus, while school leaders increasingly associated vandalism with hostility, they still proposed to calm destructive feelings through hobbies or intramural sports. "Vandalism [would be] greatly lessened," they promised, when communities "provided healthy outlets of fun and aggression for the young people." In the face of persistent property damage, however, many Americans began to doubt whether recreational opportunities could really sublimate the death instinct.[97]

As explanations of property destruction shifted from general rowdiness or malice at the turn of the twentieth century to a focus on maladjusted children by the 1950s, damage to schools seemed to represent a breakdown in cultural transmission, a rejection of normalcy, and an emerging generation gap.[98] Juvenile delinquents threatened the efficacy of public institutions and the very viability of democratic government. With totalitarian regimes lurking in the background, the destructive tendencies of teenagers seemed to raise unsettling questions about human nature under modern conditions.[99]

These fears grew more acute when misbehavior converged with actual extremism. Communism dominated the headlines, but it was fascism that attracted the most acolytes and imitators.[100] By 1960, there were over six hundred incidents of antisemitic vandalism reported each year in the United States, and many of them targeted schools. Police discovered neo-Nazi organizations at several high schools, and caught students stockpiling Nazi paraphernalia, weapons, and crude incendiary bombs. Jewish civic organizations rushed to document and interpret these incidents, and their explanations are reflective of the era's general understanding of vandalism.[101] Commentators were unsure whether swastikas in schoolrooms represented acute interpersonal hatred, a broader climate of bigotry, or merely immature provocation.[102] Some saw Nazi symbols as an opportunity for teenage boys "to express diffuse hostility toward the middle-class world." Others thought they eased "a widespread anxiety among high school youth," who, in the throes of the Cold War, "suffer[ed] diffuse forebodings about the nation's strength and [found] some reassurance in the notion of a master-race." Principals were quick to identify Nazi sympathizers as "troubled" or "oddball" students, products of "broken homes" beset with feelings of weakness and rejection. Yet they also worried about those students' appeal to mainstream students, who seemed susceptible to charismatic leaders among their peers.[103]

These eclectic explanations reflect the indeterminate theories of vandalism at the time. Experts increasingly (and perhaps mistakenly) attributed vandalism to aggression, which they proposed to mitigate through therapy and healthy recreation. Social workers cited families, clubs, and wholesome peers as the "best defense against the wanton destruction of property."[104] The same approach characterized much of the era's educational rhetoric, yet it left the roots of aggression conspicuously vague. Was vandalism fundamentally a problem of family dynamics? Economic inequality? Existential anxiety? Petty resentment? Perhaps it was the hollow materialism of postwar America, in which forced leisure played out against what the director of the US Children's Bureau described as "a background of rather constant opportunity . . . for the misuse of property"?[105]

To their credit, some social scientists recognized the gap between the unspecified causes of vandalism and its proposed remedies. Property destruction encompassed many behaviors, data were unreliable, and medical diagnoses were inconsistent. There was no guiding theory, they complained, only "arbitrary standards [of evidence]" and "general confusion" as existing research repeated a series of circular arguments.[106] As one sociologist wrote,

> Police departments, social agencies, civic groups, and organizations such as schools and churches are completely at a loss to explain [vandalism's] meaning or purpose, and equally baffled as to how such actions can be

effectively handled, controlled, or prevented. Psychiatrists, sociologists, and specialists in youth problems ponder all the known theories of causation but there is no agreement. Delinquency and crime are . . . purposeful behavior. But wanton and vicious destruction of property by teenage hoodlums reveals no purpose, no rhyme, no reason. Theories of latent aggression, paternal hostility projected against authority, frustration, rejection, lack of love—none of these can possibly furnish any reasonable clue to the meaning of such senseless and useless conduct.[107]

Some criminologists began to question whether vandalism was reducible to aggression at all, noting that "it is not at all unusual for adolescents to act out whatever is controlling them at the moment—rage, boredom, pent-up energy, or sheer joy."[108] Children seemed to have an "inner momentum, or drive, of [their] own" and were rarely able to explain their motivations.[109] In short, the field had arrived back where it started. The causes of vandalism remained obscure.

None of this is to deny that criminal subcultures or individual psychoses could provoke particular acts of vandalism. It is merely to point out that these were not the only sources of misbehavior, and that, being inscribed in social structures or individual life histories, property destruction was too entrenched to respond to superficial reforms. For all the handwringing about vandalism as a breakdown of meaning and social authority, by limiting their responses policymakers seemed unable to grasp the gravity of the issue. If wreckage was a rejection of modern conditions, surely it should have sparked criticism of those conditions rather than an adjustment to them. If it was a protest against social or economic inequality, then vandals deserved political recognition rather than patronizing dismissal. If it was a moral wrong, then it deserved punishment rather than diagnosis. By the mid-1960s, broader forms of social unrest would move each of these issues to the foreground, and vandalism would become a direct indictment of the status quo.

4

VANDALISM AND THE SECURITY STATE, 1960–2000

The film *Lean on Me* (1989) opens with an interior shot of a stately, wood-paneled school. In a time-elapsed sequence, the walls take on graffiti and unruly Black teenagers overrun the corridor. Four minutes of mayhem ensue, in which students throw a water fountain through a window, engage in multiple assaults, admit a drug dealer through a side door, and send a teacher to the hospital. Their violent misbehavior takes on a primeval quality, to the point that its specific causes not only go unmentioned but seem irrelevant. The school exists in a Hobbesian state of war, which subsides only when a no-nonsense principal overawes the students through discipline and sheer willpower.[1] This plotline reflects prevailing perceptions of urban schools since the 1960s. Images of lawless destruction seem to capture classrooms in chaos, and imply that proper education depends on strict authority and inflexible punishments. The same perceptions have yielded many of the heavy-handed policies that continue to drive school discipline today, from "zero-tolerance" suspensions to police patrols. The trouble is that *Lean on Me* is based on a true story—of principal Joe Clark and Eastside High School, in Paterson, New Jersey—in which the dynamics of segregation, underinvestment, crime, and violence were decidedly more complicated. Vandalism was convenient shorthand for these larger problems, but it was never reducible to them. Nor was it merely a result of laxity or weak leadership, to be overcome through moral reform alone. The late twentieth century did witness sharp increases in some forms of property destruction, but these are better understood as a continuation of the problems outlined in previous chapters rather than the result of suddenly uncontrollable children or unprecedented cultural upheavals.

The most visible source of vandalism during the 1960s and 1970s was ongoing racial injustice. As civil rights campaigns expanded educational opportunities for students of color (especially Black students), there was a corresponding resurgence of white populism and racist violence, which targeted both segregated and newly integrated schools. Government agencies handled this destruction differently than they had during the nineteenth century—reorganizing inequality along spatial lines to appease white parents, and confining students of color to separate schools and classrooms even in the absence of legally sanctioned segregation—but white Americans' recourse to wreckage speaks to the persistence of older forms of hostility. A newer development was property destruction as a *rejection* of unequal conditions. Whether segregated in underfunded and overcrowded buildings or made unwelcome in predominantly white institutions, students of color themselves damaged property to protest mistreatment—a form of resistance dramatically captured by riots and other forms of collective action but underlying everyday acts of defacement as well. Following the era's broader turn toward political consciousness and mobilization, property damage emerged as the voice of marginalized students.

Racial tensions were not the only source of school vandalism: many cases occurred in predominantly white suburbs and had causes that were far less distinct. The 1970s were the heyday of arson in the United States, and schools were burned as often as homes and businesses. While alarms and fire escapes kept students safer than in previous eras, fires set after hours could still overwhelm municipal budgets with catastrophic costs, pushing even affluent communities to the brink of bankruptcy while disqualifying them from insurance coverage. Meanwhile, questions about shared risk remained unresolved: most states required school districts to carry fire insurance but were reluctant to provide it themselves, and they struggled to control prices on the private market. Despite a general rise in government funding and regulatory capacity, protecting school infrastructure from unruly students seemed to overwhelm the patchwork of state, local, and private organizations that administered educational policy.

Predicting or preventing acts of vandalism through social science research continued to be ineffective as well. Academic accounts grew more sophisticated than those of the 1950s, but they still suffered from a lack of basic research and conflicting theories of causation. Sociologists replaced economic and psychological explanations of vandalism with ecological models, following the sources of misbehavior from individual students to the built environment in which it occurred. Many of these approaches were critical, comprehensive, and sensitive to student experience, but they were also complex and difficult to translate into policy.

By the late 1970s, then, voices from across the political spectrum were begging authorities to do something about school vandalism, but no one was quite sure what to do. Much like the era's "stagflation" crisis, vandalism seemed to confront local governments with a choice between skyrocketing costs and even more expensive remedies. The lack of a clear solution should remind us that there was no inevitable outcome to the crisis, but each of the factors listed above began to pull school districts in the same direction, overlaying an older paradigm of prevention and rehabilitation with a new one of deterrence and punishment. In urban schools, especially, calls for "law and order" and tax relief compelled federal and state governments to subsidize security guards, encouraged cooperation between schools and police departments, and tightened penalties for juvenile delinquency. Insurance companies forced districts to install alarm systems, floodlights, and security fencing if they expected even minimal fire and property protection. Social science surveys alerted the public to the shocking costs of vandalism, while ecological theories of crime introduced the notion of "target hardening," which controlled student behavior through architectural design and surveillance. Taken together, these changes reconfigured educational spaces and expanded rigid and discriminatory systems of punishment. Schools began to look more like prisons.[2]

Property destruction was not the sole cause of these changes. One could easily point to gangs, violence, and drug use in schools, with which vandalism was often (and sometimes wrongly) associated, and more deeply to the effects of suburbanization, demographic change, economic recession, and political polarization. As images of social disorder worsened racial and economic stratification, damaged schools heightened perceptions of danger, waste, and mismanagement in public education, reducing complicated discussions about equal educational opportunity to ostensibly simple ones about crime and taxes. Although school vandalism was only one symbol of unrest, the fact that it had quantifiable costs meant that it would play an outsize role in educational policy for decades thereafter.[3]

Racial Desegregation and the Origins of Police in Schools

Racial terrorism remained a significant source of school property destruction into the 1960s, as it had been since the nineteenth century. For African American communities, educational inequality had long been evident in the establishment of segregated schools, their placement in dangerous or unsanitary locations, their material neglect, and the secondhand textbooks and materials provided to their students. Attacks by white vandals merely punctuated these inequalities, with a shattered window or midnight fire coming as one more in a long list of indignities.[4] As civil rights activists challenged unequal accommodations, however, those attacks became more specific. Vandals and arsonists first targeted schools that expanded educational opportunities within the segregated system, particularly renovated buildings, new high schools, or elementary schools transferred from white to Black children, as well as those that fell outside the control of white school boards, such as community-based "freedom schools" and Head Start centers.[5] Across the South, fires struck dozens of these segregated institutions during the 1950s and 1960s.[6]

Federal court rulings such as *Brown v. Board of Education* (1954) also altered the dynamics of school destruction. Whereas arson attacks had previously been a gratuitous assertion of white supremacy—a low-risk undertaking for terrorist organizations or teenage hoodlums—even vague commitments to racial integration shifted the impetus from destroying segregated schools to preserving them. White political leaders could hardly claim to provide "separate but equal"

FIGURE 4.1. The Hazard Training School was one of several segregated Black institutions destroyed in arson attacks during the 1950s. Georgia Archives, Albany State College Fire Photos, ah00655. Used by permission.

accommodations or plead for gradual integration when schools for Black students kept bursting into flames. For this very reason, civil rights activists themselves occasionally burned buildings to force the hand of reluctant school boards, and several outdated schools were burned after districts committed to building more modern structures.[7] Instead, segregationists turned their attention to newly integrated buildings, hoping to intimidate parents and local authorities. The Ku Klux Klan dynamited Nashville's Hattie Cotton Elementary School in 1957 and the high school in Clinton, Tennessee, in 1958; teenagers detonated small bombs outside public school buildings in Little Rock, Arkansas, in 1959 and 1960; and unknown parties lit destructive fires elsewhere.[8] These attacks were never a uniquely Southern phenomenon. As segregation policies came under scrutiny in Northern and western cities, white residents there reacted to the prospect of redrawn attendance zones and student busing programs with the same tactics. Protesters stoned, burned, or dynamited school buses in Colorado, South Carolina, Kentucky, Massachusetts, and Michigan during the early 1970s to prevent the transportation of Black children to majority-white schools, and there were several cases of suspected arson against integrated school buildings.[9]

Burning schools and bombing buses was a dramatic demonstration of white discontent, but it was not in itself an effective means of stopping desegregation. Districts could usually reassign students to other schools, and overt violence tended to alienate middle-class white parents.[10] Instead, violence and property destruction limited the political appetite for redrawn attendance zones or equalized resources. Challenges to educational inequality met fierce resistance from white voters at every level of government, from local school boards to the US Congress, and proved more durable than executive or judicial commitments to its remediation. The result was pervasive resistance to court orders and the tacit acceptance of racial and economic inequalities, particularly between urban and suburban districts.[11]

The persistence of racial isolation and concentrated poverty in urban areas soon sparked opposition from students of color, who, as one mother put it, were fed up with "rotting conditions": "tired of the paddling, of teachers pushing children against the walls, of temporary teachers and poor buildings."[12] Many expressed their frustration by further defacing schools. Teachers and security guards regularly attributed graffiti and window breaking to overcrowding, and while some denounced the behavior as delinquency, there was a growing recognition that students were responding in kind to dilapidated and degrading environments.[13] To take one example, for decades, city school boards crammed Black students into temporary trailers rather than build them new classrooms or reassign them to integrated schools, and for decades angry students set those trailers on fire.[14]

FIGURE 4.2.   In many cities, white parents attacked school buses to stop racial desegregation during the 1970s. This shattered window was taken from a Boston school bus. National Museum of American History, Gift of Auto-Bus, Inc., through Robert E. White. Used by permission.

The same type of resistance appeared in newly integrated schools, where students of color faced inequitable course assignments, unrepresentative curricula, disproportionate punishment, disrespectful teachers, and violence from white classmates. It is unclear to what degree racist graffiti had appeared in majority-white schools before desegregation—we have already seen many examples of vandalism against Black schools—but there was plenty of it afterward, carved into bathroom walls and painted on lockers. These conditions prompted organized protests, strikes, walkouts, and petitions, but they also boiled over into rioting and unrest.[15] Waves of protest and wreckage erupted around the cancellation of Black history celebrations, offensive school mascots, segregated dances, unequal access to clubs and sports teams, and racist comments.[16] In Ann Arbor, Michigan, a group of Black students met in a high school auditorium to discuss ongoing shortages of Black teachers and counselors. When the principal ordered them to leave and escalated the situation by calling the police, the students retreated to the library, where, after some fiery speeches, they caused almost $20,000 in property damage.[17] In Ohio, a mob of four hundred white residents attacked Collinwood High School, breaking windows and forcing Black students to barricade themselves in the cafeteria until police arrived. Both sides continued to vandalize the school for weeks afterward.[18] Across the country, damage to school property became a symbol of volatility and racial tension.

All of these events played out against a broader background of destruction, which, as in earlier eras, could muddy explanations and culpability. Amid the desegregation of schools in Pike County, Mississippi, for instance, vandals broke into a Black elementary school, wrote the letters KKK on a cafeteria table, sprayed fire extinguishers around the kitchen, and tried to start an explosion with the stove. No arrests were made, but multiple sources attributed the break-in to Black teenagers rather than white terrorists.[19] A segregated school went up in flames in Cleveland, Ohio, but seems to have been the target of a random arson spree rather than political violence.[20] An attack on a school in Boston was initially attributed to white protesters, then called into question, then (without evidence) blamed

FIGURE 4.3. Ann Arbor High School Library, 1970. *Ann Arbor News.* Used by permission.

on civil rights leaders themselves by the segregationist school board president, Louise Day Hicks. The case was never solved.[21] When asked about a deliberate fire at an elementary school in Atlanta, Georgia—the fourteenth attack in the city that year—the principal denied that local desegregation efforts had anything to do with it.[22] Likewise, when a fire broke out amid protests for racial justice in New Rochelle, New York, high school activists denied responsibility. "Somebody just didn't want to go to school, understand?" one insisted. "It had nothing to do with demands."[23] There were strategic reasons for activists to downplay acts of intentional destruction, of course, just as there were for provocateurs to highlight them, but there was rarely much clarity. Even in situations of acute social unrest, school leaders were often "mystified" by particular acts of vandalism.[24]

Historians need to acknowledge the unknowable causes behind some cases of vandalism while at the same time recognizing the broader dynamics of injustice and resistance in which they were situated. Michael Katz has observed that "civil violence"—explicitly political forms of destruction—often overlaps with acts of personal vengeance and criminality. Yet he points out that powerful interests tend to exploit the ambiguity between them. One of the key tasks for the political establishment of the 1960s and 1970s was to render civil violence illegitimate by depoliticizing and criminalizing it, weakening oppressed groups' capacity for collective action and social change. In addition to various forms of political restructuring and co-optation, Katz argues, the most effective means of doing so was through police repression, particularly targeting movements for racial and economic justice. Scholars have thoroughly documented the ways in which urban police departments broke up organizations like the Black Panthers and created a power vacuum for street gangs to occupy.[25] A parallel process played out in schools. As we have seen in previous chapters, there was nothing new about students ransacking classrooms to protest perceived injustices or to make political statements. But local authorities were far less understanding when these tactics were taken up by nonwhite students. The upshot of civil rights protests during the 1960s, within schools and without, was to equate any kind of property destruction with gangs and violence, and to overreact with police supervision and spaces redesigned for security or control rather than learning.[26]

A helpful illustration of the link between property destruction and police involvement comes from the Los Angeles Unified School District (LAUSD), in California. During the first half of the twentieth century, the dynamics of vandalism in Los Angeles seemed fairly straightforward.[27] Budget cuts during the Great Depression forced the district to reduce its number of night watchmen from 336 in 1935 to only 14 in 1947. With no one patrolling the buildings, annual property damage increased from $10,000 to $215,168 over the same period. The board of education, alarmed by the spike, created a new security section to protect school property, and it seemed to work. Costs fell 32 percent by 1954, the city council awarded the security section a citation of merit, and the school board declared victory over vandalism.[28]

Yet that victory proved short lived, and it would be a mistake to assume that the LAUSD had merely restored the status quo ante. As Judith Kafka points out, the 1950s were a pivotal period for disciplinary reform in Los Angeles schools, with punishment shifting from the purview of individual teachers and principals to rules-based processes and higher levels of authority.[29] In this case, while property protection had previously been a decentralized affair, the security division standardized reporting procedures across the district and became the point of contact with the Los Angeles Police Department, to which property crimes would be referred directly.[30] Members of the board of education repeatedly blamed vandalism on the leniency of juvenile courts and pushed to tighten state and municipal laws holding minors liable for property damage and subjecting them to criminal prosecution.[31]

These changes set in motion a new policy regime. Confronted with property damage (and, later, student violence), the school district would hire more security guards and tighten its relationship with courts and the police department.[32] Criminalization aligned with conservative demands for "law and order," but it was not a one-directional march toward harsher punishments for all students. Liberals on the school board and in city government tried to pair punitive responses with preventive programs for younger children and first-time offenders, cracking down on serious crime while decriminalizing status offenses.[33] Unfortunately, this two-tiered approach was never clearly delineated in practice. Responses to vandalism, in particular, incorporated both community outreach and restitution programs on one hand, and technological deterrence, court involvement, and increased police presence on the other. Nor were they evenly applied. As Los Angeles grew more diverse in the 1950s and 1960s, schools became deeply implicated in the production of racial inequality. The divide between preventive and punitive responses to misbehavior almost immediately broke along racial lines, with Black and Latino students "regarded as hard-core offenders to be targeted for monitoring and supervision," according to Max Felker-Kantor, and white students "more likely to be treated as status offenders to be released or referred to counseling programs."[34] Despite studies that showed property damage widely distributed around the city, district officials explicitly associated vandalism with nonwhite schools, particularly after the Watts riots in 1965.[35] School buildings "represent the power, authority and the awesome forces that the alienated cannot cope with," they warned, and without opportunities for success, Black and Latino students would inevitably "'act out' their feelings of helplessness and powerlessness . . . against school facilities in their search for their primeval therapy." The board of education recommended more job-training and community-relations programs in inner-city schools, but, lest those prove ineffective, they dispatched more police officers as well.[36]

There was broad public support for these measures. Between 1965 and 1975, the LAUSD received a flood of letters and public testimony citing vandalism and violence as reasons to bring police into school buildings. These calls came from a range of groups, including parents, teachers,[37] principals,[38] PTAs,[39] community advisory councils,[40] and some civil rights organizations,[41] all of whom petitioned the school board to improve security.[42] By far the most frequent writers, however, were those who invoked their status as taxpayers to denounce vandalism as a colossal waste of money: almost $2 million per year by 1970.[43]

Many scholars have written about taxpayer revolts during the 1970s, and vandalism is relevant to these discussions in two respects.[44] First, property damage became a stand-in for a host of changes in education, essentializing students as lawless and destructive while legitimizing any number of reactionary political positions. Residents opposed to racial desegregation, for example, could argue that vandalism was the more pressing issue, or could use vandalism as a signal of poor management and an excuse to defund or withdraw their children from public schools.[45] The destruction of public property was also important because it put a price tag on social changes that would otherwise have been difficult to quantify. In lieu of a common language through which to discuss desegregation, student rights, crime, or perceived breakdowns of authority, conceiving of vandalism in dollar amounts had a common-sense political appeal. Unfortunately, reducing citizenship to taxpaying, and the public good to the protection of property, ignored countervailing appeals to justice or student welfare and often resulted in a casual cruelty, apparent in letter writers' recommendations for guard dogs, work farms, whipping posts, electrified door handles, and watchmen who would shoot vandals on sight.[46]

For all the tough talk, cost remained an impediment. Most forms of deterrence promised to increase rather than reduce taxes. Simply keeping the lights on in the district's 611 schools would add $580,000 to the annual budget.[47] Hiring round-the-clock security guards would cost an additional $30 million, twenty times the existing allocation.[48] The district installed silent alarms in several high schools, but even that investment required matching funds from the state.[49] Meanwhile, hopes of catching vandals and forcing them to pay for their actions proved overly optimistic. Criminal apprehensions rose during the 1960s but rarely exceeded half of the reported cases of serious vandalism.[50] Pursuing restitution in small claims or municipal court recovered only 1 percent of annual costs.[51] It began to dawn on local authorities that there was no affordable response to vandalism. Even when one set aside legal and safety concerns, all of the proposed remedies were significantly more expensive than the destruction itself. There was nothing for the school board to do, it seemed, but deflect criticism and plead economy.[52]

School security measures would become more affordable with subsidies from state and federal agencies. During the 1960s, Congress authorized more than forty-five programs for delinquency prevention, as well as providing funds for school security through the Omnibus Crime Control and Safe Streets Act (1968) and the Emergency Employment Act (1971). By the early 1970s, the LAUSD had secured millions of dollars in grants from these sources.[53] Some of the money went to vandalism prevention programs, but the lion's share went to the security section.[54] In a telling example, from 1974, the district superintendent praised one junior high school for its efforts "to obtain black teachers and administrators, and to present courses which meet the needs of the children no matter what their racial, educational, or economical background might be." At the same time, however, he authorized principals to reallocate "urban impact" funds earmarked for teaching positions in order to hire more guards.[55] By the end of the decade, the LAUSD was spending $5 million a year on security and employed the fourth-largest police force in Los Angeles County. Property losses continued to rise all the same, to almost $7 million a year.[56]

Fire Insurance and School Security in the Suburbs

Besides pressure from taxpayers and the allure of government funds, the strongest inducement for school districts to crack down on vandalism came from insurance companies. In 1965, the insurance supervisor for the LAUSD wrote an entire book touting the benefits of private fire insurance, which he recommended to colleagues nationwide. "Rates for school fire insurance are excessive in some areas," he conceded, but professional management and clerical services meant that coverage was almost always worth the cost.[57] Those recommendations reflected at least fifty years of best practices in educational administration, but they were outdated almost as soon as he wrote them. Over the next five years, incidents of arson in Los Angeles schools quadrupled, the district's annual insurance premiums rose from $165,000 to over $800,000, and the deductible for each claim rose from $1,000 to $100,000.[58] The installation of sprinklers, alarm systems, and security guards limited the number of catastrophic fires in city schools, but they had little effect on the overall number of attacks.[59] By 1972, the LAUSD could no longer secure any coverage for its buildings, forcing the district to budget over $1 million annually for fire damage.[60] Insurance would not have reimbursed many of the other costs anyway—most policies exempted window breaking, for example—but the loss of fire coverage exposed the district to serious financial liabilities.[61] Across the country, insurance companies had stopped writing policies for public schools. Annual losses were rising, companies claimed, and changes in social policy were altering calculations of risk. Unpredictability spooked insurers, and the prospect of unrest—whether from racist attacks, urban riots, or teenage protests—could dry up markets across entire states.[62] As one underwriter observed, "The insurance mechanism does not work in a disoriented society."[63]

One need not take the insurance industry's claims entirely at face value. As historians have reexamined the interplay of violence and capital in transforming urban space, they have challenged both the connection between arson and urban uprisings and the notion that insurers were responding to objective levels of risk in their withdrawal from urban markets.[64] Even before the protests of the 1960s, the largest insurers were reorienting their business toward comprehensive homeowner policies and more lucrative suburban markets; in the aftermath of urban unrest, they used inflated statistics to deny coverage in "riot-" or "arson-prone" areas while lobbying for federal reinsurance to backstop their losses. In doing so, insurance companies effectively redlined inner cities, worsening the outflow of capital from minority neighborhoods and condemning homeowners and businesses to lower coverage at exorbitant rates.[65] Meanwhile, the most prolific period for arson was during the 1970s, when urban unrest had already subsided and intentional fires were more likely to be set by landlords seeking to profit from insurance fraud or urban redevelopment funds.[66] One finds similar processes at work in the market for school fire insurance, particularly in the refusal of coverage and the reliance on government subsidies for high-risk pools.

That being said, given the ongoing amount of damage, the insurance industry had some basis for treating school buildings as if rioting had never really stopped. And unlike private property, which has been the sole focus of existing scholarship, the levels of risk and destruction in schools did not break clearly along urban and suburban lines, a point with important implications for school security improvements.[67] Insurance companies abandoned urban school districts just as they had private homes and businesses, but losing insurance did not necessarily determine those districts' responses to vandalism. City school boards were already investing in preventive measures and, as in Los Angeles, they could usually self-insure if rates got too high or if they were denied coverage. It was actually in the suburbs—where fires were almost as frequent and imposed higher proportional costs—that the insurance crisis reached its apex and private insurers exerted the greatest influence.[68]

A significant number of school fires broke out in smaller communities across Los Angeles County during the 1960s and 1970s. Districts such as Pomona, Bellflower, and Rowland all saw their insurance rates double after costly losses, and they were too small to self-insure.[69] If these communities expected any coverage at all, they would have to invest in deterrence technology and night watchmen, just as the LAUSD had. Even then, tightened security was not enough to stop arsonists outright. Following four intentional fires in 1966, insurers compelled Baldwin Park to allocate $80,000 a year for security guards, with costs matched by federal workforce funds.[70] Despite the new measures, the district suffered another $193,000 in fire losses by the mid-1970s, and its premiums continued to rise.[71] Other communities faced similar problems. Relative to population, suburban school districts suffered fires at significantly higher rates than Los Angeles and paid the equivalent of fifteen, twenty, or thirty times the cost, which municipal budgets struggled to accommodate. Thus, while student unrest was most visible and imposed the highest absolute costs in cities, the insurance margin fell most heavily on suburban areas.[72]

The same pattern held true elsewhere. On Long Island, where a rash of intentional fires caused millions of dollars in damage during the 1970s, increasing average insurance premiums by a factor of five, the question became how to apportion the spiraling cost of repairs between public and private entities.[73]

TABLE 4.1.   School fires in Los Angeles County, 1973–76

DISTRICT	NUMBER OF FIRES	COST ($)
Compton	22	630,000
Los Angeles	160	401,000
Rowland	2	400,000
Charter Oak	2	289,000
Long Beach	4	275,000
Inglewood	8	256,000
Azusa	3	250,000
Baldwin Park	6	193,000
Pomona	7	171,200
Norwalk–La Mirada	1	142,000
Bellflower	15	130,000
Montebello	2	123,000
Whittier Union	1	105,000
Hacienda–La Puente	3	90,000
East Whittier City	4	70,000
Covina Valley	3	62,000
Glendora	1	55,000

Sources: John Albert Anderson, "Vandalism in Unified School Districts of Los Angeles County" (PhD diss., University of Southern California, 1977), 43; supplemental information from Deming, "School Fires and Fire Recovery Procedures."

Like many other states, New York required school districts to carry fire insurance but struggled to dictate the terms under which companies would provide it. Many insurers pushed schools into the "excess-and-surplus market," where elevated risk factors allowed them to sidestep state regulation and price controls, or simply refused to write them policies at all.[74] Legislators tried to include Long Island's schools in New York's mandatory insurance pool, which required any company doing business with the state to provide coverage in unprofitable areas, but their efforts were partial and ineffective.[75] Experiments with self-insurance and group rates failed in a matter of months.[76] As in California, security systems became a prerequisite for coverage at any price. "There is no direct credit for any type of safeguard," observed an insurance broker in Massapequa, but without security improvements, a policy was simply unobtainable. To comply with insurers' demands, Nassau County considered organizing a security force to protect member districts, while local administrators authorized money for sound sensors, guards, and patrol dogs, and began exploring the legality of arresting students.[77]

These changes yielded inconsistent results. In 1979, adjoining districts in Suffolk County each used federal grants to hire security guards. One district found the guards so effective that its board budgeted an additional $50,000 to expand the program, while the other caught its new hires sleeping on the job and vandalizing the school themselves.[78] By the early 1980s, despite spending approximately $1.6 million each year on security, Nassau County's fifty-seven school districts still suffered 32,724 acts of vandalism and $1.5 million in unreimbursed damage.[79] "We always prided ourselves that suburban children didn't need to get into vandalism," said the president of the Nassau Suffolk School Boards Association. "Now we know better."[80]

Again, the point here is not that all districts adopted the same levels of surveillance or deterrence in response to property damage. From the beginning, critics rightly complained that poor and minority students were subject to policing and prison-like conditions far out of proportion to the actual incidence of vandalism in their schools, while affluent communities imposed nominal punishments and ignored or suppressed comparatively high levels of damage.[81] Rather, the point is that worsening property destruction initiated a more general turn toward social control in schools, and that the shift occurred along a variety of mutually reinforcing paths, depending on the size and demographics of particular districts. The 1970s witnessed tighter integration between schools and police departments in urban districts, the increasing influence of insurance companies in the suburbs, and the impact of municipal, state, and federal subsidies in both areas.

What was perplexing was that suburban students would engage in such high levels of destruction. "The suburban increase is largely in senseless, apparently

FIGURE 4.4. Many arson attacks had obscure causes, such as the burning of Florida's Lake Morton Elementary School in 1967. Courtesy of the State Library and Archives of Florida.

unmotivated crimes," wrote one observer.[82] It was no longer possible to attribute property damage to impoverished neighborhoods or material deprivation alone.[83] Likewise, there were far too many children involved to ascribe vandalism to abnormal psychology.[84] As had been the case since the 1920s, educators, sociologists, and law enforcement officials seemed unable to identify consistent causes of vandalism, much less prevent it.[85]

Social Science and the Rise of "Safe School" Laws

To address shortcomings in existing accounts of property damage, criminologists began to develop more sophisticated, ecological models and significantly expanded basic research and quantification of the phenomenon. These changes sometimes pulled in different directions—ecological theories tended to broaden definitions of vandalism, for example, and quantification to narrow them—but each held the promise of more tolerant responses to property crimes.[86] One question, then, is how social science also came to underwrite stricter control in schools, even against the inclination of leading researchers.

There were conceptual benefits in the shift from "strain theory" (which interpreted vandalism as a product of economic frustration) and Freudian diagnoses (which interpreted it as psychic illness) to ecological models of school crime. Fusing the child and the environment into a "sociophysical whole" extended many of the causes of vandalism back to the school itself, implicating teachers, administrators, and architects as well as students.[87] It also called into question the normative assumptions that defined delinquency, reframing rule breaking as a negotiation in which both sides exercised power.[88] The 1970s saw the first "equity models" of vandalism, which took legitimate classroom arrangements as a starting point and interpreted subsequent deviations by the teacher *or* the student as violations of an unwritten consensus, so that poor treatment or disrespect by school authorities quite understandably elicited oppositional behavior from students.[89] Equity models had a common-sense appeal, aligning with populist traditions of the nineteenth century as well as new Marxist critiques.[90] By encompassing a range of behaviors and not overdetermining their causes, they allowed for differences between similarly situated individuals. Most importantly, they asked how children themselves perceived their actions, according them a degree of agency and transforming vandalism into a form of political protest that adults needed to acknowledge.[91]

Situating children's experience of rules, authority, and culture within the built environment led to calls for structural improvements in schools.[92] Infrastructure was hardly a neutral backdrop for misbehavior. As one observer put it, "Vandalism happens because a hypocritical generation [of adults] presents opportunities for misuse, then shifts the blame for deterioration to vandalous youth. . . . Ninety percent of what is labelled vandalism can be prevented through design."[93] Architects recommended improved lighting and aesthetics, reorganized traffic patterns, moveable furniture, and open classrooms, as well as playgrounds, murals, and "graffiti walls."[94] Some went further, encouraging districts to coconstruct educational spaces with children to alleviate feelings of powerlessness and alienation.[95] Cooperation was not a cure-all, of course. As the French psychologist Claude Levy-Léboyer pointed out, "Any attempt to eliminate vandalism by 'artificially' encouraging participation in the planning and maintenance of a given environment will fail . . . if the group involved does not already share common goals and interests."[96]

The hard work of establishing common interests with students was one factor that derailed progressive responses to vandalism. While many academics interpreted property destruction as an indictment of existing arrangements, many policymakers assumed that environmental adjustments could curb vandalism without significant social change. Rather than appealing to children's consciences or cultivating community spirit, it would be far simpler to engineer spaces that reduced opportunities for destruction in the first place.[97] These ideas found their fullest voice in Oscar Newman's *Defensible Space* (1973), an influential study of housing projects in New York City, which warned that vandalism resulted from shared spaces, poor building materials, and a lack of surveillance, and that lingering damage would attract copycats.[98] Under terms such as "target hardening," "architectural determinism," and "situational crime prevention," Newman's diagnosis began to reshape schools across the country.[99] Designers replaced wood and ceramics with sturdier metal or cheaper plastic fixtures, on the assumption that, as Colin Ward puts it, "the environment . . . transmits signals to which users respond."[100] They reduced entry points; installed fencing, thorny shrubs, and floodlights around perimeters; experimented with scratchproof paint; raised or eliminated windows; replaced glass with polyurethane; and reverted to "cube structured" buildings and classrooms, noting that "nooks and crannies increase the chance of vandalism."[101] By the late 1970s, observers were complaining that vandalism prevention had transformed the modern school building into a "crime proof fortress" or, more frequently, a prison.[102]

A second way that academic scholarship influenced school security during the 1970s was through basic research and what one might describe as the allure of big numbers. Social scientists had been compiling educational datasets for over a decade, but they began tracking incidents of school crime only during the early 1970s. The result was an influx of statistics suggesting widespread property destruction, although most were snapshots rather than longitudinal data and all suffered from variations in collection, definition, and reporting that made verification difficult.[103] Federal agencies and nongovernmental organizations began to tabulate the costs of vandalism at about the same time, as did professional groups such as the National Association of School Security Directors (founded in 1970) and the National Association of School Safety and Law Enforcement Officers (founded in 1979), whose reports suffered from many of the same shortcomings.[104] The most detailed information on vandalism came from audits by large, urban districts.[105] For example, Baltimore City Public Schools, in Maryland, which had suffered unusually high levels of property damage during the 1960s, became the first district in the country to aggregate and publicize national data on the subject.[106]

All of this quantitative data was put to use in congressional hearings on school safety. In the House of Representatives, investigative committees repeatedly referenced the costs of vandalism while allocating funds for school security, culminating in the publication of the *Safe School Study* (1977).[107] In the Senate, Birch Bayh also convened hearings to publicize the problem of violence and vandalism. His committee's report was fairly measured: it denied that vandalism was "senseless" or "irrational," pointing out that too often education itself was meaningless and that many "students look[ed] upon the school as alien territory, hostile to their ambitions and hopes."[108] The report also drew attention to the effects of discriminatory rates of punishment for Black students, and cautioned that most delinquency was a product of tensions between the community and the school.[109] Nevertheless, the committee warned that property destruction had reached crisis proportions and continued to grow at an alarming rate, and it quoted statistics that jumped off the page.[110] While most reputable studies put the cost of school vandalism at about $200 million per year, the Bayh committee cited an outlying estimate of $500 million per year.[111] Elsewhere, the committee claimed that vandalism would soon cost every district in the nation an average of $63,000, and that in most urban districts the cost of broken windows alone would pay for a new school every year.[112] If these statistics were shocking, it was at least in part because they were new. The Bayh report noted sharp increases in school crime since the early 1960s, but it based that information on self-reported surveys, and critics pointed out that apparent increases could have been the result of improved reporting.[113] Even if there was a rise in property damage, other studies suggested that its causes were simply demographic, a byproduct of the baby boom and the sheer number of teenagers in school, and that vandalism costs were already plateauing or decreasing by the mid-1970s.[114]

Nationalizing the problem of school vandalism just after the issue reached its peak had the combined effect of alarming the public and giving policymakers the illusion of control. By the 1980s, a new paradigm of criminalization and punishment, only loosely related to the actual incidence of crime, had gripped school systems across the United States. Just as vandalism rates began to fall, at least a dozen states passed "Safe School Acts," which provided supplemental funds for equipment and security guards and tightened suspension policies.[115] Senate hearings included calls for federal legislation, which would eventually appear as the Safe and Drug-Free Schools and Communities Act (1994).[116]

As we have seen, public education during the 1960s and 1970s was caught up in the racial politics of "law and order," the disciplinary mechanisms of the insurance industry, and the alarmist findings of statistical surveys, all of which pushed school districts to tighten security and criminalize misbehavior. Vandalism encouraged a turn to punitive policies because it evoked pervasive social disorder and because its costs were difficult to justify in political debate. That transition, however, was neither immediate nor inevitable. Schools remained in the business of education, after all, and hopes for prevention (rather than punishment) ran high. Through the 1980s, experts continued to claim that improved job training would eliminate school crime, while urban districts poured money into antivandalism programs, hired outside firms and speakers, dedicated staff to curriculum design, and coordinated with community groups to encourage student buy-in. These programs remained largely ineffective, and their failures made it even more difficult to resist tough-on-crime reforms. Nevertheless, they persisted.[117]

The last gasps of the preventive approach were clear in the city of Baltimore. In 1980, following twenty years of arson, graffiti, and broken windows—worsened by systematic underinvestment in public buildings—Mayor William Schaefer launched a comprehensive campaign to end vandalism in the city.[118] Nobody knew what steps might work, but the mayor's task force pulled out all the stops. A local band called the Vandals recorded public service announcements.[119] A small-business owner convinced the mayor to buy his new paint-removal compound, which became the basis for a multimillion-dollar chemical firm.[120] A community theater troupe toured the city's high schools, performing interpretive dances and rap-based skits.[121] Schools tried to improve student attitudes with film strips, beautification projects, and an essay contest.[122] None of these initiatives seemed to have any impact. Structural changes fared little better. The city experimented with a decentralized management program, in which schools would tabulate their current vandalism costs and recoup any savings that they realized over the subsequent year. Unfortunately the program was incompatible with the district's funding structure, schools tried to game the system, and in the end the school board was unwilling to put up the money.[123] A student restitution program returned less than 1 percent of the district's total costs.[124] Vandalism continued unabated, and the mayor's program died with a whimper.[125] The only changes that survived were new connections between the school system, juvenile services, and the police department.[126]

Similar shifts played out in cities across the country. Preventive programs yielded to target hardening and police in schools, although these punitive approaches were not necessarily any more effective than prevention had been. Without reliable research, there was really no way to know whether the rate of vandalism was unprecedented during the early 1970s, why it declined by the end of that decade, or whether lower (but still widespread) levels of property destruction in the years since have been worth the less publicized costs of student criminalization.[127] Subsequent studies have established that school security policies responded to public perceptions of crime far in excess of actual incidence, and even at the time, critics questioned whether architectural changes actually prevented destruction.[128] Meanwhile, the same policies overwhelmingly targeted students and communities of color, criminalizing the type of misbehavior that would have been better corrected by educators and condemning students without addressing the conditions in which they were denied a meaningful education. The trend continues to the present, with reductive and overwhelmingly punitive responses to vandalism outweighing more nuanced approaches.

Part II

VANDALISM AS SELF-FASHIONING

Thus far, we have focused on vandalism as a form of political expression, inseparable from conflicts over resources, recognition, and power, and often resisting (and, in turn, tightening) systems of social control. Turning our attention to individual children raises a different set of questions, which theories of resistance are ill-equipped to answer. While many studies begin with their subjects' emotional impulses, they too quickly extrapolate them to class, race, and other categories, focusing on external factors while rendering children's internal dynamics reactive and largely one-dimensional. Current scholarship does not fully describe inducements to vandalism—its illicit thrills or emotional balms, the sulfurous joy of lighting matches—nor does it discuss the degree to which all children engage in the same behavior, which may suggest a more general impulse to destruction. Underlying both Marxist and Foucauldian theories of resistance are older, Romantic notions of "rebellion" that foreground the creative aspects of misbehavior, in which dissatisfaction, defiance, and emotional fullness become the means to selfhood. When students deface school property, the same sources should inform our understanding of their actions. In addition to focusing on the background factors that correspond with property destruction, we must also pay attention, in the words of the sociologist Jack Katz, to "those aspects in the foreground of criminality that make its various forms sensible, even sensually compelling, ways of being." That is, we should ask how individuals experience destruction, which can have not only political but profoundly personal implications. Concepts such as "moral self-transcendence," "lived mysticism," and the "magic" of perception are not typical subjects of criminology, Katz admits, yet one cannot grasp the significance of vandalism without them.[1]

Other scholars have taken a similar approach to the topic. Stanley Cohen began his career studying teenage vandals, which led him to a broader reappraisal of moral conformity and noncompliance. In *Escape Attempts* (1976), Cohen concludes that life is a series of projects "in which we either accept the arrangements that await us, or attempt to manipulate them, so that they will be more amenable, more compatible with the view that we hold of ourselves."[2] Acts of destruction often qualify as this type of manipulation: assertions of "felt individuality" through which a perpetrator establishes that he or she is irreducible to assigned social roles. While "much of the reality of everyday life already presents itself to us in a structured form," Cohen writes, there also exist "free areas" (spaces that straddle "the known and the unknown, the safe and the dangerous, the innovatory and the conventional") and "reality slips" (trances, visions, or moments of disjuncture that transcend ordinary experience), both of which allow us to stand outside everyday limitations. Breaking or defacing objects can produce the same effect, reordering our perspective of the world and ourselves. From this vantage point, vandalism becomes a useful theoretical tool: not merely something to make sense *of* but to make sense *through*.[3]

When it takes place in schools, vandalism becomes especially relevant to self-education, children's emergent ability to exercise freedom and make meaning. At first glance, destruction may seem antithetical to education, which is usually associated with order, reason, and self-control, and even more so to the childhood innocence associated with Romanticism. One might respond that damage to school property often *is* innocent and that many acts of vandalism impart sentimental lessons about coming of age, which is why adults are sometimes willing to tolerate them. But even the sort of damage that adults condemn can play an important part in children's maturation. What critics perceive as nothing more than auto-stimulation or refractory resentment, Romantics might associate with the "divine discontent" that rejects moral convention and self-estrangement. Ostensibly destructive acts can in fact impart lessons about one's sense of being.[4]

The same argument appears in existentialist thought. For Jean-Paul Sartre, for instance, freedom depends on a brooding recognition of absence. "How can we even conceive of the negative form of judgment," he asks, "if all is plenitude of being and positivity?"[5] Applied to education, Sartre's "positivity" may refer to a reliance on external sources of knowledge—the teacher or the textbook—or a refusal to acknowledge the role of boredom, doubt, or discontent in learning. If the true goal of education is for the student to recognize herself as autonomous, to discover the meeting point between the world and the individual life, then education cannot be conceived of simply as linear growth and the mastery of skills. It requires the development of interiority, the suspension of certainty, and the possibility of negation, which Sartre (following Heidegger) associates with destruction.[6]

Sartre's equation of freedom with indeterminacy brings us back to the question of wantonness, which implies students' ability to disobey not only adult authority but reason itself.[7] Philosophers have long debated whether wanton behavior is antithetical to human freedom or one of its central components. Idealists from Plato to Kant have argued against wantonness, grounding their philosophies in humanity's inborn ability to reason. While individuals may be shortsighted about the nature of the good, they claim, they are inevitably oriented toward it: one cannot embrace badness as the core of one's being.[8] That may be true, but it remains possible at any given moment for individuals to pursue courses of action that they know to be wrong, painful, stupid, or pointless, and it is a mistake to assume that, as David Sussman puts it, "a more sensible reinterpretation would appear were we just to look at these cases closely enough." Philosophers such as Arthur Schopenhauer, Friedrich Nietzsche, and Søren Kierkegaard all champion willfulness as a quintessentially human trait, and resist attempts at certainty or systematic closure in accounts of individual or social development.[9]

Wanton acts are not necessarily vicious; they may just be weird. For example, the philosopher Agnes Callard remembers cutting off her hair during her first semester of college and mailing it, wet and moldy, to her six-year-old sister. She did not have a particular reason for doing so. Callard describes her act as "unruly" and vaguely subversive. Yet while the sort of resistance outlined in part I is a *determinate* negation of the social order, a conscious rejection and a bid for some known alternative, Callard claims that mailing her hair was an *indeterminate* negation, the type that takes the form of nonsense, non sequitur, or the carnivalesque. "If unruliness exists," she observes, "then it is possible to feel a given set of rules to be false, confining, fake, alienating, in a word, exogenous, without being able to point to an alternative. Rebellion has a destination; unruliness is emigrating without having anywhere to go," with all the implications for liberation and self-determination that such wandering implies.[10] Impulsivity has never been confined to childhood, of course, but children seem particularly prone to the entwined forces of destruction and re-creation that accompany this sort of unruliness, and that underlie many incidents of vandalism.

The philosophical significance of vandalism derives not only from its sources of motivation but often from the sites in which it plays out. It matters that students engage with objects at school, against a backdrop of moral and academic authority, rather than at home or on the street, and that they do so in spaces that are simultaneously private and public, providing a field in which individuals come to recognize themselves and others.[11] Part II examines these sites through a series of essays, each of which analyzes a classroom artifact from a particular philosophical or theoretical standpoint. These pieces are meant to be suggestive rather than comprehensive, but together they advance an image of children struggling toward self-realization, with significance for contemporary interpretations of vandalism and for schooling as a whole.

"Books and Boredom" examines marginal inscriptions in nineteenth-century schoolbooks as manifestations of student boredom, raising questions about whether boredom has a history and what it can teach us about personal growth. Drawing from the *Bildung* tradition of Friedrich Schiller, Alexander von Humboldt, and Friedrich Nietzsche, the essay argues that boredom can serve educational ends, not only by dissolving and reconstituting the self but, in a culture committed to self-improvement, by encouraging students to approach the curriculum in irreverent or imaginative ways.

"Desks and Nostalgia" notes Americans' fascination with the initials carved in school furniture, which during the 1920s became the basis for widespread public nostalgia. But it identifies at least two sources of nostalgia: a reactionary impulse to romanticize the past and condemn the present, and a communitarian impulse, which uses emotional appeals to sustain continuity and foster social ties. Drawing from Wendell Berry, Christopher Lasch, and others, the essay defends the latter type of nostalgia, using scratched-up desks to explore constructions of memory in rural and African American communities, in particular.

"Walls and the Taboo" explores bathroom graffiti (or "latrinalia") during the 1950s and 1960s, which provided a basis for Marxist and Foucauldian accounts of student protest. In keeping with this book's broader attempt to expand concepts of "resistance," the essay argues that these interpretations remain too abstract to grasp the ways that students themselves made sense of dirty messages at school. Instead it returns to a different set of thinkers from the mid-twentieth century, particularly Hannah Arendt, Erik Erikson, and Paul Goodman, to explore the ways in which privacy and confrontations with the taboo helped students recognize themselves as individuals.

Like the chapters in part I, these essays are arranged in chronological order, and proceed toward less communicative and more destructive forms of damage as they go. The first three deal with graffiti—a more discernible form of vandalism than, say, arson—which they present as a means of achieving consciousness of self, class, or community. But readers should not draw too sharp a distinction between these and more destructive acts. The final essay, "Windows and Euphoria," uses Friedrich Nietzsche and Georges Bataille to suggest that window breaking, too, can teach philosophical lessons, through the aesthetics of destructive play. Breaking windows offers students a surreptitious but not necessarily political form of learning, an experience of sublimity that allows them to step outside social convention. For the same reason, the essay argues that the emergence of windowless schools since the 1970s should trouble us, because it denies children's need for both beauty and transgression.

These are philosophical issues with historical significance, especially regarding the emotions and perspectives of children. Most of what we know about childhood in the past is based on material culture, portrayals in media or literature, and the regimen of formal education, all of which adults created and imposed on the young. Less well documented are the worlds that children created for themselves.[12] Graffiti is one of the few artifacts that children produce without adult supervision, and thus it offers at least fragmentary glimpses into children's everyday frustrations and daydreams. These markings are not purely spontaneous: marginalia, latrinalia, and desk carving each have their own traditions, and each is subject to sentimental interpretation by children as well as adults. But neither are they entirely conventional. Exploring their creation opens a window onto children's individuality and their induction into broader cultural fields, a valuable perspective that remains missing from many discussions of education and resistance.

Finally, with their attention to interiority and authentic selfhood, the essays introduce an implicitly Romantic outlook that connects theoretical approaches across the book, from the celebrations of organic creativity underlying Marxist and Foucauldian studies to Nietzsche's spontaneity, Rousseau's republican virtue, Erikson's "ego psychology," and Bataille's emotionally charged "limit experiences."[13] The object is not to collapse the distinctions between these writers, who take up different questions and offer very different answers, but to suggest deeper affinities between them and to revive interpretive approaches that have fallen out of fashion in recent decades. Romantic selfhood sidesteps postmodern perspectives of the late twentieth century, which dissolve the self into a series of social constructions and intersections of power. Some postmodernists have encouraged scholars to shake off the legacy of Romanticism altogether and, in the words of Madeleine Grumet, to repudiate "the sentimental portrayals of consciousness brought to us by humanistic psychology in which true selves hovered just under the surface." The authentic self is an illusion, they write, and perpetuates the "deadly coherence" that denies multiplicity or antifoundational perspectives.[14]

In making this point, however, they may overstate the stability of earlier forms of selfhood. Chaos, absurdity, and self-loss are also legacies of Romanticism, and they persist in postmodern attachments to the sublime. By maintaining an element of incoherence in its descriptions of political power and emergent selfhood, this book emphasizes the role of interiority and indeterminacy in historical interpretation, which will be taken up further in part III.

BOOKS AND BOREDOM

There has been much written recently on the sources of boredom in the class-room, as well as on its potential remedies.[1] Although some points of consensus have emerged, the challenge remains to integrate work across a variety of disciplines, each bringing different questions, theories, and methods to the phenomenon.[2] Boredom applies a single name to a complex set of feelings, and before gauging its impact on the learner, one must understand not only proximate causes but latent meanings.[3] Unfortunately, we know little about the history of student boredom or how it might bear on current pedagogical or philosophical debates.[4] This chapter addresses that omission by examining markings in nineteenth-century schoolbooks for insights into how students may have experienced boredom in the past. In the process, it expands philosophical discussions about the relationship between boredom and maturation, and directs historians to ambiguous but potentially rich evidence of classroom experience.

I would like to open with the claim that boredom performs positive educational functions, that disaffection from course content parallels other forms of cognitive and emotional development and can actually impart independence, moral responsibility, and self-knowledge. Others have made this point before. Popular culture routinely associates boredom with creativity, and educational philosophers have recently explored how "suspended" moments in schooling may redirect learning inward.[5] The more substantive claim is that, in the nineteenth century, boredom and growth existed in a dialectic relationship, in which children navigated between private and public spaces, between fantasy and the physical world, and between spontaneity and convention. Thus, boredom stood as part of the implicit or "hidden" curriculum of schooling, but not merely as a source of alienation or oppression, as critics assume, nor entirely as a subversion of "productive" forms of learning, as proponents claim. Instead, paralleling the era's culture of self-improvement, boredom became a handmaiden of the official curriculum: classroom customs and content provided the paths along which students' minds wandered, forming necessary links between lessons and emergent selves.

A dialectic stance between the distracted child and her surroundings speaks to the educational significance of boredom, but it also raises problematic questions about historical sources. Specifically, what sort of records did student boredom leave behind? And if it was an outgrowth of the official curriculum or classroom culture, how can one distinguish boredom from other forms of learning? In some respects, the nineteenth century is the ideal setting to explore these questions, since it witnessed the emergence of modern childhood and Romantic notions of the self, as well as the textbook-centered pedagogy and rote memorization that seem to breed student detachment. Sources for this chapter include over two hundred schoolbooks from the archives of the American Antiquarian Society, published between 1780 and 1880, which contain sketches, notes, and other relevant markings in the margins. These clues, largely overlooked by historians of education, offer potentially radical insights into students' thoughts. They also remain frustratingly obscure. Students wrote in their books for many reasons, and without context it can be difficult to say whether any particular inscription signifies boredom or not. Nor do inscriptions necessarily represent unmediated glimpses into the child's mind, since they often conformed to customary modes of expression. The obscurity and conventionality of existing sources must qualify any claims about student boredom in the past, although they do not render the phenomenon completely unknowable.

This chapter rejects firm distinctions between performative and authentic expressions of boredom. Its central conjecture is that student markings provide a unique environment in which to observe the construction of subjective identity, not merely on the void of the page but within a broader cultural field—to see individuals in the process of becoming, both in spite and because of their lessons, teachers, and peers. At a point in history when children's life courses were changing, and at a point in their lives when they began to reflect on interior states of being, nineteenth-century schoolbooks became a canvas for selfhood, a site of growth and experimentation in which boredom took evolving forms, from the oppositional scratchings of confined grade-schoolers to the soul-searching queries of adolescents.

Philosophers of education have theorized about boredom since Aristotle, but until the late twentieth century, most of them conceived of it superficially and largely in opposition to student growth. Leisure stood at the apex of a classical education, insofar as learning prepared the student for contemplation, creativity, and freedom, yet philosophers relied on rigor and habituation (rather than boredom) to cultivate these traits.[6] Since the Enlightenment, educational thinkers have accorded children greater agency in their learning, but have still minimized moments of drift or inactivity. For those focused on the relationship between student attention and the learning environment—on channeling natural energies into intrinsic motivation—boredom has been useful only as a stimulus to action.[7] Most philosophers of education do not consider boredom itself educative. To the contrary, it usually signals external restraints on a child's interest or a lack of structure to help her achieve it.[8]

Meanwhile, philosophers of boredom have elaborated on its implications for cognition, freedom, and selfhood but have rarely connected it to the maturation of children. Arthur Schopenhauer, Søren Kierkegaard, Friedrich Nietzsche, and Jean-Paul Sartre all discuss the sublime melancholy underlying boredom, which they equate not only with a loss of interest but with a loss of meaning, a rupture between the mind and the world around.[9] Inability to find meaning in one's activities can alter time perception and produce feelings of disorientation and vertigo; like other forms of sensory deprivation, it ultimately effaces the ego, leaving the subject with a slipping grip on reality and a fleeting sense of self.[10] Yet the rupture between self and surroundings also offers opportunities for reflection, through which philosophers have begun to recognize boredom's educational qualities. As the psychologist Kenneth Clark points out, "the void within" can be an irresistible inducement to growth. "The sense of inner emptiness, a sense of limited experiential time, a sense of essential powerlessness . . . these are not tolerable insights. They must be compensated for with more positive, substantive concepts of self." Boredom, then, becomes an impulse not merely to activity but to self-recognition; it constitutes a distinct form of knowing.[11]

It is from this perspective that contemporary philosophers have explored the educational possibilities of boredom. "When our being . . . in the world is interrupted we have to re-order it from a new perspective," writes Jan-Erik Mansikka. "We are compelled to respond or act in a way where something unexpected, the singularity of our being, appears." When teachers determine questions and know the answers, when they preplan students' thoughts and actions, even in pedagogically constructive ways, they inhibit that singularity. Maturation requires a space where the teacher cannot offer guidance. Boredom pulls students away from the collective conscious and "leads [them], in a more reflexive way, back to themselves."[12] It does not follow that creativity or imagination necessarily spring from mindless experiences—risk taking and violence are other ways to cope with a loss of meaning—but it remains significant that boredom holds the potential for both the dissolution and the reconstruction of the self.[13]

Other scholars have made similar points about moments of drift in education, if not about boredom specifically. Sean Steel alerts educators not merely to the imaginative or playful elements of children's learning but also to the "practice of forgetting oneself, of allowing one's false sense of oneself to dissolve." Whereas schoolwork aims for constant stimulation, he writes, true contemplation "is rather a kind of unlearning than learning; it requires the emptying of the self rather than its aggrandizement."[14] Tyson E. Lewis and Daniel Friedrich likewise discuss the educational value of "tinkering" or "hacking" in the curriculum. Free time of the school, they write, provides a space in which students are momentarily detached from productive economic or political imperatives, a moment in which learning is rendered "inoperative, detached from immediate utility in daily life, its potentiality released from the need to actualize itself in socially productive forms." The resulting freedom returns agency to the student, activating curiosity, self-direction, and judgment.[15] Finally, Joris Vlieghe calls attention to rote recitation as a form of educational "practice": "a never-ending process of improving on an ability and therefore continuous work on the self." Whereas learning requires "a transition from mere possibility to actuality," he writes, "in practicing actuality gets suspended." For instance, the rhythm of reciting the alphabet or multiplication tables grants students a space to rise above application and experience potentiality, incrementally achieving self-mastery.[16]

These concepts are especially applicable to the nineteenth century, when *Bildung*, or aesthetic self-culture, animated classroom practice. To develop skill in drawing, penmanship, composition, or oratory, and from there a sense of aesthetic taste, was an exercise in individual and cultural self-formation. For that very reason, it could never be entirely predetermined. Learning required voluntary subscription and had to speak to abilities and dispositions already present in the student. It was never wholly in the teacher or even the student's control but occurred in liminal, unstructured spaces in the classroom. Insofar as *Bildung* transformed "education, indeed life itself, [into] a process of intellectual, moral, aesthetic and spiritual self-realization," notes the philosopher Alistair Miller, it demanded the cultivation of interiority. As Alexander von Humboldt wrote, "One must have a world of one's own within, which the waves of life wash over, while it quietly forms unseen."[17]

Boredom may have provided access to a "world within," but, like other aspects of school culture, its character was historically contingent. The degree and significance of that contingency have been the subject of sharp scholarly debate.[18] Some historians contend that boredom remained rare before the onset of modernity, seldom expressed or experienced outside particular contexts, and that the

FIGURE 5.1.   Marginalia from a nineteenth-century textbook. Courtesy of the American Antiquarian Society.

feeling as we know it today was an invention of the late eighteenth century. These scholars claim that most people experienced the premodern world much like a Bruegel painting: an eternal present in which one's identity derived from ritual; in which common work, humor, and sport blurred distinctions between children and adults; and in which there was little place for introspection or individuality, the preconditions of boredom. It was only with the rise of Romanticism, they contend, that boredom began to seep into the culture more broadly. Romantics accentuated emotional sensation, encouraging individuals to heights of heroism and self-perfection but also exposing them to valleys of despondency. Secular disenchantment, aspirations to happiness, and distinctions between work and leisure raised expectations for personal fulfillment far higher than could be satisfied. Beginning with the Romantics, there was a nascent sense that modernity had leached life of purpose.[19] Despite the charm of imagining a past in which boredom did not exist, other writers object that this distinction has been overdrawn. Certain *affects* can be tied to time and place, they concede, but root causes such as confinement and inactivity have always plagued mankind, engendering similar emotional or physiological responses. In their view, boredom does not have a history at all.[20]

This disagreement might be resolved with clearer conceptual categories, particularly distinctions between "simple," "situative," or "common" boredom on one hand, and "existential," "profound," or "modern" boredom on the other.[21] Simple boredom is the feeling of psychic distress that accompanies meaningless activities in the short term: waiting in line, for instance, or struggling to decipher a tax form. Existential boredom reflects a deeper loss of purpose, such as a life of forced leisure or a recognition that there are many courses of action and a reluctance to take any of them. Without oversimplifying the matter, one could say that simple boredom results from too little freedom and existential boredom results from too much. Both require a degree of self-awareness, but simple boredom, having a far lower threshold, seems more widespread and therefore less bound to a particular historical epoch. In the debate over whether boredom has a history, critics usually focus on the simple variety, while proponents focus on the existential.[22]

Yet it would be a mistake to assume that simple boredom exists entirely outside the bounds of history or that its causes are any less "modern" than those of existential boredom, and it is here that children and schools become instructive. Children may be active and easily diverted, constitutionally prone to simple boredom, but it remains difficult to separate purely physiological traits from the aesthetics of childhood innocence handed down since the eighteenth century—from William Wordsworth condemning the "prison house" of the classroom, say, or William Blake invoking the "dreary shower" of schoolwork. Romantic ideals continue to influence our understanding of simple *and* existential boredom, in ways inseparable from historical changes to childhood itself.[23] As Philippe Ariès argues, boredom became the foundation of a uniquely modern childhood, built on notions of love and tenderness but also on moralism, discipline, and confinement.[24] Michel Foucault extends that point, criticizing custodial institutions such as schools for using benevolent rhetoric and intrusive psychological methods to produce "docile," dehumanized subjects.[25] Marxist scholars have also linked boredom to the expansion of public education, which, for them, prepares students for the obeisance and alienation of the capitalist marketplace. To that end, public education since its inception has instilled tolerance of boredom, together with competitiveness and the ability to memorize, as marks of good character.[26] One could challenge each of these claims in their particulars, but they underscore the fact that both simple and existential boredom are subject to historical change and took on new meanings with the rise of modernity.[27] They also raise the possibility that boredom has performed educative functions in US history, even if those functions were only to stifle self-consciousness or class consciousness. Yet the question of intentionality here raises an element of paradox. For if the curriculum meant to impart passivity and dehumanization, surely it required students' full attention rather than their disaffection or distraction.

There have been many attempts to eliminate boredom in school. Efforts to channel children's attention began with John Locke, whose philosophy of mind emphasized sequential exposure to objects and ideas.[28] Control reached its apex with Joseph Lancaster's monitorial system during the early nineteenth century, which used rote memorization and a tightly choreographed system of commands and movements to instruct children. Through surveillance and constant activity, Lancaster sought to eliminate any space for distraction or deviance.[29] These methods softened when adapted to public schools, but attempts to engineer student engagement remained endemic, reappearing in behaviorist psychology during the twentieth century and scripted curriculum during the twenty-first. These latter approaches may dehumanize students, but boredom is as often their target as their ulterior motive. As with more progressive educational approaches, they interpret disengagement as a signal of poor design and leave little room for students' self-recognition or self-mastery. Thus, rather than aspersing teachers or textbooks as intentionally boring, as many critics do, restoring boredom as the child's prerogative may better reveal its subtleties and positive aspects.

Textbooks composed the backbone of the nineteenth-century curriculum. Most were privately owned, confining students to titles they could bring from home or borrow from a seatmate, and although some standard offerings had flooded the market by the 1830s, there remained hundreds of possibilities for individual instruction. Textbooks undergirded the practice of recitation, in which single students memorized and repeated passages while the teacher followed along. This method of instruction was a practical necessity for the ungraded classrooms of the period, in which children of all ages and abilities attended sporadically, learned at their own pace, and often lacked such basic equipment as notepaper or chalkboards. Yet recitation also spoke to the era's aspirations for self-culture and citizenship. Public performance not only provided evidence of student accomplishment but nurtured oratorical skills and encouraged students to internalize the moral sentiments they repeated. Indeed, recitation and textbooks originated as *antidotes* to student boredom, an impulse to intellectual striving and an alternative to droning lectures. But they did not always hold students' attention as intended.[30]

In reviewing nineteenth-century textbooks, one finds innumerable lines and scribbles, random shapes, and extracts of text in margins and flyleaves.[31] Students demonstrated a fascination with movement, drawing trains, carriages, and hot-air balloons, and with nature, especially flowers, trees, birds, and horses. They colored in black-and-white illustrations or embellished them in amusing ways. One boy, paging through a book about birds, put a pipe in each of their mouths. Another, reading a story about a shipwreck, drew a soldier punching a sailor in the face. A third added scatological droppings to two figures in his rhetoric book.[32] Many markings refer to the passage of time or the world outside the schoolhouse window, such as drawings of clocks, hatch marks counting the days, or inscriptions such as, "11 weeks will never go away never never never never."[33] These doodles seem in keeping with the distraction and escapism of simple boredom, yet it remains difficult to establish the intentions behind their creation.

FIGURE 5.2. Student boredom sometimes took the form of irreverent comments or inappropriate embellishments. Courtesy of the American Antiquarian Society.

For one thing, archived textbooks may suffer from forms of selection bias. Many nineteenth-century students ritualistically burned or buried their books at the end of the term.[34] As Patricia Crain points out, it may have been only certain types of students who wrote in their books in the first place. "The wild child of the nineteenth century," she writes, was "the one who [threw] his books away altogether, not the [one who] identified with their books, played in them, and treated them both as extensions of the self and as tokens and adjuncts of sociality."[35] It is also difficult to discern who made the marks inside a given book, and where or when that student did so. Most books had successive, often anonymous users, making it difficult to establish the authorship or motivation behind any given annotation, and offering few clues into the backgrounds of their readers.[36] To whatever degree a book's preservation depended on the character or social status of the owner, it may predetermine the kinds of writing found within.

Another difficulty is that many marginal inscriptions were actually sanctioned by teachers and parents as part of the era's book culture. How to differentiate between these markings and evidence of true boredom? I contend that this is a false choice, based on the assumption that boredom is entirely spontaneous, either unrelated or oppositional to one's surroundings. The lack of context for most marginal inscriptions encourages this sort of dualism, tempting the reader with glimpses of an unfiltered soul. Yet, although Crain observes that children's markings can be "ineluctably mysterious," she later contends that "there's nothing magically 'authentic' about inscriptions—or about children, for that matter"—and it would be a mistake to assume that acts of boredom were more original than other markings.[37]

When one considers two of the primary impulses for marginal inscriptions, it is possible to see how convention and spontaneity overlapped. The first is Vlieghe's concept of practice, in which students worked on penmanship and drawing in simple, repetitive ways to train their eyes and hands, outside the requirements of schoolwork but in keeping with its spirit of self-improvement. The other is the self-stimulatory behavior associated with simple boredom, in which students marked their books to occupy their minds. In both cases, as Vlieghe suggests, repetition became a point of departure to reconsider or repurpose the lesson, a parallel curriculum in which students could apply classroom skills to their own tasks of mastery. Thus, boredom could be both a rejection of assigned lessons and their offshoot, both irreverent and earnest, as students experienced distraction not only *from* but *through* their textbooks. Sanctioned markings may provide necessary context for expressions of student boredom, complicating the task of interpretation but also moving beyond simple, ahistorical forms of the phenomenon.

There were at least three types of virtues imparted in nineteenth-century schoolbook culture—ownership, friendship, and self-improvement—and each of them found parallels in unsanctioned inscriptions. All three virtues relied on the dually public and private nature of schoolbooks, which on one hand were shared between classmates, providing a space for unsupervised communication, and on the other elicited the sort of confessions and personal reflections that students associated with literary culture. In both cases, books became sites of the playfulness and knowingness that yield personal growth. M. O. Grenby illustrates the tension between public and private space by referencing a teacher's remarks in one boy's book, which contained "'the Names of several young Ladies' of the locality, along with comments on their characters and appearance, in the margins." The teacher mentioned this list not out of disapproval, but "solely to shew *Bob's* Taste"—that is, "the Meditations of his heart when wholly alone."[38] Whatever the student's original purpose for writing, he was obviously not "wholly alone" with a teacher reviewing his book. The same ambiguity, operative at the time and across the centuries, is what makes marginalia tantalizing but indeterminate evidence of student mindsets.[39]

The clearest example of the dually public and private nature of marginal annotations was the ownership inscription, written upon receipt of a book, which initiated children into a bourgeois world of private property. Books were one of the first objects to which children could stake a claim, and ownership was thick with emotional meaning.[40] Names on the flyleaf or cover were often accompanied by dedications from the giver, strengthening the transfer of property with bonds of affection. Typical examples include, "To Martha, presented by one, who most earnestly desires her perfection in virtue & goodness," or "Thankful, S. Hersey's."[41] Students were also encouraged to add propriety warnings to their books, most frequently, "Steal not this book for fear of shame, for here you see the owner's name," or "Don't steal this book my dearest friend, for fear the gallows will be your end." These poems may initially have been the product of adult guidance, but assertions of ownership encouraged originality and quickly grew into their own genre of children's writing. Clever variations include, "Steal not this book, for fear of life. / For the owner carries a butcher-knife," "This Book is one thing, Hemp is Another; / Steal not this one thing, For fear of the Other," and "Do not steal this book of knowledge, / Or you'll be sent

FIGURE 5.3. Students often wrote their names and personal ownership inscriptions in their books. Courtesy of the American Antiquarian Society.

to Sing-Sing College."[42] One student wrote a Latin version, loosely translated as "This is my book. God is my witness. / If stolen by anyone, may he be hung by the neck."[43]

Ownership inscriptions inspired other lighthearted imitation as well. Some children signed their names throughout a book, whether for practice or out of simple distraction. Others endorsed books that they enjoyed, following their names with such phrases as "very good book for you / Don't Break it," "Very good liked by little girl," or "bully good book you just bet." (To the last message a subsequent reader responded, "ha.")[44] Some poked fun at the moral tone of dedications. The owner of an 1830s geography book admonished other readers "never to scribble in books, especially if they do not belong to you," beneath which one finds scribbles in several different hands.[45] Some students turned ownership into a game and sent readers hunting for their names. One young woman wrote, "If my name you wish to see look on page 23." Then, "If my name you wish to spy look on page 35." Then, "If you like to turn pages o'er; look on Page 104." Only after reading "Turn back you big fool," does one discover the name "Jennie" tucked under some text.[46] There were some clear examples of boredom in these playful dedications. On the flyleaf of an 1816 reader is written, "Albert G. Conway's book, and go fast asleep."[47] On another is the verse, "If there should be another flood, / Then to this book I'd fly; / If all the earth should be submerged, / This book would still be dry.'" More concrete evidence of boredom would be hard to find.[48]

A second form of approved student writing was poetry dedicated to one's peers, meant to reinforce sentimental bonds in what could otherwise be a competitive classroom. Examples include "Remember me / When this you see," "Forget me not / Forget me never / Till I and you / Shall live together," and "O keep these lines to look upon / When I your friend's forever gone / Remember they were wrote by me / Who ever will prove true to thee."[49] These messages were not always in verse. Aaron Young wrote, "If you forget me it will be because you never liked me." His friend William wrote back, "O, what a lie."[50] In a similar vein, some students wrote uplifting odes or epigrams to demonstrate personal investment in their studies, such as, "That a person can pursue the study of Astronomy and not have exalted notions of the Creator is an idea not to be believed. By me at least."[51] Poetry and inspirational messages resembled the anthologized selections that most students read in class, as well as entries in commonplace books and journals.[52]

Although not products of boredom themselves, friendship poems overlapped with other peer writing to form a parallel sphere of communication in the classroom. Students often reached out to others in moments of malaise, passing notes when they should have been studying. Romance was a popular topic, especially among girls, and earnest dedications could give way to frivolous ditties. One finds poems like "Clara I love you / Clara I do / Clara believe me / for it is true / From Lettie." Or, in a similar vein, "The rose is red / the violet blue / and happy the man / who marrys you," or "May you be happie all the days of you life [sic] / and get a good husband and be a good Wife."[53] Lydia Mason wrote, "All on a summers day Lydia and Fred / went out to play / all along they gathered / roses with witch they tickled / up their noses."[54] Under the heading "Scandal" on the opening page of a science book, one finds a list of girls who hope to get married, with each respondent's reaction noted.[55] Mabel Moore, writing in the 1860s, exacted revenge on a former crush by drawing herself next to a dandy, writing, "Frank after he has been to school. We don't speak to our old friends now. to the girl he used to flirt with."[56] Others, too, drew boys in pretentious poses. One student labeled all the animals in his biology textbook with the names of classmates: D. Eckley was "The Ass," J. Clark was "The Hog," and by a nest of worms he wrote, "The whole school except me. P. D. Clarke biggest of them." He also took a moment to practice his French, relabeling the whale "La Baleine."[57]

While these poems and dedications were meant to be seen by the writers themselves and perhaps by other readers, schoolbooks also contain surreptitious notes to specific students. Besides predictable requests for pencils and paper, many feature observations about classmates' habits and relationships, the omnipresent gaze of peer pressure. "William acts queerly, don't you think so?" asked Addie Jefferson.[58] A friend criticized Louisa Stevens's handwriting as "rather inclined."[59] "You have got up quite a correspondence with Hollander," teased another student.[60] In other notes, the writers asked simply to be left alone, as did the boy listing geometry rules who paused to write, "Shoo . . . don't bother me."[61]

Geometry rules, together with lecture outlines, readers' arithmetic, underlining, and other textual annotations, represent the final type of approved textbook writing. In classrooms short of loose-leaf paper, books were used to test pens, practice handwriting, and take notes. Since most were privately owned, there was less objection to marking in them, and teachers frequently encouraged students to answer questions or summarize passages in the margins, or to reproduce math problems in copybooks. Here too, however, there was an ambiguous boundary between behaviors responding to a lesson and those resulting from self-direction or boredom. Students took seriously the era's focus on self-improvement, and practiced academic skills whenever they could.[62] Young children formed letters and wrote their names, while older students drew landscape sketches, rendered three-dimensional shapes, or recreated maps and globes from memory, often tracing the outline of a coin for their border.[63] In a book about mechanical engineering, a boy included a doodle of a train before dutifully labeling the parts of the engine.[64] In a drawing manual, a generic picture of two men talking was

Frank after he has
been to school. We
don't speak to our old
friends now, to the
girl he used to flirt
with

FIGURE 5.4. Students sometimes exacted revenge by drawing classmates in unflattering ways. Courtesy of the American Antiquarian Society.

annotated with a line from John Milton's *Paradise Lost*.[65] A book of ancient geography includes a tiny drawing of the Parthenon and the word "Athens" amid scribbles on the leaves.[66] In 1868, a student illustrated his grammar book with the capture of Confederate president Jefferson Davis in a woman's dress, a rumor that was repeated in several classroom texts of the era.[67] Another student, reviewing an index of botanical specimens, proudly wrote, "102 different kinds of flowers, plants or trees I have seen this summer in this list," an observation incidental to her lesson but attesting to content knowledge and personal interest.[68] A cheekier boy listed types of birds: "Canary. Yellowbird. Blackbird. Catbird. Jailbird."[69] Again, these self-assigned exercises suggest the admixture of educational practice and boredom, both of which increased students' self-awareness.

Given the explicitly moral content of many schoolbooks, it is interesting to see students interact with text on their own terms. Many kept running commentaries in the margin, a common academic practice, but provided more personal or oppositional observations than teachers might have preferred. Reading *The New England Primer* in the 1820s, Levi Stevens Bartlett wrote, "Some things in this book are probably false."[70] Inscriptions such as "This is not so," "No," and other contraventions also appeared frequently.[71] A younger child, reading the admonition "I must not blow the candle out," made a naughty protagonist respond, "Maybe blows is good—." A later page, with a disobedient girl sulking in front of her mother, bears the speech bubble "My name is Emma," perhaps referring to a sister or friend. Another page, in which a bad boy draws an ugly face on the wall, is copied in the front of the book, echoing the misbehavior. Meanwhile, the endleaves feature a portrait of Richard Roe, the good little protagonist, as a roguish adult.[72] Crain recounts the inscriptions of Mary Lucretia Shelton, whose remarks she finds "pertinent and responsive, engaging the text, disputing with it, idly commenting upon it, exercising her wit and intelligence upon it." After reading Isaac Watt's poem "The Sluggard," Shelton admitted, "I am a sluggard for I love / to lie abed very much in / the morning." Likewise, while Shelton sympathized with a European captive, writing, "don't you feal for them," she amended a subsequent caption to make an African a slave "of fashion." Next to a poem that offered a rhetorical choice between "dissipation" and "housewifery," she wrote, "I should chouse Dissipation."[73]

In each of these cases, we see students deploying humor, irony, and willfulness in their marginal markings. Yet there are also traces of deeper forms of self-knowledge, even despair, approaching existential forms of boredom. An unnamed boy wrote, "2 thousand 4 hundred 50 lines in this book" at the end of his Latin text. Whether in a spirit of accomplishment, humor, or depression, he had counted every one.[74] In 1856, Mary Herbert wrote in her arithmetic book, "Where shall I fly? I'm tired & sick of any thing I do and of myself."[75] Around the

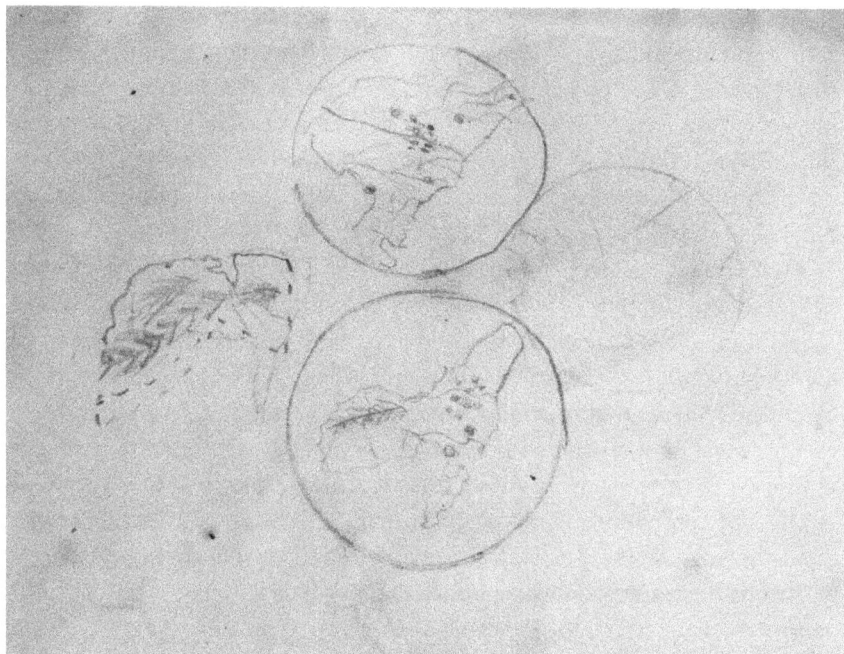

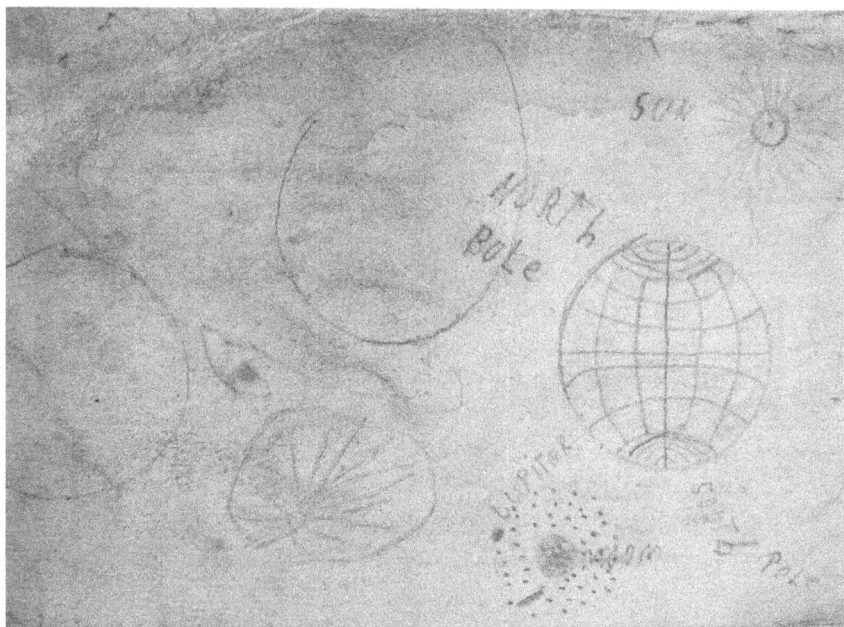

FIGURES 5.5 AND 5.6. Student drawings often imitated the academic content of their books, such as maps and charts. Courtesy of the American Antiquarian Society.

same time, Charlotte Fairbanks wrote, "I have not got any father."[76] These phrases seem to capture the laconic depression of existential boredom, or at least suggest that students were working through changes or disaffection in their own lives. If not entirely unfiltered, they do not rely on the conventions or presumed readership of other messages above, and perhaps open a space to see souls thrown back on themselves, in Heidegger's sense, to wrestle with questions of meaning and purpose.

Kierkegaard refers to boredom as a "superficial profundity," which in some ways is an apt description for students' marginal inscriptions.[77] What could be more meaningless than absent-minded phrases and free-associational drawings dredged from the drudgery of the classroom? What could better reveal the depth of students' thoughts and feelings, otherwise lost to time? In either case, however, it would be a mistake to interpret the untutored style of these markings as proof of their authenticity. As we have seen, many drawings and inscriptions reproduced conventional notions of ownership, friendship, and learning. That ambiguity suggests that boredom was not solely a product of the individual or a wellspring of creative expression, but an ongoing interaction between the "subversive and anarchic" child and the sanctioned curriculum.[78]

Touched with boredom, schoolbooks became sites of emotional immersion and intellectual striving, prompting students to reach outward (to classmates) and inward (to the emergent self), but encouraging forms of growth incidental to the book's didactic purpose. The culture of self-improvement that suffused nineteenth-century schools ensured that children's scattered thoughts returned to their lessons, even if in jest, as they became more knowing. In fact, adults expected this sort of holistic growth from their children's interactions with textbooks: in the nineteenth century, according to M. O. Grenby, "the child's hoped-for progress could be religious, moral, informational, [or] behavioural," in ways that required emotional responses to the reading, including boredom. Inscriptions "nourished children's imaginations," Grenby writes, and in the process secured "subconscious compliance with authorial hopes for children's literature," achieving growth through emulation.[79] Although the anonymous nature of textbook marginalia makes it difficult to trace the emotional development of particular students, markings do seem to show an aggregate graduation from simple to complex expressions of boredom. They were not merely therapeutic responses to confinement but, as philosophers maintain, fulfilled an educational function, paralleling the growth of children's self-consciousness.

6

DESKS AND NOSTALGIA

Desks have been ubiquitous in American schools since the mid-nineteenth century. Made of wood and iron, bolted to the floor, they began as fixtures in the truest sense of the word. So firmly did they anchor the classroom that when progressive reformers introduced movable models in the early 1900s, they complained that teachers kept lining them up as if the desks remained fastened in place, with children fastened within them.[1] Progressives worried that such arrangements would produce passive students, but as we have seen, they did not. Children simply redirected their energy toward the desks themselves, which, according to one writer in the mid-nineteenth century, were soon "adorned with every embellishment that the ingenuity of professional whittlers [could] devise."[2] While historians have analyzed desks as signals of change or consistency in teaching practices, they have yet to reckon with the significance of those illicit etchings, and particularly their place in the politics of nostalgia.[3]

By the 1920s, desks had become fixtures in the public mind, mainstays of museums and antique stores, where they derived a sort of totemic power from the figures carved into them. As the United States hurtled into the modern era, school furniture became a symbol of national innocence, satisfying a craving for simpler times. By obscuring historical realities, however, it also promoted an obnoxious brand of conservative politics, which used an imagined golden age to condemn changes in modern schools. This chapter rejects such selective, symbolic memory, although it does not reject nostalgia itself, which has never been limited to condemnation of the present or uncritical acceptance of the past.

Rather, by clarifying nostalgia's conceptual foundations, it hopes to point toward more generative forms of educational conservatism.

In recent decades, scholars from a variety of disciplines and ideological perspectives have rediscovered moral sentiments as necessary prerequisites for political association. Rather than subscribe in a purely rational way to the social contract or be blindly loyal to the state, they contend, citizens must develop tender feelings toward compatriots, communities, and common institutions like schools. Such sentimental attachments have the potential to encourage individual introspection and, from there, to widen the "circle of care" that one extends to others. Nostalgia can foster these feelings, bridging individual and collective identity to form a common culture, but only if it is taken up in the right spirit. By outlining its dual manifestations—reactionary and exclusive on one hand, sustaining and inclusive on the other—defaced desks may offer a corrective to some of the current political strife embroiling public schools.[4]

School desks became an obligatory set piece in US politics during the first decades of the twentieth century. One finds many versions of the same scene: a famous man tracing his fingers across the scarred face of his old desk, reflecting on humble beginnings, character-building lessons, mischievous scrapes, and his own good fortune.[5] When Al Smith ran for governor of New York in 1924, he returned to his Catholic school for a photograph at his desk, where an opened drawer revealed his childhood markings.[6] Walt Disney made the same pilgrimage, and his hometown museum in Marceline, Missouri, prominently displays a desk bearing his initials to symbolize the sanitized past that his theme parks would market to the masses.[7] Ironically, as desktop initials became shorthand for personal authenticity, Americans suspended doubts about the authenticity of the artifacts themselves. The John F. Kennedy Presidential Library twice courted controversy by displaying a desk from Choate, the elite New England boarding school, with the initials "JFK" scratched on the surface. Its owner, the wife of a former teacher, had been unable to convince Choate officials to accept the desk as a donation, and experts pointed out that it was not the style used during the 1930s, when Kennedy attended the school. The museum displayed it anyway, reasoning that it might "evoke Jack's life as a high school student," and Kennedy's roommate sent a letter assuring visitors that the president "carved his initials in everything," adding the thinnest veneer of credibility to an otherwise obvious fraud.[8] An even more telling example occurred in 1936, when Henry Ford took a reporter to the one-room school he had attended as a child, which he subsequently transported to Dearborn, Michigan, and reopened as a shrine to small-town America. The reporter caught his breath as Ford stood at his old desk and pointed out the initials "H. F." carved onto its surface. "For a moment he appeared lost in reverie," the reporter wrote. "It was difficult to read his thoughts."[9] The pause invited readers to juxtapose Ford's childhood with the looming burdens of greatness, the sort of cinematic move that would frame *Citizen Kane* (1941) a few years later. Yet entirely absent from the story—and probably from Ford's own inscrutable reflections—was the fact that he had carved those initials not as a boy but when the school reopened, only seven years before. Indeed, the first thing Ford did upon entering the building was to pull out a penknife. So powerful was the need to authenticate lived experience with childish scrawls that he felt obliged to do so as an adult and, at the same time, absolved himself from the implicit fraudulence of the act. This is not to say that Ford knowingly misrepresented the initials' origins. More likely he fell victim to his own mythology.[10]

That vandalized desks obscure the complexity of the past is self-evident, but the degree to which they do so is nevertheless remarkable. Historical truth does not stand a chance against the moral truths that desks seem to embody. Given the massive changes afoot in US society and in schools themselves—from progressive education and high school expansion in the first half of the twentieth century to delinquency and drugs in the second—one can appreciate why successive generations may have longed for the little red schoolhouse of their imaginations. The trouble arises when these personal musings become the basis for exclusionary politics. It is difficult to separate Henry Ford's sentimental vision of rural life from his antisemitic diatribes, or Walt Disney's folksy portrayal of Main Street, USA, from the racist policies that kept Disneyland's employees almost exclusively white for its first two decades.[11] These trends have continued and perhaps worsened in recent years. Conservative politicians have practically weaponized wistfulness, making uncritical references to the United States as a white, Christian nation; alluding to unchanging family or marital structures; and denouncing public schools as increasingly violent, immoral, and unpatriotic. These claims not only disregard historical fact but inevitably equate diversity with decline, necessitating a defense of traditional injustices and opening an unbridgeable divide between social groups. They deny the very possibility of a shared past.

Many historians have tried to counter this sort of reactionary nostalgia with fact-based arguments, hoping that evidence will impel Americans to approach the past with their heads rather than their hearts. Historical literacy is certainly a worthy goal, but it also implies a false dichotomy between thinking and feeling. One can encourage emotional attachment to the past without oversimplifying it, but doing so requires a more nuanced understanding of nostalgia itself.[12]

Nostalgia has intrigued political theorists since the term was coined in the middle of the eighteenth century, as a medical diagnosis for Swiss mercenaries pining for their mountain villages. At the time, most regarded the condition with a mixture of fascination and disgust. Why would anyone wallow in the particularism of old customs when the Enlightenment promised progress and universal truth? Nostalgia seemed like an exercise in childish self-deception.[13] Yearning for a lost place and time held a more conflicted appeal for writers like Jean-Jacques Rousseau, whose vision of republican citizenship celebrated the simplicity of the rural past but also frowned on the sort of escapism that might weaken political participation in the present. Rousseau's solution was to formulate nostalgia as a form of moral engagement, a spur to thoughtful action rather than passive brooding. By encouraging citizens to seek the past, he believed, nostalgia included a potentially critical component, inducing them, in the words of Martin McCallum, "to re-evaluate the ideas on which their sentiments depend [and] orient them towards non-alienating sentiments of the moral and political order." Nostalgia became an antidote to resignation or irony, and, by suffusing citizenship with emotion, it created a sublime attachment to the body politic.[14]

Contemporary political theorists have revived elements of Rousseau's approach. Many worry that as Enlightenment claims lose cultural authority—as abstract commitments to humanity falter along lines of race, gender, or nationality, or as science fails to establish a system of objective truth—they leave "shipwrecked minds" casting about for meaning and increasingly prone to tribalism, religious fundamentalism, or other forms of reactionary nostalgia. The latter ideologies are troubling not so much because they are retrograde but because they are superficial, offering counterfeit feelings of belonging without actually challenging the corrosive foundations of modern society. Decoupled from a particular sense of place, they sentimentalize the act of longing itself, producing an unstable and easily manipulated alternative to rationalism.[15]

Rather than this sort of "simple" or "restorative" nostalgia, which enshrines shallow feelings as unquestionable truths, scholars have offered thicker manifestations, including "reflective" nostalgia, which subjects idealized memories to a healthy dose of skepticism, and ultimately a nostalgia of "hope," which takes an emotional past not as something to be overcome but as a necessary basis for cooperative action in the future.[16] The best-known proponent of the latter type of nostalgia was the historian Christopher Lasch. In *The True and Only Heaven* (1991), Lasch argued that the uncritical embrace of a sanitized past was a corollary to the mistaken belief in unfettered progress.[17] "If the idea of progress has the curious effect of weakening the inclination to make intelligent provision for the future," he wrote, "nostalgia, its ideological twin, undermines the ability to make intelligent use of the past." For Lasch, reactionary nostalgia devitalized history, rendering it both one-dimensional and harmlessly distant from the present. Like progressive optimism, it offered little basis for criticism or redirection.[18] Lasch nevertheless maintained a central role for emotional perceptions of history, a form of nostalgia that he called "memory." "Memory may idealize the past," he wrote, "but not in order to condemn the present. . . . Rather, it sees past, present and future as continuous." Only when it was built on continuity rather than condemnation could nostalgia imbue the stewardship and judgment that Lasch found lacking in modern politics.[19]

Commitments to memory, sentiment, and historical continuity have been central to the communitarian movement, of which Lasch was a leading voice.[20] Against the paradigm of modern liberalism, communitarians emphasize context and interpersonal ties as the foundations of society, replacing the unencumbered individual with a "situated self" and the language of personal rights with one of collective duties, civic virtue, and the common good.[21] In their minds, community offers an antidote to the dissolution of modern society and, variously, a means to reaffirm personhood, democracy, environmentalism, and social justice. For example, Wendell Berry contends that civic life begins with "the mental and spiritual condition of knowing that the place is shared, and that the people who share the place define and limit the possibilities of each other's lives." Writers who do not identify as communitarians have taken similar positions. Alasdair MacIntyre writes of "[inheriting] from the past of my family, my city, my tribe, my nation, a variety of debts, inheritances, rightful expectations and obligations. These constitute the given way of my life, my moral starting point," and become the basis to forge common ground with others.[22] Martha Nussbaum agrees. "If [one] can portray the denigrated group as part of a 'we' that suffered together in the past and is working together for a future of justice," she writes, "this makes it far more difficult to continue to see the other as a contaminating and excluded outsider."[23] The argument here is that people are rooted in a particular place and cannot stand outside themselves: there is no abstract humanity, no escape from ecological limits, no "view from nowhere." In this context, nostalgia can become a source of humility rather than superiority. Fond recollections underscore one's debt to the past, prompting forbearance and mutual recognition rather than reflexive condemnation. One must beware of undue sentimentality, of course, but it is a fallacy to assume that emotional attachments necessarily foreclose critical thought or inclusivity. To say that Ford or Disney oversimplified the objects of their yearning is not to indict yearning as such, nor the conservative preference for custom and slow change that nostalgia embodies.[24]

It is exactly on this point that school desks become helpful. Transforming vandalized desks into symbols of simpler times wrenches them out of context not only because it conceals the historical realities of schooling but because it overlooks the intentions of the vandals themselves. Suffice to say that no child carved her initials into a desk to make a point about national innocence or to asperse subsequent generations of students. When children sat down at their desks, they looked at surfaces covered with a palimpsest of gouges and ink stains. These marks forged a connection between past, present, and future occupants.

They promised a degree of permanence and authenticated students' being in a particular space, inducting the individual into the lineage of those who came before.[25] Desks became a physical and heavily symbolic meeting place between the individual and the community, and children, well aware of the sentimental conventions surrounding them, performed their part in the ritual by adding their names to the list. Jonathan Zimmerman recounts the story of a Texas town in which six siblings, learning that their father had carved his initials in the schoolhouse when he was a boy, decided to follow suit over their years of attendance.[26] Carving initials into desks also came up in students' poems, essays, and speeches. For example, an outgoing student at the Colored Normal School in Richmond, Virginia, proudly recited the following poem at graduation:

> My name is still cut on the seat by the door,
> I am trying to cut it much higher, you know,
> But I wonder if fame can e'er give the joy,
> I found at old Normal when I was a boy?[27]

These quaint gestures reflected a broader romanticism developing around public education at the turn of the century. Sentimental novels and newspaper stories often remarked on "the hundred names and initials . . . scattered hither and yon about the old [school] building," which told "a tale of those who once made the walls echo with their mirth and song."[28]

Adults, too, were drawn to defaced desks, not only as symbols of times gone by but as embodied forms of community. The removal of old desks marked a moment of reflection and affirmation for citizens and could draw large crowds. In 1913, when a small town in Illinois decided to sell its desks, a local reporter carefully documented the inscriptions. He saw "designs such as two hearts intertwined, with initials in them, in some cases foreshadowing happy nuptial events; in others nuptial tragedies. There were revolvers which were carved by boys who wanted to go West to fight Indians, or who regretted that their age prevented them having participated in the battles of the Civil War, which were still recent history when the boys who are now men went to school. There were unskillful carvings of faces of boys and girls, and there were mathematical designs without number." He concluded, "From the looks of the 200 desks taken from the four rooms, every boy who attended the school must have registered his initials." More than furniture, these were cenotaphs to a town's history, and across the country, residents eagerly purchased the scarred desks that schools discarded.[29]

Nostalgia for school desks became the impetus for at least two forms of political action. The first was community mobilization. For example, in 1898, the town of Sleepy Hollow, New York, planned to demolish the one-room schoolhouse that the author Washington Irving had attended as a child and in which he had

repeatedly carved his initials. While the board cited cost savings and moderniza-
tion as reasons to raze the building, a public campaign won a referendum vote
to preserve it.[30] Forty years later, the nearby town of Stony Point likewise divided
into "warring camps" over whether to close its high school and consolidate with
the neighboring Haverstraw district. (Haverstraw had erected a new building
after its previous high school burned down under suspicious circumstances: an
investigation found that the state regents' exams had been taken from the principal's office during the evacuation.) Supporters argued that consolidation would
provide wider course offerings and better facilities, but opponents objected that
closing Stony Point High School would dishonor the legacy of James Farley, the
postmaster general (and a close ally of Franklin Roosevelt's), who had graduated in 1905. To underscore the point, they noted that Farley had inscribed his
initials into one of the desks, which was still in use. In the end, Stony Point failed
to stop the consolidation plan, and its building was reclassified as an elementary school. Yet these local movements echoed those of innumerable other small
towns, in which outdated furniture and facilities became a symbol of local control, a demand that community identity be taken into account amid the march
of educational progress and centralized governance.[31]

A second form of political engagement was the cultivation of critical memory.
Take the ten wooden desks from a segregated African American school in New-
berry County, South Carolina, currently on display at the National Museum of
African American History and Culture. According to the museum, these artifacts
are meant to demonstrate how "institutional pillars," such as schools, "have sustained and guided African American communities over the course of American
history" and, in a phrase that captures the complexity of memorializing segregation, how those communities "made a way out of no way."[32] For decades, the prevailing judgment of African American schools was the one advanced in *Brown v.
Board of Education* (1954): that they were "inherently unequal," not only because
they lacked adequate funding or facilities but because they inflicted psychological
damage on African American students. "A sense of inferiority affects the motivation of a child to learn," wrote a unanimous Supreme Court. "Segregation . . . has
a tendency to [retard] the educational and mental development of negro children
and to deprive them of some of the benefits they would receive in a racially integrated school system."[33] This claim provided a useful legal rationale, insofar as it
invalidated the principle of state-sanctioned segregation and prevented the gradual reallocation of funds to racially separate schools, but it came at a steep price.
Over subsequent decades, courts repeatedly took the superiority of white schools
for granted while ordering the closure of African American schools, which, in
turn, led to the firing of Black teachers, the transportation and dispersal of Black
students, and the dilution of many Black communities' voices in educational

politics. Nor did the purported inferiority of African American schools reflect the experience of all the parents and students that patronized them. As Vanessa Siddle Walker and others have pointed out, many viewed schools as anchors of the community, staffed by respected professionals with high expectations for behavior and corresponding records of achievement, as well as places of friendship, play, and personal growth.[34] Unequal and unacceptable as they may have been, for generations of Americans these were not inherently dysfunctional institutions but spaces imbued with warm memories. Again, those experiences were not universal and they should not blind us to inequalities of class and power within segregated institutions; nor do they prescribe a particular position on the subsequent course of school desegregation. All the same, by evoking bittersweet legacies of the past, they have the potential to heighten citizens' sensitivity and encourage a deeper form of political deliberation, within the affected communities and in the nation as a whole.[35]

FIGURE 6.1. A desk from the Hope School, a segregated institution in South Carolina, inscribed with the names of several students. Courtesy of the Smithsonian National Museum of African American History and Culture, Gift of the Hope School Community Center, Pomaria, SC.

It is hardly an accident that the paragraphs above reference rural and African American schools, which over the past century have been those most likely to suffer from unequal resources and most affected by forced closures. In both cases, educational reformers have imposed change from above, underwritten by dubious notions of local deficiency, and have done little to tap into local sources of knowledge or legitimacy. While systematically underserving communities, centralized school governance has promoted the sort of competitive striving—between both schools and individual students—that inevitably comes at the expense of collective advancement.[36] These communities "can no longer afford to be among the purveyors of this brand of individualism," argues the historian Paul Theobald. "Restoration of the shared projects that constitute community . . . is not sentimental nostalgia for the 'good old days.' Rather, it is a practical course of action for an age when resources have become seriously depleted or polluted, when hate has reemerged as an acceptable political position, and when the profit motive has proven itself capable of superseding all other pressing human and spiritual concerns." For Theobald, if schools are to become truly democratic spaces, they need not only to equalize funding or improve technologies of teaching, but to affirm the particular places in which they are embedded and which they claim to serve.[37] Common strategies for doing so have included devolving power to parents and board members, hosting community events in the school building, and incorporating local history in the curriculum. Preserving outdated facilities has been less popular, perhaps for obvious reasons. Community demographics change, and not everyone has fond memories of the local school to begin with. It can be expensive to maintain old structures, and difficult to argue that sentimental attachments outweigh access to modern amenities. Nevertheless, rural and urban communities have often demonstrated fierce allegiance to older buildings, in no small part because of the accumulated experience that they embody.

Carved desks, creaky floorboards, and weathered walls should not merely evoke the "melancholy romanticism" associated with ancient ruins, the sort of nostalgia that relies on disjuncture with lost times and fosters a shallow, voyeuristic approach to the past. Schools are "inhabited ruins," which, through continued use, impart a physical awareness of time and place, the persistence of the past in our experience of the present.[38] More than that, they exert agency as "public things," to use Bonnie Honig's term: the sort of objects that gather people together and enable "diverse peoples [to] come to see and experience themselves . . . as a collected if not a collective" public.[39] Honig argues that US democracy is in disrepair because of the neglect of these common objects and, we might add, because of their unmooring from the past. While some forms of physical degradation may undermine support for public education, there are others—such as carving one's initials on a desk—that seem to pull in the opposite direction, establishing a personal connection to shared space, which, in turn, fosters social trust, civic participation, and the many benefits that issue from them.[40]

Nostalgia grounds a collective sense of who we are and what we value. As a form of community spirit, it need not be exclusionary and cannot be relegated to bygone eras. Most parents and students retain strong support for their local schools, which remain a vital source of community cohesion.[41] It should not trouble us that sentimental memories account for some of their support—not because we condone wishful policymaking or build our politics on useful falsehoods, but because society thrives when it imbues the public good with personal meaning. Voters are not wrong in their attachment to tradition; they are wrong only when they deny others' claims to it. The choice confronting Americans, then, in schools and in general, seems to be whether our politics will be guided by a toxic, reactionary nostalgia or a nobler version, intent on preserving human connections amid change. All the children who move through our schools will one day leave a mark on our society. Let us hope, first, that they feel sufficiently invested to leave a mark next to ours on their desks.

7

WALLS AND THE TABOO

The climax of J. D. Salinger's *The Catcher in the Rye* (1951) occurs when Holden Caulfield, a troubled teenager, finds the words "Fuck you" written on the walls of his little sister's school. Having lost his own innocence and determined to preserve that of other children, he concludes that a "perverty bum" broke into the school and wrote the phrase. He fantasizes retributive violence against the man. Lost on Caulfield but obvious to the reader is that one of the students themselves probably wrote it.[1] Children seem to have an irrepressible urge to write on school walls, especially in the privacy of bathrooms, where dirty words seem most at home and punishment seems least likely. Like nineteenth-century textbooks, bathroom walls vacillate between spontaneity and convention and between public and private space, but instead of mimicking academic culture they introduce children to masturbation, defecation, sexuality, and other taboos, expounded on in foul language and surprisingly durable traditions of wit and humor. These inscriptions tend to incite moral panic when adults find them, but crackdowns are episodic and ineffective: age, gender, and status differences keep most teachers from sharing bathrooms with their students, while basic decorum limits supervision of those who enter.[2] The result is a vulnerable space, in which potentially embarrassing bodily functions are not only on students' minds but spelled out before their eyes, and also one of profound freedom, in which anonymity produces a measure of equality, privacy encourages contemplation, and students can (figuratively) speak the unspeakable. In all of these respects, bathrooms heighten self-consciousness, offering children opportunities for growth and wholeness that remain unavailable anywhere else at school.

Bathroom graffiti (or "latrinalia") emerged as a topic of scholarly inquiry during the 1950s and early 1960s, when interest in vernacular culture, taboos, and the unconscious was at its peak.[3] Subsequent studies have fallen into two broad categories. The first analyzes graffiti as a form of psychosocial development, in which instinctual forces burst forth on the bathroom wall in terms alternatively attributed to the oral, anal, and genital stages of classical Freudianism, the collective unconscious of Jung, or the underlying systems of structuralism. The second category enlists bathroom writing as a form of antirepressive politics, particularly drawing from the Marxism of Herbert Marcuse and the poststructuralism of Michel Foucault. Whereas earlier theories associated vandalism with aggression and implicitly endorsed the status quo, both of these approaches deny that latrinalia is inherently pathological or in need of correction. To the contrary, they interpret smutty scrawls as organic appeals to life.

Psychosocial and poststructural interpretations continue to dominate scholarship on latrinalia, but by framing the phenomenon as a product of subconscious drives and power structures, respectively, both tend to overlook the relationship between bathroom writing and conscious selfhood. This chapter returns to the 1950s to examine latrinalia from another perspective, using the work of Erik Erikson, Erich Fromm, Hannah Arendt, and Paul Goodman to explore the mindset of the children doing the reading and writing. It argues that the privacy of bathroom stalls provides a unique space for self-discovery: that taboo messages confront children with existential challenges, and ultimately that ridiculous, ribald, or smutty material, otherwise absent from the official curriculum, can be educational without being as tragic or corrupting as Caulfield fears.

The fact that bathroom graffiti is so often sexual or scatological makes it seem timeless, a manifestation of subconscious urges. Just as structural theories used symbolism, rules-based systems, and orderly phases of development to reveal the underlying logic of society, early studies interpreted bathroom messages as the unfolding of instinctual drives.[4] In a typical remark, the artist Brassaï argued that the transition from "supervised" schoolwork to "anonymous" graffiti opened the door to elemental self-expression. "It is about mastering the frenzy of the unconscious," he explained. "These abbreviated signs are none other than the origins of writing—these animals, monsters, demons, heroes, phallic deities are the elements of mythology, no less."[5] Brassaï was one of many commentators to compare juvenile scrawls to Paleolithic cave paintings.[6] The folklorist Alan Dundes equated dirty words with "the desire that infants allegedly have to handle and manipulate their feces."[7] Others catalogued scatological rhymes ("Push the button, pull the chain / Out comes a little black choo-choo train"), references to sexuality ("Jimmy fucked Nancy [almost]," or "I like to fuck"), self-revelations ("I like guys who are honest"), and spiritual insights ("Religion is shit").[8] Toilets elicited certain forms of humor, boasting, and confession—expressed anonymously and epigrammatically—that seemed to reflect innate impulses and predictable stages of psychological growth. Many researchers thought that bathroom graffiti could unlock the mysteries of human development.

Nevertheless, the significance of these inscriptions was debatable. Researchers struggled to establish whether anonymity made latrinalia a direct reflection of social values, in which homophobic attitudes yielded homophobic graffiti, say, and tolerance of homosexuality led to its decline, or whether the transgressive nature of vandalism suggested an inverse relationship, in which slurs once spoken publicly migrated to the bathroom as they became taboo.[9] Nor was it clear whether vandals were more likely to voice the viewpoints of dominant or minority cultures, or (mirroring broader debates in Freudian psychoanalysis) whether graffiti was implicitly sexual or aggressive.[10]

Interpreting latrinalia as the product of unchanging structures posed particular problems on the cusp of radical social change. In 1953, the sexologist Alfred Kinsey published an influential study suggesting that graffiti was less common and less explicit in women's restrooms than in men's, a result that he took as evidence of a lower sex drive in women.[11] Subsequent surveys challenged this finding, claiming that while women and girls were more likely to write about idealism and identity, they were in fact as prolific as boys and were also as likely to post messages about sexuality, iconoclasm, and rebellion. Empirical results could support both claims: it seems that, with the rise of second-wave feminism in the intervening decade, young women simply began to write more.[12] There is some truth, then, to the criticism that by obscuring individual motives and emphasizing form over content, structural explanations struggled to accommodate cultural change and subtly depoliticized children's actions—that a "deep view" of latrinalia foregrounded the psychosocial processes at work but too easily led to disempowerment or abstraction.[13]

Since the 1960s, other researchers have foregrounded student agency, interpreting bathrooms as politicized spaces and graffiti as an impetus for self-consciousness and class consciousness, incorporating dirty words into a larger form of antirepressive politics.[14] In *Eros and Civilization* (1955) and "Repressive Tolerance" (1965), Herbert Marcuse famously argued that the repression of libidinal instincts was unnecessary in an age of material prosperity—indeed, that it was nonsense for authorities to denounce sexuality or exuberance as "juvenile delinquency" while needlessly perpetuating "mature delinquency" through war and exploitation.[15] Marcuse did not address latrinalia specifically, but the phenomenon perfectly captured his admonition to call the obscene by name, to affirm organic wholeness against a mechanistic society, and to locate aggression in so-called economic and political progress rather than in acts of nonconformity. Nor was it surprising that adolescents should adopt this sort of subversive expression. Confronted with their parents' hypocrisy and the psychic damage of modern capitalism, Marcuse argued, protest became an instinctive impulse for young people. It was only natural that its expression would "assume a childlike, ridiculous immaturity," as it did in bathrooms.[16] Inscriptions from high schools at the time seemed to bear out Marcuse's point. As adolescents became more politically conscious, dirty jokes were often accompanied by activist messages such as "The principal is a pig," "Free students," "Think for yourself," "What would happen if nobody took tests," and "Join the teen-age rebellion."[17]

Political consciousness emerged not only through sexual and scatological messages but through the spatial affordances of bathroom walls themselves. Private space was inherently vulnerable to waste and damage, as both students and school authorities knew perfectly well. Beginning in the 1970s, many urban schools responded to budgetary pressures by cutting back on bathroom supplies and installing stainless-steel fixtures.[18] Some went so far as to lock bathrooms during the school day, station monitors inside, or remove doors from toilet stalls to limit graffiti.[19] Students roundly rejected these measures, which were usually imposed on poorer, nonwhite schools. Unsanitary and degrading bathroom conditions routinely appeared on lists of demands during student protests and often became the subject of bathroom graffiti itself.[20] Posting unsanctioned messages in a shared space allowed students to forge a collective identity, distinct from younger children in its vulgarity and distinct from adults in its opposition to authority.[21] In this respect, latrinalia exemplifies James C. Scott's concept of the "hidden transcript," a type of surreptitious communication that sustains collective consciousness in otherwise intrusive and authoritarian institutions.[22]

Recent interpretations of bathroom walls as spaces of resistance and group identity have come primarily from poststructural scholarship, much of it patterned on the work of Michel Foucault.[23] From Foucault's perspective, schools condition students through the endless surveillance of ostensibly nurturing teachers and counselors. By remaining relatively unobserved, school bathrooms emerge as "heterotopias," value-laden spaces associated with age or gender segregation and taboo activities, which are susceptible to forms of deviance suppressed elsewhere in society.[24] Henri Lefebvre and Edward Soja make similar arguments about "third" spaces, those in which objective or utilitarian social functions are overwritten with oppositional forms of meaning that subordinate groups can turn to their own ends.[25] Other studies have used these concepts to explore the role of latrinalia as an expression of gender and sexuality, as well as the ways in which its anonymity breeds resistance, double consciousness, and subjectivity among students. To the extent that they describe the formation of selfhood, these studies usually do so in the context of power and socially constructed identity.[26]

Surveying the field of latrinalia over the past fifty years, then, one finds two interpretative categories: the first focused on instinctual sources of the taboo, the second on space and the crosscurrents of power. There are similarities between the two. Both interpret bathroom graffiti as an expression of psychological health, both situate it in the interplay of privacy and social structures, and both see that interplay as a source of emergent selfhood. Entirely missing from the scholarly literature, however, has been any attention to the impact of graffiti on individual consciousness—the lived experience of the bathroom—which could further integrate existing accounts.

Appreciating the role of latrinalia in children's maturation requires a return to the psychological and political theories of the 1950s, as well as sustained attention to privacy as the fundamental source of bathroom writing. Especially helpful is the developmental psychology of Erik Erikson, which relied on stages of development but loosened the determinacy of earlier Freudian theories. Rather than reducing personality to the oral and genital stages of infancy, Erikson emphasized

FIGURE 7.1. Bathroom stalls provide a dually public and private space for students to exchange messages. PxHere website.

self-formation as an active and ongoing process throughout adolescence, resulting from social influences, alienation, and personal intuition. For Erikson, acts of deviance and feelings of suffering in childhood became the basis for adult freedom, "mobilizing capacities to see and say, to dream and plan, to design and construct, in new ways."[27] This sort of growth required spaces for reflection and solitary play, from which the child could stand apart from others and integrate her experiences.[28]

Like Erikson, the psychologist Erich Fromm equated freedom with the spontaneous creativity of children, which originated in the unconscious but came to fruition in moments of conscious reflection.[29] Freedom was antithetical to the repressive destructiveness, militarism, and hatred that afflicted mass society, Fromm argued, but, breaking with writers like Marcuse, he claimed that it could not be grounded in pleasure alone. Overemphasis on the instinctive sources of either aggression *or* sexuality reduced the human being to "a machine that can only produce inherited patterns of the past," who had "no part in his own life, no responsibility, and not even a trace of freedom."[30] Because Erikson and Fromm presented selfhood as more than a byproduct of instinctual or social forces—exactly the dualism underlying current theories of latrinalia—they may help reimagine the bathroom as a place of maturation and self-realization.

Probably the most important theorist of privacy and selfhood in the twentieth century was Hannah Arendt. At the center of Arendt's political theory was a strict separation of public and private spheres, the former embodied by the polis and common projects of statecraft, the latter by the home, which became both a material foundation for individuals to enter the public realm and a retreat from the rigors of political life or the glare of public scrutiny.[31] Political excellence required public performance and the recognition of one's equals, but it was also dependent on sites that remained out of view. Aaron Schutz underscores the spatial aspect of this argument: "In contrast with totalitarianism, which eliminates the capacity for individual movement and destroys all space," he notes that, for Arendt, "the public is a realm of total equality, in which each person is equal not because they are the same (as in totalitarianism) but because each has the opportunity to present themselves as equally unique."[32] Unfortunately, as modernity eroded distinctions between public and private spheres, Arendt worried that the two combined into the "social," an amorphous space that abandoned collective endeavors for private gain, replaced the freedom of equals with anonymous authority, and threatened the possibility of individual growth.[33]

Arendt concluded that children, especially, had to be shielded from the public sphere, since they could not yet be regarded as equals or enter into proper political exchanges. To grow into freedom, children first required privacy and adult authority, allowing them to learn about the cultural inheritance for which they would later assume responsibility, while simultaneously preserving their "natality" and capacity for radical change.[34] Arendt acknowledged that many aspects of education had shifted from the family to intermediate institutions such as schools, but she maintained that the latter needed to be fundamentally private spaces, in which children were protected from public scrutiny and subject to adult authority. To abandon authority or sever intergenerational ties would subject children to the worst aspects of the social—the capricious, conformist tyranny of the peer group—while destroying the shared world of tradition and denying them the freedom of individuality.[35] Thus, Arendt's dictum that "a life spent entirely in public, in the presence of others, becomes . . . shallow" rang doubly true for children: maturation and interiority required a space apart from the crowd.[36]

Is the bathroom the kind of space in which children can grow up? In some ways, it seems antithetical to Arendt's educational and political visions: an environment segregated by age and unmediated by adult authority, in which there is no collective action and the speech (such as it is) remains anonymous and often ironic.[37] Even theorists who challenge Arendt's sharp distinctions between childhood and adulthood or between education and politics tend to defend the protopolitical classroom as a respectable, constructive space in which teachers carefully inculcate democratic habits, not one in which children laugh at raunchy limericks.[38] In other respects, however, the comparison seems less far-fetched. Glossing Arendt, Gert Biesta describes the ideal school as a "worldly space" dedicated to the preservation of "otherness and difference," in which individuals become themselves by being with and valuing others.[39] Peer pressure is hardly the only threat to individualism, he points out; the increasing standardization and instrumentalism of schools themselves is also predicated on "an erasure of plurality, diversity, and difference." In that context, one might interpret latrinalia as a benign expression of deviance—an interruption of too-smooth educational processes—and the bathroom as precisely the kind of space "in which unique, singular individuals can come into the world."[40] Neil Dhingra has also argued that preserving students' natality requires not only adults' authority, as Arendt implies, but their patience. Insofar as schools seek to preserve natality, he writes, they will always be partly "the messy, somewhat indecipherable spontaneous creation of students," in which attempts at public speech are bound to include childish forms of "gibberish."[41]

Bathroom walls are certainly a worldly space, where attempts at humor (and, yes, Arendt's "virtuosity") elicit recognition and response from one's peers, and where messages can edge from private to public issues. The subversive potential of such communication is well illustrated by an incident in which a school security officer found a message in the girls' bathroom that read, "Bomb. You better get out, cuz there [*sic*] in the school." A similar message in the boys' bathroom the day before suggested an imminent threat. Upon further examination, however, it became clear not only that the two messages had different authors, but that each had taken shape in stages, with subsequent students playfully transforming their meanings into something sure to alarm school officials. The wall became a space of participation, exchange, and a playful form of collective action.[42]

At the same time, it is significant that the anonymity of the bathroom holds social standards at bay, allowing children to be in the presence of others while also, in an acute sense, being with themselves.[43] The dually public and private nature of latrinalia at least partly addresses Arendt's insistence on sincerity, in ways reminiscent of the educational critic Paul Goodman and his plea for "poetic speech."[44] Writing in the early 1960s, Goodman worried that vapid leisure and consumerism had robbed young people of the ability to express their desires and, consequently, had estranged them from themselves. Under social pressure, he wrote, "the adolescent ceases to believe in the rightness of his own wants and soon he even doubts their existence." Natural feelings of love or aspiration become sources of embarrassment, and "rebellious claims seem even to himself to be groundless, immature, ridiculous." Youth culture adopted irony and jargon to gain a measure of distance from adults, but in the process it sacrificed sincerity.[45] "Poetic speech" was authentic and spontaneous, a means of recognizing one's instinctive needs but also a point of initiation into a political community. In explicitly Arendtian terms, Goodman saw this form of speech as a means of "launching into an environment that is *unlike* oneself," of "making one's identity," and of "losing oneself with others in order to grow."[46]

One need not overstate the eloquence of bathroom inscriptions to recognize the same sort of sincerity at work. Several researchers have observed that for young women, especially those from marginalized groups, "penning and reading bathroom graffiti about sexual orientation, physical desires, and bodily functions allow girls to explore and expose complex, adult issues" in an environment sheltered from public scrutiny.[47] Others have found female students asserting personal dignity and collective power by using bathroom stalls to warn classmates about sexual predators.[48] Nor do messages need to be particularly earnest to elicit sincerity: it is hard to imagine a child reading *any* vulgar message with ironic detachment. The public nature of latrinalia may position the taboo as a signifier of adulthood—a projection of strength, knowingness, or sexual prowess—but private contemplation merely underscores its posturing externality to the self. During moments of solitude, children are likely to recognize the gap, and perhaps to ask whether they are the type of person who would write such things or, upon reading them, whether they are the type of person who finds them funny.

Ultimately, bathrooms offer the existential tests through which individual children come to know themselves.

Of course, this is precisely the challenge that confronts Holden Caulfield, and that he would mistakenly deny to other children. Staring at the phrase "Fuck you," Caulfield imagines how "all the other little kids would see it, and how they'd wonder what the hell it meant, and then finally some dirty kid would tell them—all cockeyed, naturally—what it meant, and how they'd all *think* about it and maybe even *worry* about it for a couple of days."[49] There is an understandable fear of childhood ending with lecherous leers and unsettled angst, but by the end of the book, Caulfield recognizes that it cannot be helped. One can never truly shelter children. Growing up necessarily involves risk and seeing the world as it is. Encounters with the taboo are educative not only because they elicit primal urges or challenge social authority, but because they encourage self-consciousness. That is not to say that forbidden words or images cannot be upsetting—merely that the bathroom allows children to consider them as individuals, in the safety of secrecy, and to work out the transition to adulthood on their own terms.[50]

If students are to confront these challenges, educators need to relinquish some degree of supervision. Modern education too often relies on unsparing transparency, whether in the name of disciplinary control or constructive pedagogy. Teachers patrol the aisles. Librarians track websites. Tests chart the gaps and gains in student learning. Writing prompts reward personal disclosure. As Nicole Bishop observes, there is a type of poverty that results from these efforts, from the "consistent devaluation and neglect of those distinctively and intimately personal aspects of self which cannot readily be communicated to others, or made the object of their reflected appraisal."[51] Denied other opportunities to explore who they are and who they are not, bathroom stalls may be the last place in the building where students can simply be alone with themselves.

WINDOWS AND EUPHORIA

A windowpane enchants the senses, and never more than when one is holding a brick. The delicate play of light and shadow, the crystalline expanse separating one world from the next: these visual pleasures are heightened by auditory anticipation, a longing for the whoosh, sprinkle, and spray of a waterfall spilling downward. There is an elemental joy in smashing windows, a sense of tension and release—euphoria in plane geometry. Little wonder that it stands as the most frequently reported type of vandalism in schools.[1]

Glass windows are an important artifact in the history of education, a design element crucial to children's well-being but equally vulnerable to their depredation. For much of the nineteenth century, rural schoolhouses remained dark and drafty, with sacking or scrap paper covering their windows, while city schools were hemmed in by surrounding buildings. Experts warned that poorly lit classrooms bred filth, strained students' eyes, and left them vulnerable to noxious vapors, and they encouraged school boards to construct "lightsome" schoolhouses as soon as possible.[2] The construction of larger school buildings during the late nineteenth century, together with the industrial production of glass, encouraged the installation of windows for improved lighting and airflow. By the turn of the twentieth century, officials in many cities had installed classrooms with floor-to-ceiling windows to cure tuberculosis and other ailments, and glassmakers touted their products in educational journals.[3] Architects began to design schools for maximum transparency, with windows welcoming students into fresh, home-like surroundings and providing teachers a place to display children's artwork.[4] Glass not only became a symbol of modern sanitation but composed part of the educational process itself. Sunlight would strengthen children's natural impulses to kindness, cooperation, and order, nurturing their emotions as well as their bodies.[5]

Such was the vision, at any rate. As soon as windowpanes actually appeared in schools, students seemed to take special pleasure in smashing them. A school in nineteenth-century New Hampshire responded to chronic vandalism by imposing a twenty-five-cent fine for each window broken, but students still shattered all of them, repeatedly, over subsequent years.[6] Asked why he and his friends had gone on a rampage during the 1920s, a delinquent youth shrugged. "To have fun," he said. All it took was a lighthearted suggestion—"Let's break the winders"— and his school lay in ruins. By the 1970s, the cost of such skylarking had risen to tens of millions of dollars a year.[7] Officials conceded that most of this breakage was not especially malicious: it was an unruly expression of excitement, but in the end there was really "no thought behind it."[8] Purposeless action is another way to describe play, and window breaking, like other forms of vandalism, may well be understood as a form of playfulness. The question is what that label means and what it implies about the character of property damage.

Many theorists take a constructive view of children's play, which they characterize as the development of physical dexterity, mimicry of adult behavior, or some form of experimentation, but always as a movement toward reason and maturity, "separated from violent power and firmly bound to orderly, rule-determined process."[9] In a typical comment, Jerome Bruner writes that play is "the first carrier of rule systems through which a world of cultural restraint is substituted for the operation of impulse."[10] From this perspective, even seemingly destructive acts such as window breaking are better understood as skills-based games or simple tests of cause and effect, through which children gain mastery over themselves and their surroundings.[11] Unfortunately, these explanations seem inadequate in the face of serious destruction and may fundamentally diminish play as a conceptual category. Conceiving of play as a developmental process tends to overlook children's spontaneous acts of cruelty, chaos, or irrationality, and invites adult supervision and interference when children's activities seem insufficiently wholesome.[12] Indeed, when the philosopher Jeremy Bentham coined the phrase "deep play" to describe perverse forms of risk that only children would accept, it was to justify paternalism and restraint in otherwise liberal societies. For subsequent generations of theorists, childhood became the archetype for all sorts of unreasonable behavior, and certain types of uncomfortable play remained particularly subject to correction.[13]

Taking the opposite perspective, the historian Johan Huizinga argues that play admits no end outside of itself: it cannot be attributed to instinct or subordinated to reason but is an expression of pure freedom.[14] Whereas the other chapters in this book have argued that vandalism is often mischaracterized as wanton and may be better understood as a form of emotional engagement or self-education, here we broach the possibility of legitimately senseless acts and ask whether these, too, could ever be considered properly educational, not in the constructive mode, as a move toward reason, but in some respect as a move away from it. There may not be a firm answer to that question, and, to be clear, no one is suggesting that schools should incite children to wreckage. But in approaching the boundaries between learning and play, aesthetics and destruction, ecstasy and auto-stimulation, window breaking underscores the fundamental ambiguity of vandalism. Even when stripped to its most elemental forms, children's tendency to break things remains surprisingly hard to characterize.

Modern theories of play originated with Friedrich Schiller's *On the Aesthetic Education of Man* (1795). Schiller sought to overcome what he saw as a persistent dichotomy between freedom and morality in the philosophy of education. Specifically, he hoped to teach human beings to do the right thing without relying on external authority or abstract logic.[15] Doing so requires sensuous perceptions of truth, contemplations of beauty that can reconcile reason and emotion. This sort of transcendence becomes possible only in the realm of play, Schiller argued, where one can tame desire without entirely subordinating it. Operating at a remove from physical necessity and from moral imperatives—like a lion exulting in its own strength—the individual at play engages the world actively, fully, and freely, achieving an almost divine state of potentiality—hence Schiller's famous pronouncement that "man only plays when he is in the fullest sense of the word a human being, and he is only fully a human being when he plays."[16] Play was an aesthetic and ecstatic experience, a "wonderful emotion for which reason has no conception and language no name."[17] Like the constructivists, however, Schiller considered the phenomenon "utterly formless" without the order of moral truth. Rather than "abandoning himself to the world so as to get lost in it" or dissolving in the "infinitude of phenomena," he wrote, the playful human being could elevate sensory experience only in combination with reason.[18]

The possibilities of self-abandonment and infinitude, and thus of destructive play, found fuller voice in the writings of Friedrich Nietzsche. In *The Birth of Tragedy* (1872), Nietzsche argued that aesthetic experience results from the interaction of two urges: the first an irrational ecstasy associated with the Greek god Dionysus, in which "the subjective . . . dwindle[s] to complete self-oblivion" and merges with the unity of nature, and the second a restorative illusion of selfhood, associated with the god Apollo, through which the individual can experience thought, creativity, and joy.[19] For Nietzsche, it was the struggle between these urges that allowed one to achieve an "abundance of existence," beyond reason or moral codes. In a world devoid of inherent meaning, one could exercise freedom through "self-assured recklessness," "sublime malice," and cycles of "building and destroying."[20] The Dionysian also featured prominently in the work of Georges Bataille, the twentieth-century French philosopher, who sought to heighten rather than assuage irrational forces of anger, desire, fear, and shame. For Bataille, the concept of humanity depended on the imposition of taboos, which, in turn, became operative only through transgression.[21] Individual sovereignty required emotionally charged violations of the social order, in which sublime unreason made room for rational selfhood.[22] Bataille's transgression was playful in that it served no functional ends; it was liberating precisely because it was useless, excessive, wasteful, or wanton, not something "preliminary to other and subsequent conditions grasped as beneficial" but "an irrational gesture of pure and purposeless destruction."[23]

It is hardly surprising that Nietzsche and Bataille associated the Dionysian with the unselfconsciously destructive play of young children.[24] Nietzsche wrote approvingly of the child who "throws [his] toys away from time to time and starts again in innocent caprice, beginning [his] game of creation and destruction each time anew, without remorse, in blissful self-forgetfulness."[25] In *Thus Spoke Zarathustra* (1885), he contrasted the constraining effects of the adult world—embodied in the civilizing culture of the "Fatherland" or "Motherland"—with the possibility of a far-off *Kinderland*, in which, as David Rathbone puts it, humanity discovers that "this world of purposes is not in fact grounded in any ultimate purpose" but only in "groundless meaning," as in the onrush of "infant (mute) experience," an image that Bataille would later take up as well.[26] For both writers, Dionysian impulses directed human activity toward play and spontaneous assertions of will. The trouble is that the children of these passages remain entirely metaphorical, symbols of a state to which adults should return rather than one that real children exist in or that might provide a foundation for their upbringing. Indeed, rather than embracing Dionysian abandon as a pedagogical tool, Nietzsche and Bataille both endorsed fairly conservative forms of education, through which children assimilated the cultural standards that they would later transcend or transgress.[27]

Only much later did theorists begin to explore the potential of Dionysian education. For example, the psychologist Mihaly Csikszentmihalyi has written about the trancelike state of "flow" that accompanies immersive activities. As he describes it, "One concentrates on the task at hand to the exclusion of other internal or external stimuli. Action and awareness merge, so that one simply does what is to be done without a critical dualistic perspective on one's actions. . . . In such a situation, a person has a strong feeling of control—or personal causation—yet, paradoxically, ego involvement is low or nonexistent, so that one experiences a sense of transcendence of self, sometimes a feeling of union with the environment." Echoing Schiller, Csikszentmihalyi notes that when students enjoy an activity, "they spontaneously abide by its constraints," and only when sanctioned activities lag do they seek intrinsic meaning elsewhere, for instance by breaking things.[28] It is noteworthy that Csikszentmihalyi assumes that schools are in a position to initiate such experiences—with lessons designed not merely for engagement but for transcendence—and also that he considers destructive play inferior to other forms of flow, a sensation that is based in sensory arousal but that lacks any of the specialized skills that would elevate its meaning. Property destruction is simply not the same as jazz improvisation or athletic prowess, he argues. Some types of ecstasy require tutelage and redirection.[29]

The philosopher Sean Steel comes to similar conclusions. Steel points out that modern schools are poor settings for Dionysian education. Most routinize learning through rigid curricular standards or organize the classroom around "novel stimulations" of student interest, but in neither case do they allow moments of joyful selflessness.[30] Like Csikszentmihalyi, Steel argues that irrationality must be guided if it is to hold educational value, that Dionysian learning requires a teacher to lead students "downward into death or ego-dissolution," whether through philosophical inquiries, musical crescendos, or the wonders of natural phenomena.[31] He dismisses experiences such as window breaking as "toothless imitations" of ancient ecstasies and nothing more than nihilistic sources of destruction. Rather than signifying communion with the sublime or ineffable, childhood experience is "mute" because it is nothing more than sensory stimulation.[32]

At this point, we seem to reach an impasse. On one hand, interpreting destructive play as an evolutionary imperative or a manifestation of emergent reason seems to miss the educational potential of irrationality. On the other, approaches like Csikszentmihalyi's and Steel's may leave us with a narrow vision of the Dionysian ground, which remains inaccessible to children on their own and incompatible with ecstatic forms of destruction. In either case, if play is an end unto itself and cannot be subordinated to growth or guidance, it becomes hard to see how it could be educational in any meaningful sense of the word.

Anders Schinkel arrives at a similar juncture when he considers the educational potential of "deep wonder," those moments in which individuals experience sublimity through the contemplation of nature. Schinkel notes that learning may not require interpersonal transmission—that one can be educated by experience rather than a teacher—and that it need not be purely intellectual but could result from emotional states as well. But he concludes that learning does require some degree of cognition and articulation, and by that standard awestruck wonder (or, for our purposes, ecstatic frenzy) does not seem to qualify.[33] When interpreted in the paired context of the Dionysian and the Apollonian, however, Schinkel finds the picture less clear. Feelings of wonder occupy a continuum

WINDOWS AND EUPHORIA   143

from passive contemplation to active curiosity—a "pathway from the unexpected moment of aesthetic delight through to the experience of intrinsic satisfaction and intelligibility"—and traversing that path can change one's perception of the world in ways that more progressive or linear models of learning cannot. Thus, it seems that the afterglow of sublimity may indirectly benefit students, a salutary effect that would apply to destructive play as well as deep wonder.[34]

There is a long tradition associating broken windows with intricacy, novelty, and aesthetic beauty, and it seems possible that creating or contemplating scenes of wreckage can reorient children toward the world.[35] Perhaps smashing windows allows them to marvel at their own being and power, much as Schiller's lion finds "his exuberant force rejoic[ing] in itself."[36] Perhaps, standing amid the shards, they recognize the limits of rules and routine or discover new possibilities in violation and struggle.[37] Perhaps destruction offers an erotic, emotional, and unmediated sense of being that is not merely sensationalistic but exultant. One need not overstate the point to recognize that the potential for Nietzschean self-creation is at least emergent in children's play.[38]

Unfortunately, even as scholars have rediscovered the irrational as a source of freedom and meaning for adults, most continue to suggest that children engage in risky behavior only reflexively.[39] Detaching destruction from any concept of growth has reinforced older tropes of childhood depravity, eliciting condemnation and moral panic. In the social sciences, these concerns often appear in "control theory," the study of how inhibitions and community norms limit deviant behavior, and of the outbreaks of destruction that seem to ensue in their absence. Broken windows recur throughout this research, usually as a symbol of an intoxicating and potentially contagious loss of self-control.[40] For example, during the 1950s, the sociologist Albert Cohen observed that multiple perpetrators were usually involved in acts of vandalism, which suggested that interpersonal dynamics and "group excitement" weakened children's inhibitions. A group of boys engaged in simple forms of play might undertake an "exploratory gesture," he wrote, in which one member broke a window. The initial act would cascade into "mutual conversion," as peer pressure induced others to participate and depressed feelings of individual responsibility, and "joint elaboration," in which group members tried to outdo each other. As the destruction subsided, the boys would engage in self-justification and moral minimization, telling themselves that "nothing was stolen and no one was hurt." In the wake of the Nuremberg rallies and Kristallnacht, it is understandable why this sort of frenzy would be unsettling.[41]

In 1969, Philip Zimbardo—the designer of the controversial Stanford prison experiment, in which the removal of social constraints allegedly turned normal undergraduates into depraved sadists—conducted a similar study with two

FIGURE 8.1. A broken window in the consolidated school of Coin, Iowa. Courtesy of Jo Naylor.

abandoned cars. In New York City, vandals stripped and defaced a disabled car almost immediately, while in Palo Alto, California, a similar car sat unmolested for a week, watched over by protective neighbors and passersby, a dichotomy that led Zimbardo to obvious conclusions about anonymity and urban crime. More interesting, however, was the impromptu conclusion of the experiment, when the second car was towed to the Stanford University campus. With characteristically questionable methodology, Zimbardo and two graduate students decided to provide "a better model for destruction" by attacking the car themselves and asking others to join in. After some initial reluctance, passing students did just that, smashing the car's windows, setting it on fire, and verging on riot by the time police arrived. "Once one person had begun to wield the sledge hammer, it was difficult to get him to stop and pass it to the next pair of eager hands," Zimbardo observed. "They all attacked simultaneously . . . [and] later reported that feeling the metal or glass give way under the force of their blows was stimulating and pleasurable."[42]

Zimbardo recounted this incident several times, but he wavered between contradictory interpretations of its significance. Sometimes, echoing Nietzsche and Bataille, he acknowledged the joy that the car wreckers felt, noting a "'universal need' to shatter all formal controls" or to engage in "an 'unproductive waste of energy'" in which "action precluded thought and [one] experienced total freedom of expression."[43] More often, he described the situation as dangerously antisocial, a breakdown of reason and responsibility in a society that itself was falling into hedonism and anarchy. In those cases, he would compare the melee to Albert Camus's *Caligula* (1938) and *The Stranger* (1942), or to William Golding's *Lord of the Flies* (1954).[44] In the end, however, Zimbardo downplayed the role of irrationality altogether. Extrapolating the incident to a general discussion of vandalism, he dismissed the possibility of senseless destruction, which would be almost impossible to investigate scientifically.[45] Instead Zimbardo reverted to conventional explanations of property damage as a reaction to economic frustration or political inequality. He could easily have come to the opposite conclusion: a Nietzschean vision of destruction that was healthy and rejuvenating precisely because it was mystical, universal, and antisocial.[46]

Zimbardo's car experiment would soon become the basis for the "broken windows" theory of crime, popularized by the sociologists James Q. Wilson and George L. Kelling in 1982. Whether in poor or well-to-do neighborhoods, the authors wrote, a broken window signaled apathy and a lack of community cohesion, inviting further breakage and more serious infractions. Without prompt enforcement of disciplinary norms, property crimes that seemed costless and victimless in fact eroded the trust necessary for civic space. Other forms of disorder would inevitably ensue.[47] Many of these claims seem hyperbolic in hindsight, particularly Wilson and Kelling's leap from window breaking as a form of child's play ("It has always been fun," they winked) to its creation of "an inhospitable and frightening jungle."[48] The authors' approach also relied on several theoretical premises, such as rational choice theory, that were new to criminology and have subsequently been called into question.[49] Other aspects of the argument are more familiar, particularly in the context of schools. As we have seen, the claim that degraded surroundings invite malicious damage was little different from the previous two centuries of developmental psychology (described in chapter 1) or from other ecological theories of crime (described in chapter 3). And again, it was the hope of nurturing children's souls that led schools to install so many windows to begin with.

Even if one takes the most generous reading of the broken-windows theory, however, the fact remains that, in schools, policymakers misapplied its central tenets, responding to property damage with design modifications and "target hardening" rather than community oversight and human contact. These responses also derived from older educational models. Since at least the eighteenth century, broken glass has been a quintessential example of the "natural consequences" approach to punishment, which implies that children's misbehavior is a form of rational decision-making, and that being forced to live with the consequences of their actions will curb future destruction. Critics have questioned what is so "natural" about leaving objects unrepaired—which children rightly perceive as a selective abdication of adult authority rather than an inevitable chain of cause and effect—and in this case the connection was even more tenuous.[50] No one suggested that children should sit in classrooms with the windows knocked out, which would have contradicted the entire premise of Wilson and Kelling's theory, but neither were authorities willing to pay for repairs. Instead, the "natural consequence" of broken windows became more restrictive, damage-resistant buildings. Even before Wilson and Kelling published their article, the notion that a welcoming classroom might reform children's misbehavior was in full retreat; progressive commitments to health, creativity, and sunlight had already given way to new technologies of control. Designers strengthened glass with wire mesh and urban schools began to install plastic, "break-proof" windows. When students discovered that they could melt their initials into the plastic with cigarette lighters, officials proposed buildings with no windows at all.[51] As one reporter bleakly put it, "We haven't succeeded in redesigning the young people who commit this destructive, costly, antisocial vandalism, so we will redesign the school buildings, to shut out the sunlight and thwart the delinquents."[52] Few schools did away with natural light entirely, but efforts to secure the physical plant sent a stark message to students. Windowless architecture became the concrete expression of the joyless, anti-Dionysian basis of modern schooling.[53]

The author Charles Peguy once wrote that "a society which offers to the descendants of those who built our cathedrals no other function than, at best, to be their caretakers should not be surprised if some of them, for sheer distraction, end by smashing the windows."[54] Where children are concerned, there seems to be an assumption that vandalism is nothing *but* distraction, a mindless stimulation that on one hand calls for engaging work and wholesome recreation, and on the other calls for walls, bars, and locks. Conceiving of vandalism in this way presents a false choice. Neither alternative fully captures the relationship between children's creative and destructive urges, or the ways in which deep play, exhilaration, self-loss, and spontaneity may help them come into being. Window breaking itself may not be educative—it seems unlikely to create any new cathedrals—and surely, schools should not abandon children to mindless sensation. But neither should they tame or overreact to destructive play.[55] A better approach may be to adopt what the psychologist Erik Erikson described as *spielraum*, "room for play" in the double sense of recreation and mechanical flexibility, in which schools accommodate the deviation, friction, and resistance of childhood without losing their functionality.[56] Erikson emphasized that while play is vital for maturation, it must encompass diverse motivations, including (at the boundaries) "destructive and self-destructive" varieties of discovery.[57] While maturation advances through linear stages of growth, play is necessarily recursive, a well of childish possibility to which even adults periodically return, an ontogenetic stepping stone from the past to the future.[58]

Window smashing epitomizes the difficulty of inducting children into civilized society, and as such raises ongoing questions about classroom design. What are schools to do when wholesome learning environments seem to elicit destructive behavior? Does an insistence on natural light represent a misplaced confidence in human goodness? On the other hand, can a space encourage growth while presuming the worst about its occupants? Reinterpreting breakage as a form of play may help us move beyond good and evil, to accept inexplicable outbursts not as urges to be stifled or redirected, or even as a step toward maturity, but as explorations of limits and selfhood. Doing so does not preclude punishment by school authorities, but it should temper it with a degree of forbearance. Rather than viewing windows as metaphors for children's perfectibility or depravity, as symbols of social fragility or lessons in natural consequences, we should see them as necessary investments in children's humanity—objects of beauty when whole and, in pieces, objects of the sublime.

Part III

VANDALISM AND THE HISTORICAL SUBLIME

The spontaneous nature of vandalism makes it an enticing but fundamentally ambiguous subject. Many incidents seem totally unprovoked, and even when perpetrators are caught, they cannot always account for their actions. Simply asking why someone vandalized a school may prejudice the answer, assigning forethought where none in fact existed. While political conflict and self-fashioning can shed light on some types of vandalism, the fact is that many incidents in this book remain unexplained and perhaps inexplicable. After reviewing thousands of cases of property destruction, one begins to suspect that there was something wanton about it after all, less in terms of excess aggression than of fundamental meaninglessness. Unfortunately, current scholarship is unable to speak to this aspect of vandalism. Many authors acknowledge the existence of senseless destruction, but their theoretical frameworks prevent them from assigning it any historical or philosophical significance. At a visceral level, they cannot capture the menace of a nine-year-old holding a can of kerosene. Beneath laws, institutions, and cultures of defiance and authority, primal forces eddy and flow. Readers will need to adopt a different set of perspectives to make sense of those currents.

Vandalism is often anonymous, episodic, and excessive, characteristics that it shares with the historical sublime: the irrational, impenetrable element of the past. Sublimity originated in eighteenth-century debates about human perception, perched at the tipping point between rational empiricism and the emotional fullness of Romanticism. Edmund Burke popularized aesthetic categories of the *beautiful*, which corresponded to tenderness, charm, curiosity, and order, epitomized by the image of the child in the garden; and the *sublime*,

which corresponded to intensity, wonder, and awestruck horror in the face
of nature or fate, as in Hudson River School paintings or Gothic literature.[1]
Burke attributed the sublime to deep-seated fear, which, when experienced
from a position of safety, combined shivers of pleasure with divine knowledge.[2]
"Astonishment is that state of the soul in which all its motions are suspended,
with some degree of horror," he wrote. "Hence arises the great power of the
sublime, that far from being produced by them, it anticipates our reasonings,
and hurries us on by an irresistible force."[3] The sublime revealed an existence
prior to language, reason, or individuality, a form of transcendence later captured in Friedrich Nietzsche's concept of the Dionysian and Jacques Lacan's of
the Real.[4]

Gazing on a disjointed past, detached from certainties of progress or moral
coherence, could offer the same revelations as gazing at a foaming waterfall. "We
are aided by the terrifying spectacle of change which destroys everything and creates it anew, and destroys it again," wrote the philosopher Friedrich Schiller. "We
are aided by the pathetic spectacle of mankind wrestling with fate, the irresistible elusiveness of happiness, confidence betrayed, unrighteousness triumphant
and innocence laid low; of these history supplies ample instances, and tragic art
imitates them before our eyes."[5] For Romantics such as Jules Michelet or Thomas
Carlyle, sublimity impelled readers to sympathy with and perhaps even an immediate experience of history, spanning the divide between eras by fastening on
eternal aspects of tragedy or horror.[6] Through the mid-nineteenth century, many
historians recognized the limitations of archival evidence, and tried to convey
the significance of their stories by looking beyond the written record, offering
idiosyncratic and "quasi-existential" metanarratives.[7]

Hayden White points out that during the early twentieth century, when professional historians sought to distance themselves from amateurs, sublimity was
the first thing to go. Standards of archival evidence tightened. Causal explanation
became a strictly rational affair, with little room for "the kinds of events tradi-
tionally conceived to be the stuff of religious belief and ritual [or] the kinds of
'grotesque' events that are the stuff of farce, satire, and calumny."[8] Disciplinary
history essentially subordinated the sublime to the beautiful. Historical processes
took on a "proper," comprehensible form, White continues, allowing readers to
draw political or moral lessons from the past. These lessons varied, to be sure,
but all depended on a coherent backstory, in which any "'confusion' . . . displayed by the historical record [was] only a surface phenomenon."[9] To acknowledge inexplicable events would not only undermine the historian's professional
status but lead readers toward pessimism rather than a constructive embrace of
progress and human dignity. "The sublimity of the spectacle of history had to
be transcended," argues White, "if it was to serve as an object of knowledge and

deprived of the terror it induced as a 'panorama of sin and suffering.'" Unintelligible actions simply had no place in modern historical narratives.[10]

Yet even at the height of social-scientific approaches, the specter of an unknowable past lurked at the edges of the field, suggesting the persistence of immensity and wonder in historical interpretation. "History as total actuality is chaos," wrote the American historian Charles Beard. "The human mind cannot bring [it] objectively into any all-embracing order or subjectively into any consistent system."[11] In Europe, Johann Huizinga agreed that archival evidence could take one only so far, and recommended perceiving history with emotional immediacy, as in "a moment's drunkenness."[12] Following Huizinga, the *Annales* school criticized the equation of history with short-term political change, arguing that some historical processes were so long-lived as to defy periodization or narrative, and thus called into question the penetration of Enlightenment rationality and attendant notions of political progress. Fernand Braudel noted that stretches of "immobile" time could prompt a return to the past with "new eyes [and] new uncertainties," forcing historians to recognize the necessity of "surprise, unfamiliarity, remoteness—these great ways of knowing."[13] By the 1970s, social historians began to recreate the mental landscapes of common people, dredging up stories of dead cats, doppelgängers, and village heretics to create a past that was strange and jarringly distant, casting further doubt on unified narratives of progress.[14] In the end, however, most of these studies retreated from the irrational. They achieved a degree of authority by exhaustively documenting a narrow space, but tended to resolve or domesticate the strange scenes they introduced.[15]

The fullest revival of sublime historical experience has come from postmodern theorists.[16] In *Metahistory* (1973), Hayden White argues that historians organize their work in ways that impose narrative intelligibility but do not reflect any intrinsic meaning. White does not deny the importance of facts and artifacts, but insists that historians must chart their own course out of absurdity. The past is a cacophony of conflicting voices and perspectives, and is knowable only through dissonant, fragmentary, or radically subjective accounts. It is not merely diverse but at some level remains fundamentally irreducible.[17] Just as Albert Camus's novel *The Stranger* (1942) strings together discrete, seemingly detached statements, forcing the reader to "tumble from sentence to sentence, from nothingness to nothingness," in the words of Hannah H. Kim, for theorists like White, history itself is nothing more than a compilation of meaningless moments.[18]

Postmodernists accentuate this point by foregrounding scenes that defy unitary representation. The Kennedy assassination offers one such case. Captured through cinematic fragments and conflicting witness statements, plagued by contradictions and uncanny coincidences, the shooting seems to render a comprehensive description impossible. Yet as the author John Updike notes,

"Any similar scrutiny of a minute section of time and space would yield similar strangenesses—gaps, inconsistencies, warps, and bubbles in the surface of circumstance." In history, he writes, as in physics, "investigation passes a threshold of common sense and enters a sub-atomic realm where laws are mocked, where persons have the life-span of beta particles and the transparency of neutrinos, and where a rough kind of averaging out must substitute for absolute truth."[19] Events like these achieve historical sublimity by the very fact of their indeterminacy or, in Edmund Burke's phrasing, their "obscurity."[20]

The most obscure primary sources may be the loosely contextualized anecdotes that pop up in oral histories and newspaper reports.[21] Even these must be taken up in the right spirit, of course; historians often repeat hackneyed or apocryphal stories to reinforce truths that their readers already know. Lionel Gossman argues that only when one deviates "from the classic, well-designed anecdote" can the form become "truly disruptive or disorienting." Stripped of predictability, adorned with quotidian details, it "introduces an opening into the teleological, and therefore timeless, narration of beginning, middle, and end . . . by injecting contingency and thus real, open-ended time."[22] Anecdotes constitute perhaps the most basic form of narrative. If not exactly a window into reality, they remain much closer to the uncurated facts of the medieval chronicle—which made little distinction between human endeavors and natural disasters—than to the lines of logical causation that structure modern history. Strung together, they seem to offer a glimpse into the abyss of the past.[23]

This is especially relevant to school vandalism, which usually enters the historical record in isolated incidents and can seem very much like a natural disaster. Consider the following examples from the late nineteenth and early twentieth centuries. In Michigan, an aging farmer torched the schoolhouse where his daughter taught. "I could not bear to think of her marrying and leaving me," he said, "and I thought that if I burned her school she would have to give up teaching and come back to her old dad."[24] In Illinois, a man hid dynamite in the stove of another school, hoping to murder a teacher to whom he was unhappily engaged. The explosion left the woman disfigured but alive, while the building suffered serious damage.[25] There were numerous cases in which schools were burned with the bodies of murder victims dumped inside, or burned by jealous women to avenge themselves on neighborhood rivals.[26] In West Virginia, a gang incinerated three schoolhouses and threatened to destroy more unless incarcerated members were released from the state penitentiary.[27] A Kansas man allegedly burned a school to spite his mother, who would be furious to discover that her son was prison bound.[28] On Long Island, a brigade of overzealous firemen set fire to an elementary school so they could look like heroes putting it out.[29] In New York City, four boys admitted to lighting a fire so that, presumed dead, they could run away to Florida. "We wanted to speculate in real estate down there," they told the police.[30] What is one to make of these stories? They confirm no theory, except that schools are enmeshed in the society around them and the problems of the everyday world intrude. They are all unusual, sad, or funny, but it can be hard to tell which were published with a wink and which with a straight face. They are exceptional, yet they seem to represent something quite ordinary, and while their causes were sometimes trivial, their costs were not. In short, their eclecticism does not make them historically insignificant. Rather, they remind us of the chance and absurdity that underlies much of daily life.

It is important to note, however, that there are multiple reasons that one might "idealize the fragment," as J. Drummond Bone puts it, and that the indeterminacy of anecdotes can lead to different interpretive conclusions.[31] One could easily read the incidents in this book through the lens of power and normativity (as Michel Foucault would), or the artificiality of historical narratives (as Hayden White would), or the estrangement and reengagement of the past (as Frank Ankersmit would).[32] To these I would like to add another, older perspective, more common in literature than in history: namely, the use of irrational events to convey trans- or suprahistorical meaning. Emotional eruptions *in* the past can influence our emotional perceptions *of* the past, perhaps in unsettling ways. Theorists such as Friedrich Nietzsche, Sigmund Freud, and Jacques Lacan have argued that our understanding of history often incorporates unhistorical elements, including realizations of buried trauma and recurrence, which manifest themselves in moments of sublime horror.[33] In literary narratives, these moments often appear in stories of madness or the supernatural that seem to end with logical explanations but actually contain subtle contradictions that preclude closure. Thus, as Michelle Faubert writes, readers "wade into the uncomfortable subject of insanity, confident that the new science of psychology will guarantee an explanation of this disturbing world, only to find that the mental confusion that they study is their own." The structure itself conveys a creeping (and creepy) uncertainty.[34]

Some historians have used anecdotes in exactly the same way, infusing irrational excess into their own discussions of violence or insanity.[35] Examples include Michael Lesy's *Wisconsin Death Trip* (1973), a delightfully dark compendium of small-town newspaper headlines from the 1890s, and Peter Manseau's *Melancholy Accidents* (2016), which recounts three centuries of accidental gun deaths. These authors offer relentless accounts of madness, bad luck, murder, suicide, and the occult. They provide little context for their stories, and when they do, obligatory comments about rural poverty or gun control seem insufficient and profoundly out of place.[36] In *Our Savage Neighbors* (2008), Peter Silver explores how fear of Indian raids reshaped the politics of colonial Pennsylvania. In some ways, he presents a standard political history, with competing factions cynically stoking public prejudice with rumor and sensationalism. More than that, how-ever, he offers a haunting glimpse of individuals gripped by debilitating terror and "spasm[s] of guilt fantasy."[37] *The Kingdom of Matthias* (1994), by Paul E. Johnson and Sean Wilentz, likewise introduces weird events for historical analysis—using a polyamorous, patriarchal cult to explore the social upheavals of the 1830s—but does not entirely subject its macabre sensibilities to rational scrutiny.[38] While most historians assume that their subjects acted reasonably, at least based on the information available to them and the conventions of their time, these cases sug-gest that irrationality, too, is a historical force worthy of our attention, one that should attune us not merely to the categories and experiences of the past, but to the aesthetics of the stories we tell.[39]

Elements of the irrational and uncanny are inseparable from any honest history of school vandalism. To survey US education from the perspective of discontented parents and rebellious youths is in some ways to enter a different time scale, enveloping the present in a past that is rash, unpredictable, and eerily unchanged. Significant shifts in the operation of schools fall to the side as more primal urges come into focus, producing types of breakage that remain imme-diately recognizable but fundamentally indeterminate. Part III communicates this continuity with a brief chronicle of destructive incidents across US history, presented without commentary and in no chronological order. Just as the first two parts of the book suggest that vandalism is "antieducational" in its struggle against authority and its possibilities for self-creation, the last section suggests that it may be "antihistorical" in its haunting recurrence. Presenting "shards" of history creates space for this sort of unsettling sublimity, without which earlier discussions of resistance and emotion would simply make too much sense.

SHARDS

Honolulu, Hawaii, 2012

"He walked farther toward a set of outdoor benches, then stopped and brushed the pavement with his shoe, cleaning away the daily soot. There it was, etched in block letters decades ago by a stick or index finger before the concrete had set: OBAMA.

"No historical marker designated the site. Generations of students had walked over and around it without taking notice of the name below their feet. . . . The testament of a teenage boy, and he didn't even write it himself. The story goes that one of his buddies scratched his name there to get him in trouble. But it had the same meaning nonetheless: A name etched in concrete, like *Kilroy was here* carved into rock, is an expression of time and history and fleeting existence. Looking down, I could only think: That could have been the only mark he left."[1]

Oak Grove, West Virginia, 1894

"A school house at Oak Grove, Preston county, was burned down Sunday night about twelve o'clock by some unknown person. . . . Burning school houses was certainly epidemic in the State last week."[2]

Lincoln, Nebraska, 2012

"The stress in Sharon Brewster's life had been building for months, and on the final day of school a year ago, it bubbled over, consumed her—and led her to do something she still can't fully explain. 'I wouldn't even say I had a clear, concrete plan,' Brewster, 44, said in an interview before her sentencing Wednesday for setting the $20 million blaze that destroyed the Lincoln Public Schools headquarters."[3]

Trenton, New Jersey, 1946

"Vacation time almost over, Trenton youngsters are protesting their return to the classrooms next month. Superintendent of Schools Paul Loser said pupils have been throwing stones through windows of the schools almost as fast as maintenance crews can replace them. Mr. Loser called upon parents to aid in stopping the attacks which, he complained, are putting a stiff strain on the repair budget."[4]

Emerson, Nebraska, 1920

"For the third time in a year, a rural schoolhouse near Emerson, in Dixon County, was the object of an incendiary attempt last Wednesday night. The building had been burned down twice before, and was rebuilt this fall. . . . Suspicion attaches to an Indian youth about 14 years old, who failed to get along with his teacher or schoolmates, state officials said. State Inspector Harry Hauser, who made an investigation of the second fire, was told by Indian farmers living in the district that they feared to antagonize the boy or his father as they were afraid he might set fire to their houses or barns."[5]

Sacramento, California, 1923

"Charges of first-degree murder probably will be brought against F. Padilla, who, according to the police, confessed to setting more than twenty-five fires, among them that of the Japanese mission school here, in which ten children lost their lives last April. . . .

". . . Most of Padilla's activities have been directed against the homes and business houses of Japanese, the police assert. Asked why he had set the fires, Padilla, who is a Mexican, replied through an interpreter, the officials said, that he 'liked the excitement they created.'"6

Chesterfield, Missouri, 2021

"School district officials on Tuesday said a Black student admitted writing racist graffiti in multiple bathrooms at Parkway Central High School last week.

"A Parkway School District spokeswoman said officials don't know why the student committed the acts of vandalism or used the racist slurs.

"In a letter to district parents, students and staff Tuesday, Superintendent Keith Marty said the student's race 'does not diminish the hurt it caused or the negative impact it has on our entire community.'

"'We cannot presume the reasons a student would do this and it will be important to understand why this happened as we move forward,' he added."7

Miami, Florida, 1979

"A riot had broken out at the Miami Aerospace Academy, a private military school in Little Havana, where screaming students were said to be 'possessed by spirits.' This was no trick-or-treat prank. One teenager was unconscious; others injured. Kids had smashed windows and ripped doors from their hinges. Police and firefighters who raced to the scene found hundreds of hysterical high schoolers fleeing the building as if it were ablaze. The Devil, it seemed, was to blame. . . .

"Psychologists believe that what drove the students to madness wasn't evil spirits or a weakness of heart, but pent up anger and hearts finally emboldened to do something about it."8

Hartford, Connecticut, 1766

"We hear from Hartford in Connecticut, that on Friday last the following tragical Accident happened at that Place. On hearing the joyful News of the Repeal of the Stamp Act, about 3 half Barrels of Powder were provided, and lodged in the lower Room of a Brick *School* House in the Town, where, after taking out 16 or 18 Pounds, it was locked up, and a Number of Gentlemen and others, assembled in the upper Room and were preparing Cartridges, Sky Rockets and other Fire Works, intended for the Rejoicings that Evening. While they were thus employed, a Negro Boy, seeing some Powder scatter on the Ground, scraped some of it together, and set Fire to it. This by some Means or other communicated with the Powder in the Room below, which went off with a terrible Explosion, tore the House to Pieces, scattering Part of it in the Air, and reducing the rest to a Heap of Ruins."[9]

San Francisco, California, 1959

"A 12-year-old pupil started a fire in the principal's office in the second story of a three-story, wood-framed elementary school at about 7:00 p.m. The boy had a previous record of setting fires and set this one to destroy his spelling test paper. The fire apparently smoldered for several hours and was not discovered until 5:20 a.m., when a nearby service station attendant noticed the fire and turned in an alarm. [The cost was] $343,000."[10]

Frisco, Texas, 2022

"What was supposed to be a harmless senior prank turned into a serious case of vandalism at one Texas high school. The original prank, approved by school officials, involved putting up sticky notes all over Memorial High School in Frisco, Texas. School staff members were on hand to supervise the prank, but things got out of control when a small group of seniors began setting off fire alarms, overturning furniture, spraying fire extinguishers, and damaging the school's wall and ceilings."[11]

New York City, New York, 1972

"Once I asked him why he put his name on the walls of buildings in his neighborhood. He replied, 'Because all the kids do,' and when I pressed him he had no response. Yet as he thought more about it he talked of the joy of knowing that other people see one's name and the sense of satisfaction he felt in seeing his own name next to those of his friends."[12]

Union, New Jersey, 1936

"The search for the persistent vandal who has been daubing police cars, street signs, and school walls with paint for the last month ended just before midnight last night at the rear of police headquarters here where a 20-year-old blond girl graduate of Union High School was taken into custody.

"... She is well known in the community and told police she was gathering material for a book she is writing."[13]

Columbia, Maryland, 1998

"Vandals last weekend struck two of Howard County's most diverse schools, spray painting racist, anti-Semitic, satanic and anarchist graffiti unlike anything school officials say they have ever seen. They brought to four the number of such acts at county schools in three weeks.

"'This has really got us baffled,' said Donald K. White Jr., an assistant principal who has been at Howard High School nine years and is accustomed to minor disturbances and senior pranks. . . .

"Friday's vandalism at Howard High included references such as 'White Power' and 'Satan Power.' That incident and one before it also included negative references to Howard assistant principal Steve Wallis, who is neither African American nor Jewish."[14]

Prescott, Arkansas, 1883

"The boys' preparatory department of the High School was blown up this morning at 3 o'clock by dynamite, with which experiments had been made. The explosion awakened the people of the town and produced great excitement."[15]

New York City, New York, 1917

"Richard Hippe, 13 years old . . . confessed yesterday that he had attempted four times to burn down Public School No. 10 during the past three weeks, because he had thought the destruction of the building would enable him to escape his school work. He worked out the plan, he said, while lying in bed."[16]

Pasco County, Florida, 2021

"Soap dispensers have started disappearing from several Pasco County high school restrooms. Urinals have been broken, toilet bowls filled with Kool-Aid, exit signs stolen.

"All because of a new social media craze encouraging students to perform a 'devious lick' at their schools. It started on TikTok earlier this month. . . .

"Pasco school district officials want it to stop."[17]

Collins, Mississippi, 1913

"J. C. Easterling, a wealthy planter, was arrested today charged with burning the new schoolhouse here because he did not want to pay increased taxes for its maintenance. . . .

". . . Saturday night the school was burned. Bloodhounds were put on the trail and followed it for miles through crowds of negro workers and others to Easterling's house. There they sprang upon Easterling, and with difficulty were beaten off by Sheriff Warren."[18]

Adelanto, California, 2014

"Two mothers pleaded not guilty Monday to charges they vandalized a classroom at a Mojave Desert school after losing a battle to keep it from being transformed into a charter campus under the controversial parent trigger law. . . .

"The classroom was vandalized on June 26 with ketchup, mustard and paint, causing an estimated $8,000 in damages."[19]

Milwaukee, Wisconsin, 1978

"We went to a Milwaukee Senior High School located on the border of a suburb, to present a Counter Vandalism Program; it was a pilot project. In the program, a film, 'Vandalism, Why?' was shown. In it, a small boy darts out on a bicycle from between two parked cars on the road, is hit by another car with his bicycle broken and he is lying on the road. The driver goes to the nearest pay phone and can't make a call because the dialing mechanism is ripped up. . . . At the point of the accident and the ripped out phone mechanism, there was a small group in that pilot high school audience who yelled, 'Yea! Yea!' By the next morning, the amount of vandalism at that school was almost unbelievable—everything that could be was ripped up and out and then some. Now while this took place at a high school on Milwaukee's outskirts, it could happen anywhere and does. And often more of it occurs in outer city schools than in the so-called inner city schools."[20]

Arden, North Carolina, 1995

"Two ninth-grade boys wrecked nine school buses in what one official called a 'little demolition derby thing' that produced $25,000 in damage and a string of charges against the youths. . . .

". . . The destruction began about 3 A.M. on Thursday, when the two students at T. C. Roberson school found keys in the ash trays of several school buses parked at Valley Springs Middle School. . . .

". . . They drove around the school grounds, turning circles in the lawn, running down small trees and breaking down a fence. They used the six buses they could start to ram three that they could not start. . . .

"Both boys then fled in one bus, but it slid into a ditch and became stuck. Mr. McCanless said the boys 'hunted up rocks and commenced to trash the bus.'

"The boys were picked up walking along a road some distance away and, officials said, admitted to sheriff's deputies what they had done.

"'They were going to tear up all the buses and take one of them and leave the state,' Sheriff Medford said. . . ."[21]

Epilogue

REFLECTIONS ON UNRULINESS AND EDUCATION

Thirty years have passed since I cut the seat of my school bus, and while that incident may have been oddly unmotivated, in hindsight it was not especially unusual. Schools have always been a site for pranks, score settling, and seemingly nihilistic acts of destruction, which play out in ways large and small. Tendencies to destruction have not changed much in the intervening decades. But official responses have. As early as the 1970s, state and local governments were responding to perceptions of uncontrolled vandalism, drugs, and violence in school with deterrence and inflexible forms of punishment. Beginning in urban areas and extending to the suburbs, authorities criminalized childish misbehavior, "hardened" school facilities, and increasingly outsourced punishment to police and the courts. By the late 1990s, these changes had created a regime of automatic suspensions and increasingly inaccessible buildings. Even at my high school, where damage was usually handled individually and discreetly, vandalism was increasingly linked to violence, resulting in tighter security and a police presence. In recent years, students across the country have been subject to arrest for wrongdoing as trivial as breaking signs or writing on their lockers.[1] These trends are troubling for many reasons—among them, the physical and emotional harm they cause children and their discriminatory application—but also because they seem to misunderstand vandalism's multiple meanings and its complex relationship to learning.

Education is a broadly *constructive* project, devoted to the edification or "building up" of children's moral and intellectual capacities. Vandalism seems to be a countervailing, antieducational impulse . . . but in what sense? Critics characterize the behavior as *destruction*, a violent rejection that inhibits learning and tears down moral authority. But it is rarely that simple. This book has outlined three alternative explanations, each of which offers lessons for students and educators who confront everyday acts of breakage.

Part I situates vandalism against a broader backdrop of power, and interprets it not as destruction but perhaps as a form of *deconstruction*, in that it exposes and challenges the underlying agendas of schooling. The arrangement and cleanliness of school facilities, their spatial allowances for movement, cooperation, play, or privacy—all of these are physical manifestations of how students are expected to behave, whom they are supposed to obey, and where they fit in the social order. And just as the upkeep of school buildings is a sign of inclusion, respect, and legitimacy, their neglect or defacement can convey the opposite message. School districts communicate when they make do with substandard buildings. Vandals communicate when they break windows. Interpreting vandalism as a form of political protest does not necessarily make it any more virtuous—children and adults have often attacked schools to defend unjust social arrangements—but it does lay bare the struggle. There is no neutral position from which to judge vandalism, and one cannot denounce, quantify, or control it without sanctioning particular political arrangements and technologies of power. Indeed, the difficulty of standing outside power relations is one reason that efforts to stop vandalism are doomed to fail. Schools will never exercise total control as long as conflicts persist between adults and children, between diverse segments of the public, and between competing levels of government. Smooth operations depend on a type of legitimacy and consensus that has never existed in this country. Rather than eliciting simple condemnation, however, vandalism should prompt a thoughtful search for causes and forthright attempts to recognize and remedy these sources of discontent.

Moreover, as we have seen, vandalism is not always political. Part II presents some of its *reconstructive* aspects, in which children reorder schools according to their own needs, often for purposes of growth or self-expression. Much of the damage that results is personal and only incidentally destructive. Unsanctioned inscriptions allow children to claim space as their own, to experiment with new forms of identity, and to reach out to others. Even outright breakage can teach lessons about transgression, limits, yearning, and struggle. In these cases, vandalism is antieducational only in the sense that growing up requires forging one's own path and challenging authority.[2] The development of authentic selfhood depends on interiority and hidden spaces in childhood, and in order to accommodate individual growth, adults sometimes have to relax their supervision. Experienced educators know the value of forbearance, and when sharing a space with students they permit a measure of freedom, even at the cost of some wrongdoing.

Finally, part III suggests that many types of vandalism may be fundamentally *unstructured*, meaningless in their impulsivity or their sheer variety. The anonymous nature of vandalism makes it hard to impute motives in some cases; in others the perpetrators themselves seem confused about their reasons. String enough of these incidents together and one gets a sense of irrationality as a vital historical force, of the blurred lines between accidental and intentional wreckage, of the absurdity lurking beneath much of the past. This perspective does not make vandalism any more understandable, but neither does it justify condemnation or panic. No matter how harshly they respond, authorities are unlikely to stop immature outbursts of destruction on school grounds. If anything, the fact that vandalism does not always carry some deeper meaning should remind us of the virtues of flexibility and forgiveness, and perhaps lead us to a broader acceptance of indeterminacy in educational policy. In an age of ever-tighter measurement and rationalization, the fact is that many aspects of schooling remain outside our understanding and control.

All of this is to say that we should take vandalism seriously as part of an ongoing discussion about the moral conditions of schools. If our goal is to help young people learn self-control and the responsible exercise of freedom, then rather than assuming the worst of them, we should listen to their complaints, respect their privacy, and, when they do wrong, provide them opportunities to grow into goodness. The temptation to crack down on vandalism is understandable, but if we are interested in children's long-term development then we must trust that they can learn to do the right thing, no matter how often they do not. Authorities need not stand by in the face of property damage—punishment is part of moral communication as well—but they should respond with an emphasis on growth and restitution, with the recognition that causes will often remain unclear, and ultimately with the humility that destruction will persist no matter what they do. Vandalism is ineradicable because, for better or worse, it is an expression of our unruly humanity. Born of struggle, suffused with feeling, it grasps toward the unknown, rejecting limits and reason.

Notes

INTRODUCTION

1. Michael Planty, Lenn Langton, and Joshua Hendrix, *The Cost of School Crime* (Durham, NC: RTI International, 2019).
2. Vernon L. Allen and David B. Greenberger, "An Aesthetic Theory of Vandalism," *Crime & Delinquency* 24, no. 3 (July 1978): 310.
3. William Sadler, "Vandalism in Our Schools: A Study concerning Children Who Destroy Property and What to Do about It," *Education* 108, no. 4 (1988): 557–58. A similar claim is found in J. Sélosse, "Vandalism: Speech Acts," in *Vandalism: Behaviour and Motivations*, ed. Claude Lévy-Leboyer (New York: Elsevier Science, 1984), 30–49.
4. Kathleen Cushman, *Fires in the Bathroom: Advice for Teachers from High School Students* (New York: New Press, 2003), ix.

VANDALISM AS POLITICAL RESISTANCE

1. For a more detailed discussion of wantonness, will, and reflexivity, see Harry Frankfurt, "Freedom of the Will and the Concept of a Person," in *Agency and Responsibility: Essays on the Metaphysics of Freedom*, ed. Laura Waddell Ekstrom (Boulder, CO: Westview, 2001), 77–91. On questions of culpability for vandalism, see Jeri J. Goldman, "Restitution for Damages to Public School Property," *Journal of Law and Education* 11, no. 2 (April 1982): 150.
2. Stanley Cohen, "Sociological Approaches to Vandalism," in *Vandalism: Behaviour and Motivations*, ed. Claude Lévy-Leboyer (New York: Elsevier Science, 1984), 55.
3. See E. P. Thompson, *The Making of the English Working Class* (New York: Vintage Books, 1966), 9–12; and Eric Hobsbawm, *Bandits* (New York: W. W. Norton, 2000). Like resistance theorists, these authors were far from doctrinaire in their interpretation of class formation and left more room for individual agency than Marxist scholars had done theretofore. See Mary Fulbrook, *Historical Theory* (New York: Routledge, 2002), 64–65.
4. Robin D. G. Kelley, "'We Are Not What We Seem': Rethinking Black Working-Class Opposition in the Jim Crow South," *Journal of American History* 80, no. 1 (June 1993): 76.
5. Early examples include Henry Giroux, *Theory and Resistance in Education: Towards a Pedagogy for the Opposition* (South Hadley, MA: Bergin and Garvey, 1983); Michael Apple, *Ideology and Curriculum* (Boston: Routledge and K. Paul, 1979); and Paul Willis, *Learning to Labor: How Working-Class Kids Get Working-Class Jobs* (New York: Columbia University Press, 1981). A more recent example is Carla Shedd, *Unequal City: Race, Schools, and Perceptions of Injustice* (New York: Russell Sage Foundation, 2015). For specific insight into vandalism as resistance, see Stanley Cohen, "Property Destruction: Motives and Meanings," in *Vandalism*, ed. Colin Ward (London: Architectural Press, 1973), 51.
6. Eric Toshalis, *Make Me! Understanding and Engaging Student Resistance in School* (Cambridge, MA: Harvard Education Press, 2015), 43–46.
7. Colin Ward, "Notes on the Future of Vandalism," in Ward, *Vandalism*, 284–85.
8. Ken McGrew, "A Review of Class-Based Theories of Student Resistance in Education: Mapping the Origins and Influence of 'Learning to Labor' by Paul Willis," *Review of Educational Research* 81, no. 2 (June 2011): 234–66. Similar criticisms can be found

in James C. Walker, "Rebels with Our Applause? A Critique of Resistance Theory in Paul Willis's Ethnography of Schooling," *Journal of Education* 167, no. 2 (1985): 63–83; Paul William Kingston, "Resistance Theory: How Marxists Interpret Student Life," *Sociological Forum* 1, no. 4 (Autumn 1986): 717–25; and Kathleen Abowitz, "A Pragmatist Revisioning of Resistance Theory," *American Educational Research Journal* 37, no. 4 (Winter 2000): 877–907.

9. Foucault drew this argument largely from Philippe Ariès, *Centuries of Childhood: A Social History of Family Life*, trans. Robert Baldick (New York: Alfred A. Knopf, 1962).

10. See Michel Foucault, *Discipline and Punish: The Birth of the Prison*, trans. Alan Sheridan (New York: Pantheon, 1977); and Michel Foucault, *Madness and Civilization: A History of Insanity in the Age of Reason*, trans. Richard Howard (New York: Vintage Books, 1973).

11. On Foucault's influence on historical research, see Mark Poster, "Foucault and History," *Social Research* 49, no. 1 (Spring 1982): 116–42. For examples from the history of education, see David Hogan, "The Market Revolution and Disciplinary Power: Joseph Lancaster and the Psychology of the Early Classroom System," *History of Education Quarterly* 29, no. 3 (Autumn 1989): 381–417; and Benjamin Justice and Tracey Meares, "How the Criminal Justice System Educates Citizens," *Annals of the American Academy of Political and Social Science* 65, no. 1 (January 2014): 159–77.

12. Michel Foucault, "The Subject and Power," *Critical Inquiry* 8, no. 4 (Summer 1982): 790.

13. Foucault, "Subject and Power," 785, 794–95.

14. Ivan Jablonka, "When History Flows through Us: An Interview with Philippe Artières," trans. Kate McNaughton, *Books & Ideas*, June 12, 2014, http://www.booksand ideas.net/When-History-Flows-Through-Us.html.

15. See the "Rethinking the History of Childhood" exchange in *American Historical Review* 125, no. 4 (October 2020): 1260–322, particularly Sarah Maza, "The Kids Aren't All Right: Historians and the Problem of Childhood," 1261–85, and Steven Mintz, "Children's History Matters," 1286–92. A similar critique of the missing perspective of children in the history of education appears in the introduction to Kyle P. Steele, *Making a Mass Institution: Indianapolis and the American High School* (New Brunswick, NJ: Rutgers University Press, 2020), 1–7.

1. POPULISM AND PROPERTY DESTRUCTION, 1790–1890

1. Michael J. Pfeifer, *The Roots of Rough Justice: Origins of American Lynching* (Urbana: University of Illinois Press, 2011), 7. See also Pauline Maier, "Popular Uprisings and Civil Authority in Eighteenth-Century America," in *Colonial America: Essays in Politics and Social Development*, ed. Stanley Nider Katz (Boston: Little, Brown, 1971), 308–38; William Pencak, Matthew Dennis, and Simon P. Newman, eds., *Riot and Revelry in Early America* (University Park: Pennsylvania State University Press, 2002), 4–5; Benjamin H. Irvin, "The Streets of Philadelphia: Crowds, Congress, and the Political Culture of Revolution, 1774–1783," *Pennsylvania Magazine of History and Biography* 129 (2005): 7–44; Benjamin H. Irvin, "Tar, Feathers, and the Enemies of American Liberties, 1768–1776," *New England Quarterly* 76 (2003): 197–238; and Steven J. Stewart, "Skimmington in the Middle and New England Colonies," in Pencak, Dennis, and Newman, *Riot and Revelry*, 41–86.

2. Paul A. Gilje, *Rioting in America* (Bloomington: Indiana University Press, 1996), 6. For nineteenth-century examples, see James C. Scott, *Domination and the Arts of Resistance* (New Haven, CT: Yale University Press, 1990), 150–51; and Paul Johnson, *Sam Patch: The Famous Jumper* (New York: Hill and Wang, 2003), 50–52.

3. Similar questions appear in Alexis de Tocqueville, *Democracy in America*, trans. Arthur Goldhammer (New York: Library of America, 2004), chaps. 7–9.

4. Thomas Jefferson to William Stephens Smith, November 13, 1787, *Papers of Thomas Jefferson*, ed. Julian P. Boyd (Princeton, NJ: Princeton University Press, 1955), 12:355–57. See also John Phillip Reid, "In a Defensive Rage: The Uses of the Mob, the Justification in Law, and the Coming of the American Revolution," *New York University Law Review* 49 (1974): 1043–91; Richard Slotkin, *Gunfighter Nation: The Myth of the Frontier in Twentieth-Century America* (New York: Atheneum, 1992); Patrick Griffin, Robert G. Ingram, Peter S. Onuf, and Brian Schoen, eds., *Between Sovereignty and Anarchy: The Politics of Violence in the American Revolutionary Era* (Charlottesville: University of Virginia Press, 2015); and Michael Kazin, *The Populist Persuasion: An American History* (Ithaca, NY: Cornell University Press, 1995).

5. Gilje, *Rioting in America*, 7.

6. Keach Johnson, "Elementary and Secondary Education in Iowa, 1890–1900," *Annals of Iowa* 45, no. 2 (Fall 1979): 107. For other descriptions of ramshackle schools, see Paul Theobald, *Call School: Rural Education in the Midwest to 1918* (Carbondale: Southern Illinois University Press, 1995), 89; and Reverend S. J. May, "Dedication of a Schoolhouse," *Common School Journal* 2, no. 14 (July 1840): 302.

7. Alfred Holbrook, *School Management* (New York: A. S. Barnes, 1872), 161–62.

8. *Twenty-Third Annual Report of the State Board of Health* (New Haven: Connecticut State Board of Health, 1901), 28.

9. Barbara Finkelstein, *Governing the Young: Teacher Behavior in Popular Primary Schools in Nineteenth-Century United States* (New York: Falmer, 1989), 219–21, 275.

10. On youth politics, see Jon Grinspan, *The Virgin Vote: How Young Americans Made Democracy Social, Politics Personal, and Voting Popular in the Nineteenth Century* (Chapel Hill: University of North Carolina Press, 2016).

11. Finkelstein, *Governing the Young*, 214–15.

12. Joseph F. Kett, *Rites of Passage: Adolescence in America, 1790 to the Present* (New York: Basic Books, 1977), 47.

13. Untitled article, *Pennsylvania Gazette*, January 11, 1744, 1.

14. Theobald, *Call School*, 88.

15. For a few examples, see "Incendiarism," *San Francisco Evening Bulletin*, November 20, 1873, 3; "High School Burned," *Grand Forks Daily Herald*, March 30, 1893, 1; "Howard County," *Baltimore Sun*, May 17, 1895, 2; "Public School Burned," *Duluth Daily News*, November 20, 1888, 1.

16. "Simeon Sulks," *Current Local* (Van Buren, MO), July 1, 1893, 3; "Said by Children," *Caldwell (ID) Tribune*, February 13, 1904, 3; untitled article, *Galveston Daily News*, October 22, 1895, 4.

17. "St. Anna Girls' School," *New Orleans Republican*, June 21, 1870, 1. The trope was widespread among adults too. For instance, in a debate about burning land contracts to halt western speculation, the Pennsylvania legislature made a casual comparison to schoolboys burning their textbooks. Untitled article, *Pennsylvania Gazette*, March 9, 1796, 1.

18. "Schoolhouse Burned," *Dallas Morning News*, November 11, 1888, 4.

19. "Schoolhouse Burned," *Daily Olympian*, September 9, 1896, 1.

20. "Church and School Burned," *Daily Inter-ocean* (Chicago), December 9, 1888, 5.

21. "School-House Burned," *Knoxville Journal*, September 6, 1889, 8; "Incendiaries," *Idaho Tri-weekly Statesman*, January 15, 1876, 1.

22. "Parkersburg," *Wheeling Register*, May 13, 1886, 1.

23. Theobald, *Call School*, 70.

24. Jonathan Zimmerman, *Small Wonder: The Little Red Schoolhouse in History and Memory* (New Haven, CT: Yale University Press, 2009), 44.

25. "A School House on Wheels," *Washington (DC) Evening Star*, October 25, 1895, 12.

26. Theobald, *Call School*, 79.

27. R. M. Marshall, "The School Vandalism Trial of 1867," *Daily Record* (Kittanning, PA), April 8, 1901. For a broader discussion of factions occupying schoolhouses, see Benjamin Justice, *The War That Wasn't: Religious Conflict and Compromise in the Common Schools of New York State, 1865–1900* (Albany: SUNY Press, 2005), chap. 5.

28. See John Locke, *Some Thoughts concerning Education* (Indianapolis: Hackett, 1996); and Jean-Jacques Rousseau, *Emile, or On Education*, trans. Allan Bloom (New York: Basic Books, 1979). Secondary sources include Sarah Anne Carter, *Object Lessons: How Nineteenth-Century Americans Learned to Make Sense of the Material World* (New York: Oxford University Press, 2018); and Gerald L. Gutek, *Joseph Neef: The Americanization of Pestalozzianism* (Tuscaloosa: University of Alabama Press, 1978).

29. Henry Barnard, *Practical Illustrations of the Principles of School Architecture* (Hartford, CT: Case, Tiffany, 1851), 13, 17–18; Rebecca Noel, "'No Wonder They Are Sick, and Idle of Study': European Fears for the Scholarly Body and Health in New England Schools before Horace Mann," *Pedagogica Historica* 54, no. 1–2 (February 2018): 134–53.

30. Josiah Holbrook, "Democracy of Science," *National Era*, March 17, 1853, 1.

31. Barnard, *Practical Illustrations*, 28. See also Frederick S. Jewell, *School Government: A Practical Treatise* (New York: A. S. Barnes, 1875).

32. Barnard, *Practical Illustrations*, 28.

33. Thomas H. Burrowes, *Pennsylvania School Architecture: A Manual of Directions and Plans for Grading, Locating, Constructing, Heating, Ventilating and Furnishing Common School Houses* (Harrisburg: Pennsylvania Department of Public Instruction, 1856), 251. For similar sentiments, see Kett, *Rites of Passage*, 120–23; Francis Parker, "Report of the Superintendent," *Annual Report of the Town of Quincy, Massachusetts, 1875–1876* (Boston: White and Potter, 1876), 121–22; and "Debate on the Destruction of Small Birds," *National Era*, August 21, 1851, 1.

34. Jacob R. Freese, *Report on Schoolhouses, and the Means of Promoting Popular Education* (Washington, DC: US Government Printing Office, 1868), 8.

35. Burrowes, *Pennsylvania School Architecture*, 189; *Records of the Columbia Historical Society, Washington D.C.*, vol. 1 (Washington, DC: Columbia Historical Society, 1897), 138–39.

36. Horace Mann, "Report of the Secretary on the Subject of Schoolhouses, Supplementary to His First Annual Report," *Common School Journal* 1, no. 19 (October 1839): 291–92.

37. Barnard, *Principles of School Architecture*, 28, 164–65; Henry Barnard, "Damage to School Property," *American Journal of Education* 19 (1870): 436. See also "Fundamental Rules of Brookeville School, 1811," *Brookville Academy Minute Book*, vol. 1, *1810–1831*, Montgomery County (MD) Historical Society Library, accessed October 6, 2022, http://townofbrookevillemd.org/brookeville-academy-2/history.

38. Lander v. Seaver, 32 Vt. 114 (1859).

39. Board of Education v. Frank Helston, 32 Ill. App. 300 (1889).

40. Sanford Harwood v. Independent District of Charles City, Iowa (1874), in C. W. von Coelln, *School Law Decisions* (Des Moines: F. M. Mills, 1880), 68–71. On the general effects of litigation on school governance, see Tracy L. Steffes, *School, Society, and State: A New Education to Govern Modern America, 1890–1940* (Chicago: University of Chicago Press, 2012).

41. John Demos: *The Heathen School: A Story of Hope and Betrayal in the Age of the Early Republic* (New York: Knopf, 2014), 181–82, 191.

42. "Willful Damage," *San Francisco Bulletin*, September 22, 1866, 2.

43. Amanda Beyer-Purvis, "The Philadelphia Bible Riots of 1844: Contest over the Rights of Citizens," *Pennsylvania History* 83, no. 3 (Summer 2016): 367; Vincent P. Lannie and Bernard C. Diethorn, "For the Honor and Glory of God: The Philadelphia Bible Riots of 1840," *History of Education Quarterly* 8, no. 1 (Spring 1968): 75; "Another Bible Excitement," *Frederick Douglass Paper*, December 2, 1853, 1; "In the District," *Washington Evening Star*, April 13, 1895, 4.

44. For sporadic examples of publicly funded schools for African Americans in the antebellum South, see Camille Walsh, *Racial Taxation: Schools, Segregation, and Taxpayer Citizenship, 1869–1973* (Chapel Hill: University of North Carolina Press, 2018), chap. 1; and Walter C. Stern, *Race and Education in New Orleans: Creating the Segregated City, 1764–1960* (Baton Rouge: Louisiana State University Press, 2018), chaps. 1–2.

45. Hilary Moss, *Schooling Citizens: The Struggle for African American Education in Antebellum America* (Chicago: University of Chicago Press, 2009), chap. 1. See also Zöe Burkholder, *An African American Dilemma: A History of School Integration and Civil Rights in the North* (New York: Oxford University Press, 2021), chap. 1; Stephen Kantrowitz, *More Than Freedom: Fighting for Black Citizenship in a White Republic* (New York: Penguin Books, 2013).

46. Kyle G. Volk, *Moral Minorities and the Making of American Democracy* (New York: Oxford University Press, 2014), 119.

47. Iver Bernstein, *The New York City Draft Riots: Their Significance for American Society and Politics in the Age of the Civil War* (New York: Oxford University Press, 1990); "The Thriving Little Village of Cox," *National Era*, July 20, 1854, 1; untitled article, *Emancipator and Republican*, September 8, 1842, 1.

48. "Eyewitness Account of the Snow Riot," August 1835, Special Collections, George Mason University; "Colored Public Schools," *National Republican* (Washington, DC), May 8, 1876, 1.

49. Volk, *Moral Minorities*, 116.

50. Kabria Baumgartner, "Love and Justice: African American Women, Education, and Protest in Antebellum New England," *Journal of Social History* 52, no. 3 (2019): 667–68.

51. "Proscription," *Anti-slavery Bugle* (Salem, OH), December 16, 1818, 1; "Preachers' Association," *Christian Recorder*, September 5, 1878, 1.

52. W. E. B. Du Bois, *Black Reconstruction in America: An Essay toward a History of the Part Which Black Folk Played in the Attempt to Reconstruct Democracy in America, 1860–1880* (New York: Harcourt, Brace, 1935); Steven Hahn, *A Nation under Our Feet: Black Political Struggles in the Rural South from Slavery to the Great Migration* (Cambridge, MA: Belknap Press of Harvard University Press, 2003); Eric Foner, *Reconstruction: America's Unfinished Revolution* (New York: Harper, 2002).

53. James C. Scott, *Seeing like a State: How Certain Schemes to Improve the Human Condition Have Failed* (New Haven, CT: Yale University Press, 1998), chap. 9. The collection of (and contention around) federal educational statistics began in 1869. By the 1930s, the NAACP and other advocacy organizations would use extensive state and federal data on facilities, funding, and curriculum to underscore racial inequalities in public education. It was not until the early 1960s, however, that the federal government systematically investigated damage to African American schools as a civil rights violation. See, respectively, Janet A. Weiss and Judith E. Gruber, "The Managed Irrelevance of Federal Education Statistics," in *The Politics of Numbers*, ed. William Alonso and Paul Starr (New York: Russell Sage Foundation, 1987), 363–91; James T. Patterson, *Brown v. Board of Education: A Civil Rights Milestone and Its Troubled Legacy* (New York: Oxford University Press, 2001), chaps. 1–2.

54. For local studies that discuss school destruction, see Joseph Browne, "'The Expenses Are Borne by Parents': Freedmen's Schools in Southern Maryland, 1865–1870,"

Maryland Historical Magazine 86, no. 4 (1991): 407–22; Michael Goldhaber, "A Mission Unfulfilled: Freedmen's Education in North Carolina, 1865–1870," *Journal of Negro History* 77, no. 4 (1992): 199–210; Alton Hornsby Jr. "The Freedmen's Bureau Schools in Texas, 1865–1870," *Southwestern Historical Quarterly* 76 (April 1973): 397–417; Barry A. Crouch, "Land, Lumber, and Learning: The Freedmen's Bureau, Education and the Black Community in Post-emancipation Maryland," in *The Freedmen's Bureau and Reconstruction: Reconsiderations,* ed. Paul A. Cimbala and Randall M. Miller (New York: Fordham University Press, 1999), 288–314; James Smallwood, "Black Education in Reconstruction Texas: The Contributions of the Freedmen's Bureau and Benevolent Societies," *East Texas Historical Journal* 19, no. 1 (1981): 17–40.

55. The leading sources consulted for this study include the state educational reports of the Bureau of Refugees, Freedmen, and Abandoned Lands, available on microfilm at the National Archives and Records Administration in Washington, DC; the *Report of the Joint Select Committee to Inquire into the Condition of Affairs in the Late Insurrectionary States,* available online at http://onlinebooks.library.upenn.edu/webbin/ metabook?id=insurrection1872; and exhaustive search terms in the following newspaper databases: "Chronicling America: Historic American Newspapers" (https://chronicling-america.loc.gov); Newspapers.com; "America's Historical Newspapers" (infoweb.news-bank.com); "African American Newspapers" (infoweb.newsbank.com); and "Portal to Texas History" (https://texashistory.unt.edu/search/advanced_search/). As noted below, the numbers included in this survey put the most conservative construction on the evidence available. For instance, a textual reference to "several" schools destroyed has been quantified as 3, though it could easily have been more. The only incidents included on maps or tables are those that specifically mention arson or vandalism, or those that reference suspicious circumstances, such as schools burning at night. Church burnings were included only if they specifically referenced education. There were dozens more African American schools that burned down under circumstances that seem accidental or that were attributed to children or to intraracial feuds. These have been excluded. It is possible that sporadic references exist elsewhere in the Freedmen's Bureau records, but the sheer volume of the records limited my research to educational reports.

56. Current histories of African American education in the South generally follow James Anderson's *The Education of Blacks in the South* (Chapel Hill: University of North Carolina Press, 1988). More recent additions have emphasized community education and self-education, as in Heather Andrea Williams, *Self-Taught: African American Education in Slavery and Freedom* (Chapel Hill: University of North Carolina Press, 2005); Black voters' role in securing public education systems, as in Christopher M. Span, *From Cotton Field to Schoolhouse: African American Education in Mississippi, 1862–1875* (Chapel Hill: University of North Carolina Press, 2014); and the role of urban educational spaces, as in Hilary Green, *Educational Reconstruction: African American Schools in the Urban South* (New York: Fordham University Press, 2016); and Stern, *Race and Education.* A second strand of research, tangential to this study, has drawn from Du Bois and Carter Woodson's *Miseducation of the Negro* (1933) to focus on philanthropy and the inequitable systemization of African American education. In addition to James Anderson, see Robert Francis Engs, *Educating the Disenfranchised and Disinherited: Samuel Chapman Armstrong and the Hampton Institute* (Knoxville: University of Tennessee Press, 1999); William H. Watkins, *The White Architects of Black Education: Ideology and Power in America, 1865–1954* (New York: Teachers College Press, 2001); Eric Anders and Alfred A. Moss, *Dangerous Donations: Northern Philanthropy and Southern Black Education, 1902–1930* (Columbia: University of Missouri Press, 1999); Robert J. Norrell, *Up from History: The Life of Booker T. Washington* (Cambridge, MA: Belknap Press of Harvard University Press, 2011).

57. For a full discussion of conceptualizing silence in the Freedmen's Bureau archives, see Jim Downs, "Emancipating the Evidence: The Ontology of the Freedmen's Bureau Records," in *Beyond Freedom: Disrupting the History of Emancipation*, ed. David W. Blight and Jim Downs (Athens: University of Georgia Press, 2017), 160–80. See also Hannah Rosen, "In the Moment of Violence: Writing the History of Postemancipation Terror," in Blight and Downs, *Beyond Freedom*, 145–59; and Elaine Frantz Parsons, *Ku-Klux: The Birth of the Klan during Reconstruction* (Chapel Hill: University of North Carolina Press, 2015).

58. Jacqueline Jones, *Soldiers of Light and Love: Northern Teachers and Georgia Blacks* (Chapel Hill: University of North Carolina Press, 1980), 224; "Negro Education," *New York Times*, July 1, 1875, 1. The ways in which the readmission of secessionist states depended on establishing systems of public education remains a contested (and legally significant) point. See Derek W. Black, "The Constitutional Compromise to Guarantee Education," *Stanford Law Review Online* 70 (2018): 735–837, https://www.stanfordlawreview.org/print/article/constitutional-compromise-guarantee-education/; and Joshua E. Weishart, "The Compromised Right to Education," *Stanford Law Review Online* 71 (2018): 123–31, https://www.stanfordlawreview.org/online/the-compromised-right-to-education/.

59. Ronald Butchart, *Schooling the Freed People: Teaching, Learning, and the Struggle for Black Freedom, 1861–1876* (Chapel Hill: University of North Carolina Press, 2010), chap. 6; Jones, *Soldiers of Light and Love*, 80–81.

60. The multiple uses of African American church buildings complicate efforts to quantify educational property destruction, for several reasons. First, while church burnings also appear in Freedmen's Bureau records, they were tracked even less systematically than schoolhouses, sometimes appearing in reports on general crime, legal proceedings, or other correspondence having nothing to do with education. Likewise, while district agents occasionally referred to a building as a "church and school-house" or "churches, also used for school purposes," more often they used nomenclature that referenced a school's name without mentioning that it met in a church, or a church's name without mentioning that it held classes. Finally, churches could host different types of schools, including evening and Sabbath schools. In reviewing the bureau's educational reports, this study includes attacks on buildings referred to as any type of "school" or that included specific references to teaching. To be conservative and consistent, it does not include church burnings without mention of educational activities. This methodological choice obviously lowers the number of documented cases significantly. (The phrases above are taken from *Monthly Narrative Report of Operations and Conditions* [New Orleans, LA], September 1867, Records of the Assistant Commissioner for the State of Texas, Bureau of Refugees, Freedmen, and Abandoned Lands, 1865–69, National Archives Microfilm Publication M821, roll 26, Records of the Bureau of Refugees, Freedmen, and Abandoned Lands, RG 105, National Archives and Records Administration, Washington, DC (hereafter BRFAL); and US Congress, *Report of the Joint Select Committee to Inquire into the Conditions of Affairs in the Late Insurrectionary States* (hereafter JSC) (Washington, DC: US Government Printing Office, 1972), 9:1025.

61. Jones, *Soldiers of Light and Love*, 77–81.

62. The same sort of vigilantism had targeted African American schools in the North since the 1830s. These incidents were not systematic, and riotous behavior was condemned by civic leaders and the press and was usually portrayed as the work of misguided individuals. Nevertheless, targeted property destruction reinforced the actions of city and state governments—which segregated schools by law and custom, systematically under-resourcing those attended by African American students—and contributed to a broader culture of white supremacy. See Pencak, Dennis, and Newman, *Riot and Revelry*; Moss, *Schooling Citizens*; Kantrowitz, *More Than Freedom*.

63. Green, *Educational Reconstruction*, 97.

64. Subdistrict report [Washington Parish, LA], November 1865, Records of Superintendent of Education for the State of Louisiana, Bureau of Refugees, Freedmen, and Abandoned Lands, 1865–69, M1026, roll 3, BRFAL.

65. Subdistrict report [Circleville, TX], April 1868, Records of the Assistant Commissioner for the State of Texas, Bureau of Refugees, Freedmen, and Abandoned Lands, 1865–1869, M821, roll 26, BRFAL.

66. *JSC*, 8:140.

67. *JSC*, 2:98.

68. *JSC*, 11:333.

69. J. Goins, "Labors and Sufferings for African M.E. Church," *Christian Recorder*, December 1, 1881, 1; untitled article, *San Francisco Chronicle*, July 13, 1873, 6.

70. Subdistrict report [Greenville, AL], December 1868, Records of the Assistant Commissioner for the State of Alabama, Bureau of Refugees, Freedmen, and Abandoned Lands, 1865–70, M809, roll 18, BRFAL.

71. *JSC*, 6:402.

72. In addition to Green, *Educational Reconstruction*, and Stern, *Race and Education*, see Amy Louise Wood, *Lynching and Spectacle: Witnessing Racial Violence in America, 1890–1940* (Chapel Hill: University of North Carolina Press, 2009), chap. 1.

73. State report [GA], November 1866, Records of the Assistant Commissioner for the State of Georgia, Bureau of Refugees, Freedmen, and Abandoned Lands, 1865–69, M798, roll 32, BRFAL; *JSC*, 1:279.

74. Nearly a century of historiographic neglect undoubtedly squandered primary sources, especially oral histories and physical structures, leaving subsequent generations with less to work with. See John David Smith and J. Vincent Lowery, *The Dunning School: Historians, Race, and the Meaning of Reconstruction* (Lexington: University Press of Kentucky, 2013). For an example of the Dunning School's approach, which makes no reference to educational destruction or intimidation, see E. Merton Coulter, *The South during Reconstruction* (Baton Rouge: Louisiana State University Press, 1947), 322–25.

75. John Cox and LaWanda Cox, "General O.O. Howard and the 'Misrepresented Bureau,'" in *The Freedmen's Bureau and Black Freedom*, ed. Donald G. Nieman (New York: Garland, 1994), 105–34; David Tyack and Robert Lowe, "The Constitutional Moment: Reconstruction and Black Education in the South," *American Journal of Education* 94, no. 2 (February 1986): 236–56; Robert C. Morris, "Educational Reconstruction," in *The Facts of Reconstruction: Essays in Honor of John Hope Franklin*, ed. Eric Anderson and Alfred A. Moss Jr. (Baton Rouge: Louisiana State University Press, 1991), 141–66.

76. Richard White, *The Republic for Which It Stands: The United States during Reconstruction and the Gilded Age* (New York: Oxford History of the United States, 2017), 70.

77. Goldhaber, "Mission Unfulfilled," 200.

78. "The Memphis Riot," *Cleveland Daily Leader*, May 7, 1866, 2.

79. Gregory P. Downs, *After Appomattox: Military Occupation and the Ends of War* (Cambridge, MA: Harvard University Press, 2015), 142–43.

80. State report [NC], December 1867, Records of the Assistant Commissioner for the State of North Carolina, Bureau of Refugees, Freedmen, and Abandoned Lands, 1865–70, M843, roll 22, BRFAL; Subdistrict report [Pulaski, VA], March 1867, Records of Superintendent of Education for the State of Virginia, Bureau of Refugees, Freedmen, and Abandoned Lands, 1865–70, M1053, roll 13, BRFAL; Albert C. Smith, "'Southern Violence' Reconsidered: Arson as Protest in Black-Belt Georgia," *Journal of Southern History* 51, no. 4 (November 1985): 527–64.

81. I have found only one case in which vandals were successfully caught and fined. Subdistrict report [Noxubee County, MS], May 1868, Records of the Assistant Commissioner

for the State of Mississippi, Bureau of Refugees, Freedmen, and Abandoned Lands, 1865–69, M826, roll 32, BRFAL; Subdistrict report [Eufala, AL], February 1868, Records of the Assistant Commissioner for the State of Alabama, Bureau of Refugees, Freedmen, and Abandoned Lands, 1865–1870, M809, roll 18, BRFAL.

82. Subdistrict report [Greensboro, AL], October 1868, M809, Roll 18, BRFAL.

83. State report [Mississippi], March, 1867, Records of the Education Division of the Bureau of Refugees, Freedmen, and Abandoned Lands, 1865–1871, M803, roll 33, BRFAL.

84. State report [KY], February 1867, Records of the Education Division of the Bureau of Refugees, Freedmen, and Abandoned Lands, 1865–1871, M803, roll 33, BRFAL.

85. State report [MD and DE], April 1867, Records of the Education Division of the Bureau of Refugees, Freedmen, and Abandoned Lands, 1865–1871, M803, roll 33, BRFAL.

86. Subdistrict report [Eufala, AL], March 1868, Records of the Assistant Commissioner for the State of Alabama, Bureau of Refugees, Freedmen, and Abandoned Lands, 1865–1870, M809, roll 18, BRFAL.

87. JSC, 1:280.

88. State report [LA], June 1867, Records of the Education Division of the Bureau of Refugees, Freedmen, and Abandoned Lands, 1865–1871, M803, roll 33, BRFAL.

89. Subdistrict report [Paris, TX], October 1866, Records of the Assistant Commissioner for the State of Texas, Bureau of Refugees, Freedmen, and Abandoned Lands, 1865–1869, M821, roll 24, BRFAL.

90. Subdistrict report [Brazos, TX], April 1868, Records of the Assistant Commissioner for the State of Texas, Bureau of Refugees, Freedmen, and Abandoned Lands, 1865–1869, M821, roll 28, BRFAL.

91. JSC, 1:279.

92. Parsons, Ku-Klux, 181.

93. Parsons, Ku-Klux, 196.

94. Parsons, Ku-Klux, 182.

95. For broader discussions of misinformation, education, and politics, see Richard D. Brown, Knowledge Is Power: The Diffusion of Information in Early America, 1700–1865 (New York: Oxford University Press, 1989), chap. 1; and A. J. Angulo, ed., Miseducation (Baltimore: Johns Hopkins University Press, 2016).

96. JSC, 5:1611.

97. JSC, 3:460–64.

98. JSC, 8:179–81.

99. JSC, 8:236.

100. JSC, 11:260; State report [TN], May 1867, Records of the Assistant Commissioner for the State of Tennessee, Bureau of Refugees, Freedmen, and Abandoned Lands, 1865–69, M999, roll 18, BRFAL.

101. JSC, 6:524, 3:462.

102. JSC, 3:68.

103. JSC, 9:1026.

104. JSC, 1:377–78; 12:901.

105. JSC, 12:640.

106. Camille Walsh, Racial Taxation: Schools, Segregation, and Taxpayer Citizenship, 1869–1973 (Chapel Hill: University of North Carolina Press, 2018), chap. 1.

107. Untitled article, National Republican, August 8, 1868, 2.

108. "The Louisiana Bolt," Rutland (VT) Herald, August 1, 1872, 6.

109. "Gen. Grant's Position," Daily Phoenix (Columbia, SC), December 25, 1866, 2.

110. "Political," The Clarion (Jackson, MS), November 8, 1872, 1.

111. "The Case of Mr. Work," Galveston Daily News, December 12, 1889, 4.

112. Untitled article, Whig and Tribune (Jackson, TN), May 8, 1875, 4.

113. Notably, many Southerners opposed public education outright, and burned both white and Black schools. Untitled article, *Memphis Daily Appeal*, July 23, 1873, 2; *JSC*, 9:747, 11:478.

114. For example, see Jill Lepore, *New York Burning: Liberty, Slavery, and Conspiracy in Eighteenth-Century Manhattan* (New York: Alfred A. Knopf, 2005).

115. "South Carolina," *New York Times*, February 25, 1868, 2.

116. "Tennessee," *New Orleans Times-Picayune*, May 31, 1868, 7; "Both Races Charge Each Other with Incendiarism," *Charleston Daily News*, November 2, 1871, 1.

117. When an African American minister testified that these charges were baseless, Democratic congressmen undermined his credibility, noting that he had a "reputation for romancing," such that "small events that would not be noticed by other men his imagination and fancy work into terrorism." *JSC*, 8:156, 179–80.

118. "Incendiarism," *Daily Phoenix*, May 18, 1869, 3.

119. "Disgraceful Conduct," *The Southerner* (Tarboro, NC), May 12, 1866, 2.

120. *JSC*, 2:72, 83.

121. On Southern whites' perceptions of arson, militias, and the prospect of racial warfare, see Hahn, *Nation under Our Feet*, chap. 6.

122. *JSC*, 8:236.

123. *JSC*, 12:640; untitled article, *Georgia Weekly Telegraph*, March 27, 1877, 6.

124. *JSC*, 12:650.

125. *JSC*, 5:1611.

126. For example, see untitled article, *Baltimore Sun*, March 14, 1901, 7; "Two Schoolhouses Burnt," *Virginia Dispatch*, September 18, 1902, 6.

127. *JSC*, 9:765.

128. *JSC*, 2:133–34.

129. Subdistrict report [Greene County, AL], July 1868, Records of the Assistant Commissioner for the State of Alabama, Bureau of Refugees, Freedmen, and Abandoned Lands, 1865–1870, M809, roll 18, BRFAL.

130. On local compromise in nineteenth-century education, see Justice, *War That Wasn't*; Robert N. Gross, *Public vs. Private: The Early History of School Choice in America* (New York: Oxford University Press, 2018).

131. See Anderson, *Education of Blacks*, chap 3.

2. MODERN EDUCATION AND ITS DISCONTENTS, 1890–1930

1. "Crazy Man, Not Reds, Held to Be Firebug," *New York Times*, December 12, 1920, 3.

2. "Wholesale Arson Ascribed to Reds; Loss of $4,000,000 Near Uniontown, Pa.," *New York Times*, December 9, 1920, 1.

3. "Firebug Destroys $200,000 Building," *New York Times*, December 28, 1920, 12.

4. "Hold Pole as Arson Head," *New York Times*, January 13, 1921, 4.

5. "Crazy Man, Not Reds."

6. "Boys Burned School House to Bring End to Study," *New York Times*, April 17, 1925, 1. For other examples, see "Boys Set School Ablaze," *New York Times*, May 24, 1900, 7; "Delavan School Destroyed by Fire," *Duluth (MN) News Tribune*, October 18, 1904, 7; "Dunmore High School Destroyed by Fire," *Wilkes-Barre Times-Leader*, June 1, 1908, 1; "Many Injured in California School Incendiary Fires," *Medford (OR) Mail*, December 31, 1923, 1.

7. "A Fire Detective," *New York Times*, May 7, 1911, 57. On the shifting science of criminology during the nineteenth and twentieth centuries, see Stephen Jones, *Criminology* (New York: Oxford University Press, 2013). On the shifting lexicon of evil, see Andrew

Delbanco, *The Death of Satan: How Americans Have Lost the Sense of Evil* (New York: Farrar, Straus and Giroux, 1995).

8. "Firebug Tries to Burn School," *San Francisco Call*, May 6, 1908, 24; "Dynamite Bomb Damages High School," *New York Times*, November 11, 1927, 9.

9. Charles Tilly, *The Politics of Collective Violence* (New York: Cambridge University Press, 2003), 47; James C. Scott, *Seeing like a State: How Certain Schemes to Improve the Human Condition Have Failed* (New Haven, CT: Yale University Press, 1998), chap. 5.

10. Relevant statistics are available through the US Census Bureau. See working paper and attached tables at Campbell J. Gibson and Emily Lennon, "Historical Census Statistics on the Foreign-Born Population of the United States: 1850-1990," United States Census Bureau, February 1999, https://www.census.gov/library/working-papers/1999/demo/POP-twps0029.html.

11. Zoë Burkholder, *Color in the Classroom: How American Schools Taught Race, 1900–1954* (New York: Oxford University Press, 2011); Diana Selig, *Americans All: The Cultural Gifts Movement* (Cambridge, MA: Harvard University Press, 2008).

12. "Fiery Cross Prompts Boy to Arson," *New York Times*, February 26, 1925, 5; "The Riot in Boston," *New York Times*, July 6, 1895, 4.

13. "Ohio School Dynamite," *New York Times*, October 21, 1918, 15; "Sets Fires, Loss $5,000,000," *New York Times*, August 18, 1923, 4.

14. Julia Grant, *The Boy Problem: Educating Boys in Urban America, 1870–1970* (Baltimore: Johns Hopkins University Press, 2014), 73.

15. These fears were not entirely without basis. There were incidents in which mobsters took potshots at school buildings, and in which the bombing of nearby businesses blew out the windows of public schools. "Fear-Crazed Women Besiege Harlem School," *New York Times*, October 4, 1904, 16; "Black Hand Rumor Causes School Panic," *New York Times*, April 9, 1908, 9; "Panic in a School," *Morning Astorian* (Astoria, OR), May 29, 1908, 1; "Young Mayors Govern a Once Unmanageable School," *New York Times*, May 29, 1910, 12; "Powder Bomb Jars a Downtown Block," *New York Times*, November 5, 1911, 11.

16. David B. Tyack, *The One Best System: A History of Urban Education* (Cambridge, MA: Harvard University Press, 1974), 179.

17. "The Negro in Illinois," *Evergreen (AL) Courant*, June 25, 1902, 1; "Miami Negro Schoolhouse Blown Up by Dynamite," *Warren (OH) Tribune*, June 28, 1926, 1. For an overview of the Great Migration, see Isabel Wilkerson, *The Warmth of Other Suns: The Epic Story of America's Great Migration* (New York: Vintage, 2011); and Nell Irvin Painter, *Exodusters: Black Migration to Kansas after Reconstruction* (New York: W. W. Norton, 1992).

18. It was not uncommon for schools to fall victim to more general racial violence, as in the mob attack in Tulsa, Oklahoma, in 1921, or the "Rosewood Massacre" in Levy County, Florida, in 1923. See Tim Madigan, *The Burning: Massacre, Destruction, and the Tulsa Race Riot of 1921* (New York: St. Martin's, 2001); and Michael D'Orso, *Like Judgment Day: The Ruin and Redemption of a Town Called Rosewood* (New York: G. P. Putnam's Sons, 1996).

19. "Negro Burned to Death by Missouri Mob," *Tampa (FL) Tribune*, January 13, 1931, 2.

20. "Schoolhouse Dynamited," *Kansas City (KS) Gazette*, March 10, 1896, 1.

21. For an overview, see Judith Kafka and Cici Matheny, "Racial Integration, White Appropriation, and School Choice: The Demise of the Colored Schools of Late Nineteenth Century Brooklyn," *Journal of Urban History* 48, no. 1 (January 2022): 1–28.

22. Burkholder, *Color in the Classroom*, 35.

23. Tyack, *One Best System*, 114–19.

24. "Arson Follows Race War," *New York Times*, January 3, 1904, 7; "Burning a School-House," *New York Times*, February 26, 1881, 2. For other examples, see Zöe Burkholder, *An African American Dilemma: A History of School Integration and Civil Rights in the North* (New York: Oxford University Press, 2021), 31–35, 41–44.

25. Burkholder, *Color in the Classroom*, 114–16; untitled article, *Morning Astorian*, October 27, 1905, 2; "Students in Race Riot," *Perth Amboy (NJ) Evening News*, January 26, 1916, 10; "Fear of Race Riot," *St. Tammany (LA) Farmer*, September 12, 1908, 1; untitled article, *Watauga (NC) Democrat*, April 21, 1904, 3; "Social Uplift Show Wrecked in Jersey," *New York Times*, March 13, 1914, 1; "Daily Doings in Judge Foley's Police Matinee," *Columbus (GA) Inquirer*, March 1, 1916, 12.

26. "Bound Not to Have a Colored Teacher," *St. Paul (MN) Globe*, November 7, 1902, 1. For other examples of racist student uprisings, see David J. Peavler, "Drawing the Color Line in Kansas City," *Kansas History* 27 (Autumn 2005): 188–201; and Burkholder, *Color in the Classroom*, 114–15.

27. Claudia Goldin, "A Brief History of Education in the United States," in *Historical Statistics of the United States*, vol. 2, ed. Susan Carter (New York: Cambridge University Press, 2006), part B, 480.

28. "Angry Father Burns School," *Fairmont West Virginian*, October 21, 1913, 8; untitled article, *Daily Public Ledger* (Maysville, KY), December 20, 1901, 1; "Schoolhouse Burned in Catahoula," *Daily Picayune* (New Orleans), June 13, 1888, 2; "Feudists in Battle," *Emporia (KS) Gazette*, September 5, 1904, 1; untitled article, *Clarksburg (WV) Telegram*, November 30, 1894, 1; "Two Schoolhouses Burned on Saturday," *Indiana Progress*, September 6, 1911, 1; "Schoolhouse Burned," *Louisville Courier-Journal*, August 1, 1899, 1; "Confederate Veterans," *Emporia Gazette*, June 14, 1904, 1.

29. Campbell F. Scribner, *The Fight for Local Control: Schools, Suburbs, and American Democracy* (Ithaca, NY: Cornell University Press, 2016), chap. 2; Goldin, "Brief History," 398.

30. "Schoolhouse Burned," *Louisville Courier-Journal*, June 2, 1903, 3; "Building in Place of One Recently Burned," *Idaho Daily Statesman*, January 27, 1920, 7; "Trailed by Bloodhounds," *New York Times*, September 16, 1913, 11.

31. "Verndale School Destroyed by Fire," *Grand Forks (ND) Daily Herald*, May 29, 1915, 2; "Consolidated School Destroyed by Fire," *Grand Forks Herald*, February 19, 1918, 2.

32. "Attempt to Burn School," *Evening Times-Republican* (Marshalltown, IA), August 21, 1915, 3.

33. "Dynamite in a School," *Topeka State Journal*, May 17, 1895, 6.

34. Monty J. Ellsworth, *The Bath School Disaster* (Bath, MI: self-pub., 1927); Anne Bernstein, *The Bath School Disaster* (Ann Arbor: University of Michigan Press, 2009). For additional coverage, see "Survivors Recall 1927 Michigan School Massacre," National Public Radio, April 17, 2009, https://www.npr.org/templates/story/story.php?storyId=103186662.

35. William J. Reese, *America's Public Schools: From the Common School to "No Child Left Behind"* (Baltimore: Johns Hopkins University Press, 2011), 181.

36. Goldin, "Brief History," 421–22. On debates about the high school curriculum, see Diane Ravitch, *Left Back: A Century of Battles over School Reform* (New York: Simon and Schuster, 2000); David L. Angus and Jeffrey Mirel, *The Failed Promise of the American High School, 1890–1995* (New York: Teachers College Press, 1999); and Kyle P. Steele, *Making a Mass Institution: Indianapolis and the American High School* (New Brunswick, NJ: Rutgers University Press, 2020).

37. "Big School Building Blown Up," *New York Times*, April 16, 1896, 1.

38. "Authorities Probe Wrecking of School by Dynamite Blasts," *Richmond (IN) Palladium and Sun-Telegram*, October 30, 1922, 1.

39. "Dynamite under a School," *New York Times*, October 23, 1896, 1. Principals, eager to soothe public nerves, often attributed these incidents to careless workmen. For examples of high school fires, see "Schoolhouse Burned," *San Jose Evening News*, July 21, 1894, 1; "Reward of $6,000 for Lewistown Firebug," *Montana Standard*, May 13, 1918, 3.

40. Goldin, "Brief History," 411.

41. "Say Mother Set Fire to Daughter's School," *New York Times*, September 12, 1929, 23.

42. "High School Vandalism," *Grand Rapids Herald*, November 25, 1900, 4; "Fire Follows Prank," *New York Times*, July 6, 1913, 2; "Four Young Fire-Bugs," *New York Times*, December 12, 1883, 5. Pranks had long been part of the classroom culture, but they became more elaborate as teenagers patterned their clubs after college fraternities and engaged in daring acts of theft or sabotage. Popular culture made light of these hijinks, with films and comic strips about booby-trapping teachers' desks and packing their pipes with gunpowder. See Heather A. Weaver, "'The Teacher's Unexpected Bath': Plumbing the Meaning of Mayhem in the Celluloid Classroom," *History of Education Quarterly* 54, no. 2 (May 2014): 145–71.

43. "Wrecked a Public School," *New York Times*, January 19, 1897, 4.

44. "1,000 Pupils Riot against Gary Plan," *New York Times*, October 17, 1917, 6.

45. "Pupils Besiege Board Meeting," *New York Times*, April 10, 1913, 11.

46. "Boys Wreck High School," *Morning Oregonian*, March 26, 1920, 7.

47. "Student Strikers Wreck Lunchroom," *New York Times*, May 7, 1913, 5.

48. Grant, *Boy Problem*, 73.

49. "Town Was Fired by Boy," *Oakland Tribune*, November 28, 1908, 1. For a similar case, see "Boy Set Fire to School," *New York Times*, May 9, 1903, 6.

50. "Vandals Wreck a School," *New York Times*, November 11, 1902, 1.

51. "Say Schoolboy Set Fire to Burn His Bad Marks," *New York Evening World*, February 18, 1921, 25.

52. Untitled article, *Denison (TX) Gazetteer*, April 5, 1891, 2; "3 Arson Attempts Made in School Building," *New York Times*, January 18, 1929, 16; "Boys Burned Down Obnoxious School," *Duluth News Tribune*, March 23, 1904, 2; "Arrested on Arson Charge," *Philadelphia Inquirer*, January 20, 1911, 3.

53. "Yoncalla Church Burns," *Morning Oregonian*, April 29, 1916, 6.

54. "Boy, Disliking School, Fires Two," *New York Times*, February 16, 1928, 47; "Third Attempt to Burn Building," *Lincoln (NE) Star*, November 26, 1920, 1; "Boy Tries to Burn School," *New York Times*, May 9, 1917, 7.

55. An incomplete list of incidents at boys' schools includes "Boys Fight Barn Fire," *Baltimore Sun*, April 7, 1916, 16; "Four Very Bad Boys Are These," *New York Times*, August 10, 1893, 5; "A Reform School Burned," *Daily Ohio Statesman*, December 21, 1865, 3; "Lancaster, Ohio," *Pittsburgh Daily Commercial*, November 14, 1874, 1; "Industrial School Burned," *Macon (GA) Telegraph*, February 4, 1887, 1; "Handsome Reform School Destroyed," *Wheeling (WV) Register*, June 25, 1891, 1; "Territorial Reform School at Ogden Burned," *San Francisco Bulletin*, June 25, 1891, 3; "Sent to State Prison," *Los Angeles Times*, July 28, 1897, 2; untitled article, *Burlington (VT) Free Press*, March 22, 1900, 5; "Oregon Institution Burned," *Idaho Daily Statesman*, December 19, 1901, 2; "Bad Boys Narrowly Escape," *Duluth News Tribune*, March 21, 1902, 5; "Tries to Burn Boys' School," *Des Moines Register*, February 28, 1906, 7; "Boys Try to Burn House of Refuge," *New York Times*, June 20, 1907, 5; "Boy Fires Building on Randall's Island," *New York Times*, April 7, 1915, 9; "Bits of News," *Day Book* (Chicago), March 3, 1916, 31; "Fire of Incendiary Origin," *New*

Journal and Guide (Norfolk, VA), October 25, 1924, 9; "Firebug, 16, Confesses in Lynn," *New York Times*, December 29, 1927, 10. Incidents at girls' schools include untitled article, *True Northerner* (Paw Paw, MI), October 31, 1888, 6; "Burning of a Prison," *Idaho Daily Statesman*, March 2, 1892, 1; "Seven Perish in Flames," *Omaha World-Herald*, October 7, 1897, 1; "Fire at a Reform School," *Washington (DC) Times*, July 21, 1897, 2; *School Fires* (Boston: National Fire Protection Association, 1931), 15.

56. In addition to the titles described below, see Tera Eva Agyepong, *The Criminalization of Black Children: Race, Gender, and Delinquency in Chicago's Juvenile Justice System, 1899–1945* (Chapel Hill: University of North Carolina Press, 2018); Geoff K. Ward, *The Black Child-Savers: Racial Democracy and Juvenile Justice* (Chicago: University of Chicago Press, 2012); and Jason Mayernick, "Segregated Young Men's Reformatories in Maryland during the Great Depression," *Journal of the History of Childhood and Youth* 15, no. 1 (Winter 2022): 7–28.

57. Michael B. Katz, *The Irony of Early School Reform: Educational Innovation in Mid-Nineteenth Century Massachusetts* (New York: Teachers College Press, 2001); Grant, *Boy Problem*, chap. 1.

58. Karin Zipf, *Bad Girls at Samarcand: Sexuality and Sterilization in a Southern Juvenile Reformatory* (Baton Rouge: Louisiana State University Press, 2016), 1–3.

59. David Wallace Adams, *Education for Extinction: American Indians and the Board School Experience, 1875–1928* (Lawrence: University Press of Kansas, 1995); Adrea Lawrence, *Lessons from an Indian Day School: Negotiating Colonization in Northern New Mexico, 1902–1907* (Lawrence: University Press of Kansas, 2011); Kim Cary Warren, *The Question for Citizenship: African American and Native American Education in Kansas, 1880–1935* (Chapel Hill: University of North Carolina Press, 2010).

60. "Whipped Boy Starts a Fire," *Kansas City (MO) Star*, February 2, 1909, 1; "A Disastrous Fire," *Daily Inter Ocean* (Chicago), June 23, 1888, 3; "Indian Girls Homesick," *Wichita Beacon*, February 9, 1898, 3; "Friends' Indian School Burned," *Philadelphia Inquirer*, February 26, 1886, 1. In one exceptional case, in 1919, the Haskell Indian School in Kansas had a full-scale rebellion, in which students ransacked the classrooms and threatened to lynch the principal. Brenda Child, "Runaway Boys, Resistant Girls: Rebellion at Flandreau and Haskell, 1900–1940," *Journal of American Indian Education* 35, no. 3 (Spring 1996): 49–57.

61. "Indian School House Burned," *La Plata (MO) Home Press*, March 4, 1892, 6.

62. "President Befriends an Indian Girl," *New York Times*, September 11, 1906, 12.

63. "Boy Gets Failing Grade, Sets School on Fire," *San Antonio Register*, December 28, 1962, 7. Lacking adequate playgrounds, children often played on construction sites, discovered sticks of dynamite or glycerin blasting caps, pocketed them, brought them to school, and, out of boredom, began pricking them with safety pins, horrifically maiming themselves in the process. See, for instance, "Dynamite Blows Off Fingers," *New York Times*, September 17, 1936, 25.

64. "Children Have Dynamite," *New York Times*, May 11, 1908, 1.

65. "To Dynamite School," *Columbia (TN) Herald*, January 18, 1907, 8; "Enough Dynamite to Blast a Block Found on Roof of Jewish School," *New York Times*, August 24, 1949, 27.

66. Kate Rousmaniere, *City Teachers: Teaching and School Reform in Historical Perspective* (New York: Teachers College Press, 1997), 116.

67. "Blow Up School House," *Emporia Gazette*, September 13, 1906, 1.

68. Rousmaniere, *City Teachers*, 77.

69. For earlier examples of ideology inscribed in architecture, see Augustín Escolano Benito, "The School in the City: School Architecture as Discourse and as Text," *Pedagogica Historica* 39, no. 1/2 (2003): 53–64; Dell Upton, "Lancasterian Schools, Republican Citizenship, and the Spatial Imagination in Early Nineteenth-Century America," *Journal of the*

Society of Architectural Historians 55, no. 3 (September 1996): 238–53. On the persistence of the environmental interpretation of student misbehavior, see *Addresses and Proceedings of the NEA* (Washington, DC: National Education Association, 1911), 367–68.

70. William George Bruce, *School Architecture: A Handy Manual for the Use of Architects and School Authorities* (Milwaukee: American School Board Association, 1910), 87–89; "Boy Tries to Fire School," *New York Times*, January 14, 1914, 1; "School Officials Sift Cause of Fire," *Chicago Defender*, September 29, 1928, 11; "Boys Suspected of Starting School Fires," *New York Times*, January 10, 1904, 13; "Started Two Fires in School," *New York Times*, February 17, 1904, 5.

71. "Central High School Scene of Fire Scare," *Pueblo (CO) Chieftain*, May 10, 1918, 4; "Didn't Like Teacher; Tried to Burn School," *New York Times*, March 10, 1927, 6; "Set Fires to See Pupils in Drill," *New York Times*, May 5, 1914, 5; "Negro Children Start Fire," *Lexington (KY) Herald*, March 20, 1920, 1.

72. "Boy Arrested for Arson," *New York Times*, January 12, 1904, 18; "Insurance Matters in and around Boston," *Insurance Press*, October 23, 1895, 5.

73. "Lad Who Put Burning Film under Desk Convicted," *New York Sun*, April 1, 1919, 18; "Too Many School Fires," *Baltimore Sun*, April 15, 1919, 6.

74. "A Schoolhouse Burned," *New York Daily Herald*, December 21, 1875, 7; "Michigan City," *Insurance Press*, January 29, 1896, 5. Without zoning provisions, there were also several cases in which explosives were stored in or adjacent to school buildings, which were accidentally destroyed. "Exploding Fireworks Kill Many Persons," *New York Times*, June 22, 1901, 1; "Telegraph Briefs," *Day Book*, March 3, 1915, 31; "Terrific Explosion," *Cleveland Gazette*, November 15, 1884, 2.

75. To take one example of the cost that districts bore, a high school in Parkersburg, West Virginia, burned at a total loss of $30,000. Only a year later, it burned again at an additional cost of $10,000, with only $5,000 insured. "Schoolhouse Burned," *Washington Post*, December 8, 1905, 4.

76. On the history of insurance, see Jonathan Levy, *Freaks of Fortune: The Emerging World of Capitalism and Risk in America* (Cambridge, MA: Harvard University Press, 2012); Tom Baker and Jonathan Simon, eds., *Embracing Risk: The Changing Culture of Insurance and Responsibility* (Chicago: University of Chicago Press, 2002); Barbara Young Welke, "The Cowboy Suit Tragedy: Spreading Risk, Owning Hazard in the Modern American Consumer Economy," *Journal of American History* 101, no. 1 (June 2014): 97–121; Hannah Farber, *Underwriters of the United States: How Insurance Shaped the American Founding* (Chapel Hill: University of North Carolina Press, 2021); and Caley Dawn Horan, "Actuarial Age: Insurance and the Emergence of Neoliberalism in the Postwar United States" (PhD diss., University of Minnesota, 2011).

77. Deborah Stone, "Beyond Moral Hazard: Insurance as Moral Opportunity," in Baker and Simon, *Embracing Risk*, 52–53.

78. Carol A. Heimer, "Insurers as Moral Actors," in *Risk and Morality*, ed. Richard V. Ericson and Aaron Doyle (Toronto: University of Toronto Press, 2003), 284–85.

79. Tracy Steffes, *School, Society, and State: A New Education to Govern Modern America, 1890–1940* (Chicago: University of Chicago Press, 2012). See also Karen Benjamin, "The Limits of Top-Down versus Bottom-Up Educational Reform during the Great Depression," in *The Shifting Landscape of the American School District: Race, Class, Geography, and the Perpetual Reform of Local Control*, ed. David Gamson and Emily Hodge (New York: Peter Lang, 2018), 143–68.

80. For contemporary conceptions of the insurance market, see Henry R. Gall and William George Jordan, *One Hundred Years of Fire Insurance: Being a History of the Aetna Insurance Company* (Hartford: Aetna Insurance Company, 1919); *The Fire Insurance Contract: Its History and Interpretation* (New York: Insurance Society of New York,

1922). Readers can find relevant policies for schools at the Philadelphia Contributorship, https://1752.com/.

81. Actuarial tables had been applied to property losses only over the previous twenty years. Mark Tebeau, *Eating Smoke: Fire in Urban America, 1800–1950* (Baltimore: Johns Hopkins University Press, 2003), 265. Cataloguing safety features led to the fire insurance maps that have become vital tools for other forms of urban history. For example, see the Sanborn fire insurance maps at the Library of Congress, https://www.loc.gov/collections/sanborn-maps.

82. For examples, see *Occupancy Fire Record* (Boston: National Fire Protection Association, 1957).

83. Harvey A. Smith, *Economy in Public School Fire Insurance* (New York: Teachers College Press, 1930), 15; Milton Henry Steinhauer, "Fire Insurance on Public School Property in Pennsylvania" (PhD diss., University of Pennsylvania, 1939), 41–43.

84. For instance, see *American School Board Journal* 6, no. 1 (1894): 7.

85. *School Fires* (Boston: National Fire Protection Association, 1927), 183; untitled article, *American School Board Journal* 45, no. 4 (October 1912): 16; untitled article, *American School Board Journal* 44, no. 2 (February 1912): 52.

86. Smith, *Economy*, 20; "Uninsured School Buildings Noted," *Baltimore Sun*, April 20, 1926, 3.

87. "The School Insurance," *St. Paul (MN) Daily Globe*, October 9, 1891, 8; "Powell Bros. Propose to Keep Insurance," *Daily Press* (Newport News, VA), February 23, 1907, 3; untitled article, *American School Board Journal*, 6, no. 11 (1894): 3; "Selling to the Schools," *American School Board Journal* 45, no. 5 (November 1912): 9; untitled article, *American School Board Journal* 44, no. 1 (January 1912): 39.

88. On financial malfeasance related to insurance, see Fred M. Warner, *General School Laws of Michigan* (Lansing: Wynkoop Hallenbeck Crawford Company, 1901), 90; *Public School Laws of Missouri* (Jefferson City: Department of Education, 1921), 76; Francis Blair, *The School Law of Illinois* (Springfield: State Journal Company, 1910), 21–22.

89. "The Burned High School," *San Francisco Bulletin*, January 17, 1890, 2.

90. Untitled article, *American School Board Journal* 45, no. 6 (June 1912): 29; "Board Lets Contracts for Two New Schools," *Dallas Morning News*, July 1, 1909, 9; *Fire Tragedies and Their Remedy* (Providence, RI: Grinnell Company, 1919).

91. Smith, *Economy*, 89.

92. *Some Recent School Fires* (Boston: National Fire Protection Association, 1933), 5.

93. Untitled article, *American School Board Journal* 20, no. 3 (March 1900): 3; "Among Boards of Education," *American School Board Journal* 41, no. 3 (September 1910): 19; "Board of Education," *American School Board Journal* 41, no. 5 (November 1910): 20; "School Administration," *American School Board Journal* 32, no. 1 (January 1906): 5; *Some Recent School Fires*, 6.

94. Betty J. Annis, "A Plan for Fire Insurance on Public School District Property in the State of Nebraska," PhD diss. (University of Nebraska, Lincoln, 1978), 21–23; untitled article, *American School Board Journal* 32, no. 2 (February 1906): 15; "Concrete Schoolhouses vs. Fire Traps," *American School Board Journal* 42, no. 2 (February 1911): 12; untitled article, *American School Board Journal* 23, no. 5 (November 1901): 29; "Uninsured School Buildings Noted," *Baltimore Sun*, April 20, 1926, 3; Steinhauer, "Fire Insurance," 42; *Some Recent School Fires*, 6.

95. Smith, *Economy*, 100; *Some Recent School Fires*, 5.

96. "Buffalo Public Buildings," *Insurance Press*, February 11, 1914, 7.

97. "Among Boards of Education," *American School Board Journal* 41, no. 3 (September 1910): 19; "Board of Education," *American School Board Journal* 41, no. 5 (November 1910): 20.

98. Untitled article, *American School Board Journal* 40, no. 2 (February 1910): 14.

99. *The Fire Insurance Contract: Its History and Interpretation* (New York: Insurance Society of New York, 1922), 7; "School House Fires," *American School Board Journal* 38, no. 2 (1909): 8; "Concrete Schoolhouses vs. Fire Traps," 12; "School House Fires," *American School Board Journal* 10, no. 3 (March 1895): 8; *Some Recent School Fires*, 65. On other aspects of rural infrastructure and state support, see Andrew Needham and Allen Dieterich-Ward, "Beyond the Metropolis: Metropolitan Growth and Regional Transformation in Postwar America," *Journal of Urban History* 35, no. 7 (January 2009): 943–69.

100. William George Bruce, "School Building Insurance," *American School Board Journal* 32, no. 2 (February 1906): 3.

101. In Wisconsin, 205 unincorporated towns saved an average of $10,000 over five years after moving to mutual insurance. On mutual insurance, see Newton Edwards, *The Courts and the Public Schools*, 3rd ed. (Chicago: University of Chicago Press, 1971), 165–66. For particular states adopting the reform, see "School Laws," *American School Board Journal* 31, no. 6 (December 1905): 2; untitled article, *American School Board Journal* 35, no. 2 (August 1907): 15; "School House Fires," *American School Board Journal* 38, no. 2 (1909): 8. A similar system remains popular today, often coordinated by state board of education associations. Julie Blair, "Liability Insurance's Skyrocketing Costs Confound Districts," *Education Week*, February 6, 2002, 1.

102. *Some Recent School Fires*, 4.

103. Insurance File Photographs, ca. 1935–52, South Carolina Archives, accessed August 16, 2022, http://www.archivesindex.sc.gov/SeriesDescriptions/S112113.html. Oklahoma maintained a school insurance fund while still a territory, but it seems to have reverted to a mutual insurance model upon gaining statehood. "Oklahoma Territory," *Dallas Morning News*, July 31, 1898, 22; Clinton Orrin Bunn, ed., *Supplement to the Revised Laws of Oklahoma of 1910* (Ardmore, OK: Bunn, 1918), 435.

104. Smith, *Economy*, 102–5; *Wisconsin Blue Book* (Madison: Industrial Commission of Wisconsin, 1966). Even today, less populous states tend to provide insurance coverage only through quasi-public entities, such as school board associations or interdistrict cooperatives, rather than through the legislature itself.

105. James K. Lathrop, ed., *Life Safety Code Handbook* (Boston: National Fire Protection Association, 1991).

106. "Perils of School House Construction," *American School Board Journal* 42, no. 4 (April 1911): 2.

107. *Addresses and Proceedings of the NEA* (Washington, DC: National Education Association, 1911), 1010. On the transmission of urban reforms, see Tyack, *One Best System*; and David Gamson, *The Importance of Being Urban: Designing the Progressive School District, 1890–1940* (Chicago: University of Chicago Press, 2019).

108. Edwards, *Courts and the Public Schools*, 104–5; Kansas City v. School District of Kansas City, 356 Mo. 364, 201 S.W. (2d) 930 (1947); Pasadena School District v. City of Pasadena, 166 Calif. 7, 134 Pac. 985, 47 L.R.A. (N.S.) 492 (1913); Community Fire Protection District of St. Louis County v. Board of Education, 315 S.W. (2d) 873 (Mo.) (1958). For a general discussion of the issue, see Lee O. Garber and Newton Edwards, *The Law Governing School Property and School-Building Construction* (Danville, IL: Interstate, 1964).

109. Kentucky Institution for Blind v. City of Louisville, 123 Ky. 767, 8 L.R.A. (N.S.) 553, 97 S.W. 402 (1906); Salt Lake City v. Board of Education, 52 Utah 540, 175 Pac. 654 (1918); Hall v. City of Taft (CA), 302 P.2d 574 (1956).

110. "Education in Fire Prevention," *American School Board Journal* 43, no. 5 (November 1911): 12; "School House Fires," *American School Board Journal* 28, no. 3 (March 1904): 8.

111. Robert Wiedrich, "Boy Denies Setting School Fire," *Chicago Tribune*, February 24, 1962, 7.

112. "Hundred and Sixty-Seven Dead," *Omaha Daily Bee*, March 7, 1908, 1; Irvin May, "New London School Explosion," Texas State Historical Association, last updated June 9, 2020, https://tshaonline.org/handbook/online/articles/yqn01. See also untitled article, *Bridgeport (CT) Evening Farmer*, December 19, 1913, 19; "Schoolhouse Burned," *Dallas Morning News*, March 4, 1889, 6; Robert J. Quinn, "Tragedy in Chicago," *Fire Engineering* 112, no. 1 (January 1959): 30–36; Adam Groves, "Our Lady of Angels School Fire: 50 Years Later," *Fire Engineering* 161, no. 12 (December 2008): 59–66; *Occupancy Fire Record FR 57–1* (Boston: National Fire Protection Association, 1957), 3, 18.

113. Findings ranged between 4.8 percent and 25 percent; the total was 160 out of 2,057, or 7.8 percent. *School Fires* (Boston: National Fire Protection Association, 1927), 183; *School Fires* (Boston: National Fire Protection Association, 1931), 39–40; Steinhauer, "Fire Insurance," 3, 85–86; "Protecting Schoolhouses against Fire," *American School Board Journal* 53, no. 1 (July 1916): 55; "Annual Schoolhouse Fires," *American School Board Journal* 35, no. 6 (1907): 36; *Fire Tragedies and Their Remedy*, 38–47.

114. *A Study of School Fires* (Boston: National Fire Protection Association, 1973), 2, 18.

3. DIAGNOSING DELINQUENCY, 1930–60

1. While this chapter focuses on juvenile delinquency, school vandalism also resulted from the contentious adult politics of the Depression. For example, in Harlan County, Kentucky, a contested school board election, following close on the heels of the region's deadly coal strike, led to the dynamiting of the winner's car. In New York City, striking workers stoned school buses and beat up their drivers, and either Communist agitators or the police wrecked a building that they were occupying. "Blow Up Car in Evarts, KY," *New York Times*, July 10, 1932, 23; "Buses Are Stoned in Queens Strike," *New York Times*, October 24, 1939, 1; "3 WPA Teachers Deny They Wrecked Office," *New York Times*, July 13, 1937.

2. Despite the subject's importance, historians have written surprisingly little about schools during the Depression. Exceptions include David B. Tyack, Robert Lowe, and Elizabeth Hansot, *Public Schools in Hard Times: The Great Depression and Recent Years* (Cambridge, MA: Harvard University Press, 1984); Andrew Hartman, *Education and the Cold War: The Battle for the American School* (New York: Palgrave Macmillan, 2008), chap. 2; Thomas Fallace, *In the Shadow of Authoritarianism: American Education in the Twentieth Century* (New York: Teachers College Press, 2018); Britt Haas, *Fighting Authoritarianism: American Youth Activism in the 1930s* (New York: Empire State Editions, 2017); and Kyle Steele, *Making a Mass Institution: Indianapolis and the American High School* (New Brunswick, NJ: Rutgers University Press, 2020), chap. 3.

3. Tyack, Lowe, and Hansot, *Public Schools in Hard Times*, 27–41.

4. *Final Report on the WPA Program, 1935–1943* (Washington, DC: US Government Printing Office, 1943), 52.

5. Richard A. Reiman, *The New Deal and American Youth: Ideas and Ideals in a Depression Decade* (Athens: University of Georgia Press, 1992), chaps. 4–6.

6. *Historical Statistics of the United States, Colonial Times to 1970* (White Plains, NY: Kraus International, 1989), 379.

7. William Graebner, *Coming of Age in Buffalo: Youth and Authority in the Postwar Era* (Philadelphia: Temple University Press, 1990), 88.

8. Eleanor T. Glueck, "Coping with Wartime Delinquency," *Journal of Educational Sociology* 16, no. 2 (October 1942): 86–98; Milton Lessner, "Controlling War-Time Juvenile Delinquency," *Journal of Criminal Law and Criminology* 35, no. 4 (1945): 242–48.

9. "Five Boys Arrested for Firing School," *Philadelphia Inquirer*, March 21, 1939, 3; "Hate Led to Vandalism," *New York Times*, July 6, 1944, 17; *Schools: Occupancy Fire Record* (Boston: National Fire Protection Association, 1965), 4–5.

10. "School Bell Was Stolen," *Gate City and Constitution-Democrat* (Keokuk, IA), March 8, 1920, 2; "Bell That Tolled School Hours Years Ago Is Mysteriously Missing in White Plains," *New York Times*, February 9, 1938, 21; "Slides to His Death Down Pole at School," *New York Times*, December 9, 1938, 2; "Underwear Replaces the Flag at Canal Zone School," *New York Times*, November 20, 1932, E7; "Student, 19, Is Slain in Hallow-een Prank," *New York Times*, November 2, 1935, 16; "School Pranksters Pass by Guards-men," *Oklahoma City Times*, May 30, 1919, 2; "Arrested in School Prank," *New York Times*, November 7, 1931, 2; Judson Jerome, *Flight from Innocence: A Memoir, 1927–1947* (Fay-etteville: University of Arkansas Press, 1990), 182; "Playing with Dynamite," *Newsweek*, April 5, 1954, 89.

11. Brian Sutton-Smith, *The Ambiguity of Play* (Cambridge, MA: Harvard Univer-sity Press, 1997), 217–19; *Children's Folklore: A Sourcebook* (Logan: Utah State University Press, 1999), 217–18; Ralph Linton and Adelin Linton, *Halloween through Twenty Centu-ries* (New York: Schuman, 1950), 100–104; Gillian Brockell, "The Frightening History of Halloween Haunted Houses," *Washington Post*, October 26, 2019, https://www.washing tonpost.com/history/2019/10/26/frightening-history-halloween-haunted-houses/. Other examples include "School Windows Replaced," *New York Times*, November 29, 1950, 35; "Vandals Force School to Close," *New York Times*, November 2, 1951, 37; Nelson E. Viles, *The Custodian at Work* (New York: University Publishing, 1941), 151; Johnathan Croyle, "1934: Flap over a Broken Flagpole Draws Nation's Eyes to a One-Room Schoolhouse in Pompey Hollow," Syracuse.com, November 12, 2019, https://www.syracuse.com/ living/2019/11/1934-flap-over-a-broken-flagpole-draws-nations-eyes-to-a-one-room-schoolhouse-in-pompey-hollow.html.

12. "'Shots' Break School Windows," *New York Times*, April 24, 1940, 11; "Girl Wounded in Classroom; Two Boys Arrested in Shooting," *New York Times*, May 13, 1959, 29.

13. John Donner, *A Professional's Guide to Pyrotechnics* (Boulder, CO: Paladin, 1997), 53–66; Ronald Lancaster, *Fireworks: Principles & Practice* (New York: Chemical Publish-ing, 1998), chap. 1; "Firecracker Inquiry On," *New York Times*, November 25, 1949, 18; "Student Maimed by Firecracker," *New York Times*, June 13, 1958, 48.

14. Jason Barnosky, "The Violent Years: Responses to Juvenile Crime in the 1950s," *Polity* 38, no. 3 (July 2006): 339–40. See also "Teenage Delinquency" (ca. 1955), "Draft of Senator Kefauver's Statement on Bill Providing Assistance to State and Local Juvenile Delinquency Programs" (1956), and "President's Committee on Juvenile Delinquency and Youth Crime" (1961), Crime Documents from the Estes Kefauver Collection, Special Col-lections, University of Tennessee, Knoxville, https://digital.lib.utk.edu/collections/crimed-ocumentscollection?_ga=2.264095876.904583663.1627515204-1814573517.1627515204.

15. On anxiety and deviance, see Daniel Immerwahr, "The Thirty Years' Crisis: Anxiety and Fear in the Mid-century United States," *Modern Intellectual History* 13, no. 1 (2016): 287–98; Louis Menand, "Freud, Anxiety, and the Cold War," in *After Freud Left: A Cen-tury of Psychoanalysis in America*, ed. John Burnham (Chicago: University of Chicago Press, 2012), 199–200; James Gilbert, *A Cycle of Outrage: America's Reaction to the Juvenile Delinquent in the 1950s* (New York: Oxford University Press, 1986), 3–9, 14–19; Elaine Tyler May, *Homeward Bound: American Families in the Cold War Era* (New York: Basic Books, 2008), chap. 1; Margot A. Henriksen, *Dr. Strangelove's America: Society and Cul-ture in the Atomic Age* (Berkeley: University of California Press, 1997), 81–182; Leerom Medovoi, *Rebels: Youth and the Cold War Origins of Identity* (Durham, NC: Duke Univer-sity Press, 2005); Ronald D. Cohen, "The Delinquents: Censorship and Youth Culture in Recent U.S. History," *History of Education Quarterly* 37, no. 3 (Autumn 1997): 251–70. On

"containment theory" and delinquency, see Walter C. Reckless, "A New Theory of Delinquency and Crime," in *Readings in Juvenile Delinquency*, ed. Ruth Shonie Cavan (New York: J. B. Lippincott, 1964), 158–67.

16. "Symposium: Secondary Schools and Juvenile Delinquency," *California Journal of Secondary Education* 30, no. 8 (December 1955): 473–507.

17. Gilbert, *Cycle of Outrage*, 29.

18. For instance, see Ernst Wenk and Nora Harlow, eds., *School Crime and Disruption* (Davis, CA: Responsible Action, 1978); "School Forum Views Teen-Age Vandalism," *New York Times*, March 24, 1953, 35.

19. Abe Stein, "Adolescent Participation in Co-ordinating Councils," *Journal of Educational Sociology* 21, no. 3 (November 1947): 177–83.

20. Jesse G. Fox and Alex H. Lazes, "Children, Spare That Window!," *Clearing House* 29, no. 5 (January 1955): 287–89.

21. Michael D. Casserly, Scott A. Bass, and John R. Garrett, *School Vandalism: Strategies for Prevention* (Lexington, MA: Lexington Books, 1980), 40–41.

22. "Symposium: Secondary Schools and Juvenile Delinquency"; Dorothy Barclay, "Destructiveness in Children," *New York Times*, March 7, 1954, SM56; Charles H. English, "What to Do without Facilities," *The Playground* 18, no. 9 (December 1924): 514.

23. "Ex-vandals Urge Family Pledges as a Way to Curb Destruction Evil," *New York Times*, May 30, 1953, 17; *Schools: Occupancy Fire Record* (Boston: National Fire Protection Association, 1965), 41.

24. Viles, *Custodian at Work*, 5, 97–98; Fox and Lazes, "Children, Spare That Window!," 287–90.

25. Examples include "Every Room Crowded," *Dallas Morning News*, October 15, 1901, 10; "School Affairs," *Grand Forks (ND) Daily Herald*, May 28, 1885, 1.

26. Fox and Lazes, "Children, Spare That Window!," 287; Gerard Zwier and Graham Vaughan, "Three Ideological Orientations in School Vandalism Research," *Review of Educational Research* 54, no. 2 (Summer 1984): 263–92.

27. "School Vandalism Showing Decrease," *Philadelphia Inquirer*, December 3, 1922, 20; "Ex-vandals Urge Family Pledges."

28. Jeri J. Goldman, "Restitution for Damages to Public School Property," *Journal of Law & Education* 11, no. 2 (April 1982): 158–59. On district-level debates, see Ruth Olson to Sen. Horace Wilkie, January 27, 1957, Horace Wilkie Papers, Wisconsin Historical Society, Madison (hereafter WHS); school board minutes, August 11, 1955, collection 1923, box 1459, and Association of Elementary School Administrators, June 24, 1954, collection 1923, box 2036, Los Angeles Unified School District Board of Education Records, Special Collections, UCLA (hereafter LAUSD).

29. Linda A. Chapin, "Out of Control? The Uses and Abuses of Parental Liability Laws to Control Juvenile Delinquency in the United States," *Santa Clara Law Review* 37, no. 3 (1997): 629–38; Toni Weinstein, "Visiting the Sins of the Child on the Parent: The Legality of Criminal Parent Liability Statutes," *Southern California Law Review* 63, no. 3 (March 1991): 863–64.

30. Chapin, "Out of Control?," 633.

31. Lamro Ind. Consolidated School District v. Cawthorne, 76 S.D. 106 (1955); Board of Education v. Hansen, 56 N.J. Super. 567 (1959).

32. Arenson v. National Automobile and Casualty Insurance Co., 45 Cal. 2d 81, 286 P.2d 816 (1955).

33. *Board of Education v. Hansen*, 567.

34. Board of Education v. Caffiero, 86 N.J. 308 (1981); Goldman, "Restitution for Damages," 147–70.

35. Courts insisted from the beginning that districts take into account parents' ability to pay. Allen v. Chacon, 449 S.W.2d 289 (1969).

36. Horace Wilkie to Ben Lang, February 1, 1957, Horace Wilkie Papers, WHS; "Proposed Amendment to Los Angeles Municipal Code," June 22, 1954, collection 1923, box 2036, LAUSD; "Vandalism Curb Urged," New York Times, October 23, 1959, 9.

37. See Superintendent of Schools to Mrs. Willard Murray and Mrs. Hilda Nigro, May 7, 1971, box 2037, folder 2, LAUSD; Zwier and Vaughan, "Three Ideological Orientations," 275.

38. A review of Los Angeles's restitution program during the 1970s found that only 10 percent of vandals were caught, and of those, only 20 percent repaid anything at all to the school system. Association of Elementary School Administrators, June 24, 1954, collection 1923, box 2036, LAUSD; Zwier and Vaughan, "Three Ideological Orientations," 275. For similar results in Wisconsin, see Stevens Point Chamber of Commerce, February 11, 1957, and Lloyd H. Swanson to Horace Wilkie, May 7, 1957, Horace Wilkie Papers, WHS.

39. On racially disproportionate punishments, see Tera Agyepong, The Criminalization of Black Children: Race, Gender, and Delinquency in Chicago's Juvenile Justice System (Chapel Hill: University of North Carolina Press, 2018); Carl Suddler, Black Youth and the Justice System in Postwar New York (New York: New York University Press, 2019); and Khalil Gibran Muhammad, The Condemnation of Blackness: Race, Crime, and the Making of Modern America (Cambridge, MA: Harvard University Press, 2010), 123.

40. "School Wrecked by 3 Small Boys," New York Times, March 28, 1945, 1.

41. Fox and Lazes, "Children, Spare That Window!," 288; Charles G. Spiegler, "An Apple for the Teacher?," New York Times, April 4, 1943, SM14. See also Eric C. Schneider, Vampires, Dragons, and Egyptian Kings: Youth Gangs in Postwar New York (Princeton, NJ: Princeton University Press, 1999).

42. For an overview, see Stephen Jones, Criminology (New York: Oxford University Press, 2013). There were some lingering attempts to establish physiological types among juvenile delinquents. See Sheldon Glueck, "On the Causes of Crime," in The Problem of Delinquency, ed. Sheldon Glueck (Boston: Houghton Mifflin, 1959), 52–53; William H. Sheldon, Varieties of Delinquent Youth (New York: Harper and Brothers, 1949); Sheldon Glueck and Eleanor Glueck, Physique and Delinquency (New York: Harper and Brothers, 1956); and Earl Moses, The Negro Delinquent in Chicago (Washington, DC: Social Science Research Council, 1936).

43. Paul J. Brantingham and Patricia Brantingham, Environmental Criminology (London: Sage, 1981), 12–13; Gary Alan Fine, A Second Chicago School? The Development of Postwar American Sociology (Chicago: University of Chicago Press, 1995), ix–xii.

44. Frederic M. Thrasher, The Gang: A Study of 1,313 Gangs in Chicago (Chicago: University of Chicago Press, 1927). For an overview of the book's influence on the field, see David C. Brotherton, Youth Street Gangs (New York: Routledge, 2015), chap. 1.

45. Bernard Lander, Towards an Understanding of Juvenile Delinquency (New York: Columbia University Press, 1954), 4.

46. Thrasher, Gang, 20.

47. Greg Dimitriadis, "The Situation Complex: Revisiting Frederic Thrasher's The Gang: A Study of 1,313 Gangs in Chicago," Cultural Studies/Critical Methodologies 6, no. 3 (2006): 340; Jones, Criminology, 94–95; Robert Wiebe, The Search for Order, 1877–1920 (Westport, CT: Greenwood, 1967).

48. Thrasher, Gang, 30, 46.

49. Thrasher, Gang, 28, 95, 375–76, 519; Frederic M. Thrasher, "School Backgrounds and School Problems," Journal of Educational Sociology 1, no. 3 (November 1927): 121–30.

On the history of playground reform, see Michael Hines, "'They Do Not Know How to Play': Reformers' Expectations and Children's Realities on the First Progressive Playgrounds of Chicago," *Journal of the History of Childhood and Youth* 10, no. 2 (Spring 2017): 206–27; and Dominick Cavallo, *Muscles and Morals: Organized Playgrounds and Urban Reform, 1880–1920* (Philadelphia: University of Pennsylvania Press, 1981).

50. Graebner, *Coming of Age*, 88.

51. Schneider, *Vampires*, 12–13.

52. Gresham M. Sykes and David Matza, "Techniques of Neutralization: A Theory of Delinquency," *American Journal of Sociology* 22, no. 6 (December 1957): 664–70; David Matza, *Delinquency and Drift* (New York: Wiley, 1964); Donald J. Shoemaker, *Juvenile Delinquency* (New York: Rowman and Littlefield, 2009), 119; Matt Long and Roger Hopkins Burke, *Vandalism and Anti-social Behavior* (New York: Palgrave Macmillan, 2015), 31; Jones, *Criminology*, 92.

53. Thrasher, *Gang*, 69–71, 519.

54. "Boys Prepare Survey of Teachers; Find Them the Cause of Disorders," *New York Times*, December 30, 1942, 25.

55. "School in Orange Curbs 'Terrorists,'" *New York Times*, May 19, 1936, 25.

56. Frederic Wertham, *Seduction of the Innocent* (New York: Rinehart, 1954).

57. Quoted in Dimitriadis, "Situation Complex," 344–45.

58. Thrasher, *Gang*, 94–95, 113.

59. Jane Addams, *The Spirit of Youth and the City Streets* (Urbana: University of Illinois Press, 1972), 3–4, 6, 15. For a discussion of Addams and a critique of her silence on racial issues, see Muhammad, *Condemnation of Blackness*, 118–23.

60. Edwin H. Sutherland, *Principles of Criminology*, 4th ed. (Philadelphia: J. B. Lippincott, 1947), 6–7; Frank Tannenbaum, *Crime and the Community* (Boston: Ginn, 1923).

61. Martin R. Haskell, "Toward a Reference Group Theory of Juvenile Delinquency," *Social Problems* 8, no. 3 (December 1960): 220–30; Shoemaker, *Juvenile Delinquency*, 97.

62. Clifford R. Shaw and Henry D. McKay, "Are Broken Homes a Causative Factor in Juvenile Delinquency?," *Social Forces* 10, no. 4 (May 1932): 514–24; Clifford R. Shaw and Henry D. McKay, *Juvenile Delinquency and Urban Areas* (Chicago: University of Chicago Press, 1942); F. Ivan Nye, "Socioeconomic Status and Delinquent Behavior," *American Journal of Sociology* 63, no. 4 (January 1958): 381–89; Lewis Yablonsky, *The Violent Gang* (Baltimore: Penguin Books, 1970).

63. Pauline Lee to Los Angeles School Board, March 15, 1971, collection 1923, box 2037, folder 1, LAUSD; Ruth Shonie Cavan, "The Concepts of Tolerance and Contraculture as Applied to Delinquency," in Cavan, *Readings in Juvenile Delinquency*, 16.

64. Marshall B. Clinard, "Toward the Delineation of Vandalism as a Sub-type in Juvenile Delinquency," *Journal of Criminal Law and Criminology* 48, no. 5 (1958): 493–99; Travis Hirschi, *Causes of Delinquency* (Berkeley: University of California Press, 1969); Travis Hirschi, "Hellfire and Delinquency," *Social Problems* 17, no. 2 (October 1969): 202–13; Richard A. Kulka and David M. Klingel, "School Crime and Disruption as a Function of Student-School Fit: An Empirical Assessment," *Journal of Youth and Adolescence* 9, no. 4 (1980): 353–70. Subsequent research did not always bear out these claims. See Shoemaker, *Juvenile Delinquency*, 141.

65. Robert Merton, *Social Theory and Social Structure* (Glencoe, IL: Free Press, 1957); Shoemaker, *Juvenile Delinquency*, 130; Jones, *Criminology*, 121–23.

66. Richard Cloward and Lloyd Ohlin, *Delinquency and Opportunity: A Theory of Delinquent Gangs* (Glencoe, IL: Free Press, 1960); Jones, *Criminology*, 143.

67. John M. Martin, *Juvenile Vandalism: A Study of Its Nature and Prevention* (Springfield, IL: Thomas Books, 1961), 123–25; Steven Mintz, *Huck's Raft: A History of American Childhood* (Cambridge, MA: Belknap Press of Harvard University Press, 2004), 294–95.

68. For a thorough discussion of subcultural theory and its connection to later notions of "resistance," see Ken McGrew, "A Review of Class-Based Theories of Student Resistance in Education: Mapping the Origins and Influence of *Learning to Labor* by Paul Willis," *Review of Educational Research* 81, no. 2 (June 2011): 234–66.

69. Albert K. Cohen, *Delinquent Boys: The Culture of the Gang* (Glencoe, IL: Free Press, 1955), 28. See also Martin, *Juvenile Vandalism*, 110; William H. Sheldon, *Varieties of Delinquent Youth* (Darien, CT: Hafner, 1949); Shaw and McKay, *Juvenile Delinquency and Urban Areas*; John M. Martin, "The Vandals: A Study of Malicious Mischief" (PhD diss., New York University, 1959); John M. Martin and Joseph P. Fitzpatrick, *Delinquent Behavior: A Redefinition of the Problem* (New York: Random House, 1966); Walter B. Miller, "Lower-Class Culture as a Generating Milieu of Gang Delinquency," *Journal of Social Issues* 14, no. 3 (Summer 1958): 5–19; William C. Kvaraceus and Walter B. Miller, "Norm-Violating Behavior and Lower-Class Culture," in Cavan, *Readings in Juvenile Delinquency*, 56–65. On Cohen's continuing influence, see Long and Burke, *Vandalism and Anti-social Behavior*, 3–4, 31.

70. Talcott Parsons, "Age and Sex in the Social Structure of the United States," *American Sociological Review* 7, no. 5 (October 1942): 604–16; Herbert A. Bloch and Arthur Niederhoffer, *The Gang: A Study in Adolescent Behavior* (New York: Philosophical Library, 1958), chap. 5.

71. Martin, *Juvenile Vandalism*, 73, 108.

72. Casserly, Bass, and Garrett, *School Vandalism*, 15.

73. Casserly, Bass, and Garrett, *School Vandalism*, 2–3.

74. Shaw and McKay, "Broken Homes," 514–24; Charles A. Murray, *The Link between Learning Disabilities and Juvenile Delinquency* (Washington, DC: US Government Printing Office, 1976).

75. Andrew Greeley and James Casey, "An Upper Middle Class Deviant," *American Catholic Sociological Review* 24, no. 1 (Spring 1963): 33–41; Ralph W. England Jr., "A Theory of Middle Class Juvenile Delinquency," in Cavan, *Readings in Juvenile Delinquency*, 66–75; John M. Martin, "Some Characteristics of Vandals," *American Catholic Sociological Review* 20, no. 4 (Winter 1959): 319; Martin, *Juvenile Vandalism*, 111; Albert Deutsch, *Our Rejected Children* (Boston: Little, Brown, 1950), 184.

76. Martha M. Eliot, "What Is Vandalism?," *Federal Probation* 18, no. 1 (March 1954): 3–5; Casserly, Bass, and Garrett, *School Vandalism*, 17; Arnold P. Goldstein, *The Psychology of Vandalism* (New York: Plenum, 1996), 27; Alan T. Sohn, "An Analysis of School and Classroom Discipline Practices and Their Relationship to School Property Loss" (PhD diss., Temple University, 1983), 16–17.

77. Martin, *Juvenile Vandalism*, 73.

78. Long and Burke, *Vandalism and Anti-social Behavior*, 5; Zwier and Vaughan, "Three Ideological Orientations," 264–65.

79. Zwier and Vaughan, "Three Ideological Orientations," 267.

80. Sol Cohen, "In the Name of the Prevention of Neurosis," in *Regulated Children, Liberated Children: Education in Psychohistorical Perspective*, ed. Barbara Finkelstein (New York: Psychohistory Press, 1979), 184–219; Deborah Blythe Doroshow, *Emotionally Disturbed: A History of Caring for America's Troubled Children* (Chicago: University of Chicago Press, 2019); Stephen Petrina, "The Medicalization of Education: A Historiographic Synthesis," *History of Education Quarterly* 46, no. 4 (Winter 2006): 503–31.

81. Robert L. Woolfolk, *The Value of Psychotherapy* (New York: Guilford, 2015), 2–3; Nathan G. Hale Jr., *The Rise and Crisis of Psychoanalysis in the United States: Freud and the Americans, 1917–1985* (New York: Oxford University Press, 1995), 85–88; Sarah Igo, *The Known Citizen: A History of Privacy in Modern America* (Cambridge, MA: Harvard University Press, 2018), 129–31; James Bennett, *Oral History and Delinquency: The Rhetoric*

of Criminology (Chicago: University of Chicago Press, 1981), chap. 5; Cohen, "Prevention of Neurosis," 187.

82. Hale, *Rise and Crisis*, 87, 89.

83. Donald W. Robinson, "Psychoanalysis and Education," *Phi Delta Kappan* 43, no. 7 (April 1962): 292–99; William McCord and Joan McCord, *Psychopathy and Delinquency* (New York: Grune and Stratton, 1956), ix; Michael A. Sulman, "The Humanization of the American Child: Benjamin Spock as a Popularizer of Psychoanalytic Thought," *Journal of the History of Behavioral Sciences* 9, no. 3 (1973): 258–65; John Burnham, introduction to Burnham, *After Freud Left*, 12.

84. Martin, *Juvenile Vandalism*, 38, 44–45.

85. Bruno Bettelheim and Emmy Sylvester, "Delinquency and Morality," *Psychoanalytic Study of the Child* 5, no. 1 (1950): 329–42. See also Anna Freud, *Normality and Pathology in Childhood* (London: Karnac Books, 1989), 18–19; and Fritz Redl and David Wineman, *Children Who Hate: The Disorganization and Breakdown of Behavior Controls* (New York: Free Press, 1960).

86. Ernst Simmel, "Incendiarism," in *Searchlights on Delinquency: New Psychoanalytic Studies*, ed. K. R. Eissler (New York: International Universities Press, 1949), 90–101.

87. August Aichhorn, *Wayward Youth: A Psychoanalytic Study of Delinquent Children* (New York: Viking, 1935), 173–74. Some educators suggested similar leniency in public schools, writing that "a wholesome environment [with] plenty of outlets for energies and anger . . . [would] ease the pressures on those . . . children who now cause so much of the current school and park damage." Suffice to say, that argument did not get far. Barclay, "Destructiveness in Children."

88. For overviews of art therapy, see Francis Reitman, *Psychotic Art* (New York: International Universities Press, 1951); and Cathy A. Malchiodi, *Handbook of Art Therapy* (New York: Guilford, 2003).

89. Edith Kramer, *Art as Therapy for Children* (New York: Schocken Books, 1971), 9–11, 26.

90. For more on the Wiltwyck School, see Doroshow, *Emotionally Disturbed*, chap. 2. On art therapy and Holocaust refugees, see Kramer, *Art as Therapy*, xiv–xv; "Children's Drawings from the Terezín Ghetto," Jewish Museum in Prague, accessed August 16, 2022, https://www.jewishmuseum.cz/en/collection-research/collections-funds/visual-arts/children-s-drawings-from-the-terezin-ghetto/.

91. Quoted in Louise E. Hoffman, "War, Revolution, and Psychoanalysis: Freudian Thought Begins to Grapple with Social Reality," *Journal of the History of the Behavioral Sciences* 17, no. 2 (1981): 252, 254–55. For Freud's theory of the death instinct, see Sigmund Freud, *Beyond the Pleasure Principle* (New York: Boni and Liveright, 1920). On responsibility during the Cold War, see Hartman, *Education and the Cold War*, chap. 3; Cohen, "Prevention of Neurosis," 185, 206; and Dorothy Ross, "Freud and the Vicissitudes of Modernism in the United States, 1940–1980," in Burnham, *After Freud Left*, 168–71.

92. *Historic Psychology: Boredom* (Asheville, NC: Quality Information Publishers, 1961); *A Chance to Play* (New York: General Electric, 1950); *Boredom at Work: The Empty Life* (Norman: University of Oklahoma, 1961).

93. *Why Vandalism?* (Encyclopaedia Britannica Films, 1955), Internet Archive, https://ia601305.us.archive.org/25/items/WhyVandalism_201512/WhyVandalism.m4v. See also *Vandalism Story: The Clubhouse* (San Francisco: McDonald and Crain, 1973).

94. "Vandalism (*I Led Three Lives* #68B)," United Artists Corporation, ZIV-TV Script Files, box 92, folder 4, WHS.

95. Woolfolk, *Value of Psychotherapy*, 33; McCord and McCord, *Psychopathy and Delinquency*, 2, 24–25, 99; Freud, *Normality and Pathology*, 166.

96. Freud, *Normality and Pathology*, 12–13.

97. Eli M. Bower, "Vandalism: An Outgrowth of Hostility, Aggression, and Frustration," *Federal Probation* 18, no. 1 (March 1954): 12–14; Hale, *Rise and Crisis*, 84, 90; Hyman S. Lippman, "Vandalism as an Outlet for Aggression," *Federal Probation* 18, no. 1 (March 1954): 5–6.

98. Karl Mannheim, "The Problem of Generations," in *Karl Mannheim: Essays*, ed. Paul Kecskemeti (New York: Routledge, 1952), 276–322; Margaret Mead, *Culture and Commitment: A Study of the Generation Gap* (Garden City, NY: Natural History Press, 1970); Lewis S. Feuer, *The Conflict of Generations: The Character and Significance of Student Movements* (New York: Basic Books, 1969).

99. Gilbert, *Cycle of Outrage*, 3–4; Anthony Chaney, *Runaway: Gregory Bateson, the Double Bind, and the Rise of Ecological Consciousness* (Chapel Hill: University of North Carolina Press, 2017), 58–59.

100. Teresa Lenox, "The Carver Village Controversy," *Tequesta: The Journal of the Historical Association of Southern Florida* 50 (1990): 39–51; "Dynamite-by-Night Calendar: Bomb-by-Bomb Review of Blasters' Acts," *Norfolk (VA) Journal and Guide*, October 18, 1958, B1.

101. "Add Philly to US Bomb Towns," *New York Amsterdam News*, February 16, 1952, 16; *Why the Swastika? A Study of Young American Vandals* (New York: Institute of Human Relations Press, 1961); David Caplovitz and Candace Rogers, *Swastika 1960: The Epidemic of Anti-Semitic Vandalism in America* (New York: Anti-defamation League, 1961); Martin Deutsch, "The 1960 Swastika Smearings: Analysis of the Apprehended Youth," *Merrill-Palmer Quarterly of Behavior and Development* 8 (1960): 99–120.

102. "Add Philly to US Bomb Towns."

103. Caplovitz and Rogers, *Swastika 1960*, 39–41.

104. Chester C. Scott, "Vandalism and Our Present-Day Pattern of Living," *Federal Probation* 18, no. 1 (March 1954): 12.

105. Eliot, "What Is Vandalism?," 3–5. See also Scott, "Present-Day Pattern of Living," 10–12; Joseph P. Murphy, "The Answer to Vandalism May Be Found in the Home," *Federal Probation* 18, no. 1 (March 1954): 8–10.

106. Sheldon Glueck, "Cause and Effect in Biosocial Problems Involving Delinquency," in Glueck, *Problem of Delinquency*, 20; Zwier and Vaughan, "Three Ideological Orientations," 263–64; K. R. Eissler, "General Problems of Delinquency," in Eissler, *Searchlights on Delinquency*, 5; J. P. Shalloo, "Youth and Crime," *Annals of the American Academy of Political and Social Science* 194, no. 1 (1937): 79–86.

107. J. P. Shalloo, "Vandalism: Whose Responsibility?," *Federal Probation* 18, no. 1 (March 1954): 6–8.

108. Center for Juvenile Delinquency Prevention, *Vandalism: A Study of School Vandalism* (San Marcos: Southwest Texas State University, 1979), 4.

109. Murphy, "Answer to Vandalism," 10; Lowell J. Carr, "Cause-Mindedness," in Glueck, *Problem of Delinquency*, 26–27.

4. VANDALISM AND THE SECURITY STATE, 1960–2000

1. *Lean on Me*, directed by John G. Avildsen (1989; Burbank, CA: Warner Home Video, 2010), DVD.

2. For overviews of the interrelationship between punitive policies and restrictive architecture, see Damien M. Sojoyner, *First Strike: Educational Enclosures in Black Los Angeles* (Minneapolis: University of Minnesota Press, 2016); Lizbet Simmons, *The Prison School: Educational Inequality and School Discipline in the Age of Mass Incarceration* (Oakland: University of California Press, 2017); Victor M. Rios, *Punished: Policing the Lives of Black and Latino Boys* (New York: New York University Press, 2011); Kathleen Nolan,

Police in the Hallways: Discipline in an Urban American High School (Minneapolis: University of Minnesota Press, 2011); Aaron Kupchik, *Homeroom Security: School Discipline in an Age of Fear* (New York: New York University Press, 2010).

3. Historians of education have thoroughly described the euphemisms surrounding racial desegregation, as well as its myriad effects on educational politics in the United States. For some examples, see Robert Hampel, *The Last Little Citadel: American High Schools since 1940* (Boston: Houghton Mifflin, 1986); Judith Kafka, *The History of "Zero Tolerance" in American Public Schooling* (New York: Palgrave Macmillan, 2011); Judith Kafka, "'Sitting on a Tinderbox': Racial Conflict, Teacher Discretion, and the Centralization of Disciplinary Authority," *American Journal of Education* 114 (May 2008): 247–70; Ansley Erickson, *Making the Unequal Metropolis: School Desegregation and Its Limits* (Chicago: University of Chicago Press, 2016); Douglas Reed, *Building the Federal Schoolhouse: Localism and the American Educational State* (New York: Oxford University Press, 2014); Walter C. Stern, *Race and Education in New Orleans: Creating the Segregated City* (Baton Rouge: Louisiana State University Press, 2020).

4. An interesting analysis of the spatial aspects of school segregation can be found in Mark Fiege, *Republic of Nature: An Environmental History of the United States* (Seattle: University of Washington Press, 2012), chap. 8.

5. For example, see "Fire at Moultrie and Woman's Death," *Vienna (GA) News*, October 16, 1924, 1; "Fire Sweeps Wendell Phillips School," *Chicago Defender*, February 2, 1935, 2; "$40,000 High School Destroyed by Vandals," *Kansas City (KS) Plain Dealer*, October 12, 1951, 1; Sam Grayson and Logan Smith, oral history with Virgil Adams, April 20, 2011, https://faculty.mercer.edu/davis_da/fys102/Virgil_Adams.pdf; "Fire Damages School Recently Converted for Negroes," *Kansas City Plain Dealer*, September 25, 1953, 1.

6. For examples, see "Nab Klansmen, Dynamite at Negro School," *Chicago Tribune*, February 17, 1958, 16; Ronald Smothers, "School Fire Fuels Passions in Racially Torn Town," *New York Times*, August 8, 1994, A10; "$40,000 High School."

7. Arthur L. Littleworth, *No Easy Way: Integrating Riverside Schools* (Riverside, CA: Inlandia Institute, 2014); Irving G. Hendrick, *The Development of a School Integration Plan in Riverside, California: A History and Perspective* (Washington, DC: US Department of Health, Education and Welfare, 1968); Jeff Nesbit, "Separate High Schools, Unequal Everything," *U.S. News & World Report*, March 29, 2016, https://www.usnews.com/news/articles/2016-03-29/delayed-desegregation-separate-sc-high-schools-unequal-everything; Ray Paul, "Ohio Town to Keep Its Segregated School," *Cleveland Call and Post*, August 7, 1954, 1A; Gary Abernathy and Jeff Gilliand, "'Learning Together' Was a Hard-Fought Right Here," *Hillsboro (OH) Times-Gazette*, February 26, 2016, https://www.timesgazette.com/news/5890/learning-together-was-a-hard-fought-right-here; "All-Negro School in Mt. Sterling, KY, Destroyed by Fire," *North Adams (MA) Transcript*, August 31, 1964, 1; "DuBois School (Mt. Sterling, KY)," Notable Kentucky African Americans Database, last modified October 21, 2020, https://nkaa.uky.edu/nkaa/items/show/1990; "School Burned," *Dade County (GA) Times*, November 25, 1954, 1.

8. Neil McMillen, "Organized Resistance to School Desegregation in Tennessee," *Tennessee Historical Quarterly* 30, no. 3 (Fall 1971): 315–28; Wilma Dykeman and James Stokely, "Clinton, Tennessee: A Town on Trial," *New York Times*, October 26, 1958, 9; Ansley T. Erickson, *Making the Unequal Metropolis: School Desegregation and Its Limits* (Chicago: University of Chicago Press, 2016), chap. 2; "Blast in Little Rock," *New York Times*, August 25, 1959, 10; US Department of Justice, Federal Bureau of Investigation, memorandum, July 12, 1960, 157-CG-53 v1, National Archives and Records Administration (hereafter NARA); Claude Sitton, "Since the School Decree: Decade of Racial Ferment,"

New York Times, May 18, 1964, 1; John Dittmer, oral history interview with Julia Matilda Burns, Library of Congress, March 13, 2013, https://www.loc.gov/item/2015669172/.

9. Gareth Davis, *See Government Grow: Education Politics from Johnson to Reagan* (Lawrence: University Press of Kansas, 2007), 130; George Lipsitz, *How Racism Takes Place* (Philadelphia: Temple University Press, 2011), 27; A. S. Young, "Bigotry Raises Ugly Head in Anti-busing Campaigns," *Los Angeles Sentinel*, September 16, 1971, A1; Kathryn A. Schumaker, "The Politics of Youth: Civil Rights Reform in the Waterloo Public Schools," *Annals of Iowa* 72, no. 4 (Fall 2013): 353–85; Natasha Gardner, "The Legacy of Denver's Forced School Busing Era," *5280*, June 2018, https://www.5280.com/2018/05/the-legacy-of-denvers-forced-school-busing-era/; Karen Balmer, "CORK Leader Denies School Arson Plot," *Cleveland Call and Post*, January 6, 1979, 1A; Matthew F. Delmont, *Why Busing Failed: Race, Media, and the National Resistance to School Desegregation* (Berkeley: University of California Press, 2016), 39.

10. US Commission on Civil Rights, *Civil Rights U.S.A.: Public Schools in Southern States, 1962* (Washington, DC: US Government Printing Office, 1962), 96; Matthew Lassiter, *The Silent Majority: Suburban Politics in the Sunbelt South* (Princeton, NJ: Princeton University Press, 2006).

11. In addition to the examples in note 3, see Ronald P. Formisano, *Boston against Busing: Race, Class, and Ethnicity in the 1960s and 1970s* (Chapel Hill: University of North Carolina Press, 2004); Howell S. Baum, *"Brown" in Baltimore: School Desegregation and the Limits of Liberalism* (Ithaca, NY: Cornell University Press, 2010); and James Ryan, *Five Miles Away, a World Apart: One City, Two Schools, and the Story of Educational Opportunity in Modern America* (New York: Oxford University Press, 2010).

12. Joette Chancy and Brenda Franklin, "Report from Boston: The Struggle for Desegregation," *Black Scholar* 7, no. 4 (December 1975): 19–27; Elijah Anderson, "The Devolution of the Inner-City High School," *Annals of the American Academy of Political and Social Science* 673 (September 2017): 67; *Report of the National Advisory Committee on Civil Disorders* (New York: Bantam Books, 1968); G. G. Labelle, "Cost: $1 Billion in '74," *Charleston (WV) Gazette-Mail*, June 8, 1975, 55.

13. "Death of a High School," Spring 1973, series 47, box 1913, folder 17, National Education Association Archives, George Washington University, Washington, DC (hereafter NEA); "What Causes Negro Juvenile Delinquency," *Arkansas State Press*, April 16, 1954, 4.

14. This was most famously the case in Chicago, where "Willis Wagons" became a rallying cry for student resistance and grassroots activism. John L. Rury, "Race, Space, and the Politics of Chicago's Public Schools: Benjamin Willis and the Tragedy of Urban Education," *History of Education Quarterly* 39, no. 2 (Summer 1999): 132. Other examples include "Seven Boys Confess to Arson Charges," *Philadelphia Tribune*, September 17, 1936, 1; "School Conditions at Washington Hit by Civic Leader," *Atlanta Daily World*, November 18, 1943, 1.

15. In addition to the examples below, see Mary Haywood Metz, *Classrooms and Corridors* (Berkeley: University of California Press, 1978), 235; George W. Noblit and Thomas W. Collins, "Order and Disruption in a Desegregated High School," *Crime & Delinquency* 24, no. 3 (July 1978): 277–89; "Vandalism and Violence: Innovative Strategies Reduce Cost to Schools," 1971, series 40, box 4207, folder 1, NEA; William P. Gullng to Richard M. Nixon, May 6, 1969, RG 12, "Records Concerning the Desegregation of Public Schools, 1968–1970," box 1, folder July 1969, NARA.

16. Kathryn Schumaker, *Troublemakers: Students' Rights and Racial Justice in the Long 1960s* (New York: New York University Press, 2019), chaps. 2–3; Wayne King, "Racial Animosity Turns to Violence in Pensacola, Fla.," *New York Times*, March 7, 1976, 33; Virginia E. Causey, "The Long and Winding Road: School Desegregation in Columbus, Georgia: 1963–1997," *Georgia Historical Quarterly* 85, no. 3 (Fall 2001): 398–434.

17. Jan Stucker, "Pioneer Reconvenes Quietly; Vandals' Prosecution Vowed," *Ann Arbor News*, October 1, 1970, 1.

18. Heidi Fearing, "The Collinwood High School Riots," Cleveland Historical, January 12, 2012, https://clevelandhistorical.org/items/show/392#.WBFP46OZOu4.

19. *Vandalism at Taggert Elementary*, RG 65, Case 157–11679; report by Pike County Deputy Sheriff John Sharpling, RG 65, FBI Case 157–11521, Federal Bureau of Investigation, NARA.

20. Alvin Ward, "Fire Destroys Giddings," *Cleveland Call and Post*, April 15, 1967, 1A.

21. "Boston School Arsons Ignite Race Tinderbox," *Chicago Daily Defender*, June 3, 1965, 12.

22. "Fire Closes School in Columbus," *Atlanta World*, March 30, 1972, 7.

23. Ralph Blumenthal, "Fire Ruins School in New Rochelle," *New York Times*, May 18, 1968, 1.

24. "Blast Shatters Windows of Academy for Dropouts," *New York Times*, July 14, 1968, 39.

25. Michael B. Katz, *Why Don't American Cities Burn?* (Philadelphia: University of Pennsylvania Press, 2012), 86, 93. On the racial politics of policing throughout the twentieth century, see Khalil Gibran Muhammad, *The Condemnation of Blackness: Race, Crime, and the Making of Modern America* (Cambridge, MA: Harvard University Press, 2010); Simon Balto, *Occupied Territory: Policing Black Chicago from Red Summer to Black Power* (Chapel Hill: University of North Carolina Press, 2019).

26. Kathryn Schumaker, *Troublemakers: Students' Rights and Racial Justice in the Long 1960s* (New York: New York University Press, 2019); Michael W. Flamm, *In the Heat of the Summer: The New York Riots of 1964 and the War on Crime* (Philadelphia: University of Pennsylvania Press, 2017).

27. For an overview of Los Angeles schools during the 1930s, see Judith Raftery, *Land of Fair Promise: Politics and Reform in Los Angeles Schools, 1885–1941* (Stanford, CA: Stanford University Press, 1992), chaps. 5–6.

28. Committee of the Whole report, No. 2, July 29, 1948, and "Recommendations re: Property Protection Section" (ca. 1947), box 234, folder 1; LA Board of Education Emergency Communication to the Committee of the Whole, July 29, 1948, box 1459, folder 1; Business Division to the Insurance Committee, April 27, 1953, box 2036, folder 1; Auxiliary Services Division to the Committee of the Whole, February 14, 1955, and R. O. Graham to Guy M. Hoyt, April 27, 1955, box 2036, folder 4; Don C. Allen, resolution, November 8, 1954, box 2036, folder 1; Los Angeles City Schools, Division of Elementary Education, August 11, 1955, box 2036, folder 1, LAUSD.

29. Kafka, *History of "Zero Tolerance,"* chap. 3.

30. Portion of transcription of recording of regular board meeting, August 11, 1955, box 1459, folder 1, LAUSD.

31. "Proposed Amendment to Los Angeles Municipal Code," June 22, 1954, and Association of Elementary School Administrators, June 24, 1954, box 2036, folder 2, LAUSD.

32. Los Angeles Board of Education, "Motion," March 29, 1971, box 2037, folder 1; "Campus Safety," April 25, 1974, box 1459, folder 1, LAUSD.

33. Max Felker-Kantor, *Policing Los Angeles: Race, Resistance, and the Rise of the LAPD* (Chapel Hill: University of North Carolina Press, 2018), 87–88. On vandalism prevention programs in California, see Ernst Wenk and Nora Harlow, eds., *School Crime and Disruption* (Davis, CA: Responsible Action, 1978).

34. Felker-Kantor, *Policing Los Angeles*, 87. On the effects of racial diversity on schooling in Los Angeles and surrounding areas, see Jack Schneider, "Escape from Los Angeles: White Flight from Los Angeles and Its Schools, 1960–1980," *Journal of Urban History* 34, no. 6 (August 2008): 995–1012; Becky Nicolaides, *My Blue Heaven: Life and Politics in the*

Working-Class Suburbs of Los Angeles, 1920–1965 (Chicago: University of Chicago Press, 2002); and Emily Straus, *Death of a Suburban Dream: Race and Schools in Compton, California* (Philadelphia: University of Pennsylvania Press, 2014). On police discrimination against Black students outside school, see Dorothy Lawrence, "Some Problems Arising in the Treatment of Adolescent Negro Girls Appearing in the Los Angeles Juvenile Court" (MA thesis, University of Southern California, 1941), 3, 14–20, 34–38.

35. "Violence and Education: A Position Paper," n.d., box 1335, folder 3; Board of Education minutes, June 24, 1954, box 2036, folder 1, LAUSD; John Albert Anderson, "Vandalism in Unified School Districts of Los Angeles County" (PhD diss., University of Southern California, 1977), 3–4, 24.

36. "Violence and Education."

37. Statement of Robert Ransom, president of UTLA, n.d., box 2037, folder 2; Mrs. Leon Chernick to Dr. Julian Nava, n.d., box 2037, folder 1, LAUSD.

38. Sylvia Levine to LA Board of Education, February 26, 1974, box 1459, folder 1, LAUSD.

39. Grape Street School Faculty Association to LA Board of Education, March 24, 1971, box 2037, folder 1; LA Board of Education minutes, June 11, 1973, box 1459, folder 1; Superintendent of Schools to LA Board of Education, November 24, 1975, box 1459, folder 1, LAUSD.

40. San Jose Street Elementary School Community Advisory Council to LA Board of Education, May 19, 1981, box 2037, folder 4, LAUSD.

41. Barbara Matsui to Dr. Robert Doctor, president, LA Board of Education, November 6, 1975, box 1459, folder 1, LAUSD.

42. There were also objections to the police presence from the outset, particularly complaints that guards were "abusive and officious" toward students. "Violence and Education." See also Michael D. Casserly, Scott A. Bass, and John R. Garrett, *School Vandalism: Strategies for Prevention* (Lexington, MA: Lexington Books, 1980), 28–31.

43. Mrs. Willard Murray and Mrs. Hilda Nigro to Dr. Julian Nava, March 5, 1971, box 2037, folder 2; "Vandalism Seminar," August 3, 1972, box 1440, folder 3; Report of Correspondence: Bertha Credilla to Phillip G. Bardos, president, Board of Education, April 18, 1974, box 1459, folder 1, LAUSD.

44. For representative discussions of tax politics in California, see Robert Self, *American Babylon: Race and the Struggle for Postwar Oakland* (Princeton, NJ: Princeton University Press, 2003); Robert Self, "Prelude to the Tax Revolt: The Politics of the 'Tax Dollar' in Postwar California," in *The New Suburban History*, ed. Kevin M. Kruse and Thomas J. Sugrue (Chicago: University of Chicago Press, 2006), 144–60; and Isaac Martin, *The Permanent Tax Revolt: How the Property Tax Transformed American Politics* (Stanford, CA: Stanford University Press, 2008), chap. 5. On the relationship between school taxes and systemic racism, see Camille Walsh, *Racial Taxation: Schools, Segregation, and Taxpayer Citizenship, 1869–1973* (Chapel Hill: University of North Carolina Press, 2018).

45. E. M. Moore to LA Board of Education, March 2, 1977, box 2037, folder 4; Louise W. Hadley to LA Board of Education, February 27, 1970, box 2037, folder 2, LAUSD.

46. "Recommendations re: Property Protection Section" (ca. 1947), and Board of Education, "Emergency Communication to the Committee of the Whole," July 29, 1948, collection 1923, box 1459, folder 4; Dwight E. Lyons to Mrs. M. C. Wright, June 14, 1963, box 2037, folder 3; Mrs. H. S. Gillies to LA Board of Education, February 26, 1971, box 2037, folder 2; Charles H. Sach to LA Board of Education, April 10, 1962, box 2037, folder 1; Ida Levin to LA Board of Education, July 19, 1971, box 2037, folder 1; Mr. Alwood to LA Board of Education, April 8, 1953, box 2037, folder 3, LAUSD.

47. R. W. Jarrett to Mr. M. J. Seelbach, May 12, 1970, box 2037, folder 2, LAUSD.

48. Superintendent of Schools to Mrs. Willard Murray and Mrs. Hilda Nigro, May 7, 1971, box 2037, folder 2, LAUSD. Local residents suggested using welfare recipients, retirees, the American Legion, and even the Boy Scouts as night watchmen. A plan to house janitors in trailers on campus won nationwide publicity but proved short lived. John Zeisel, *Stopping School Property Damage* (Arlington, VA: American Association of School Administrators, 1976), 59; "Act to Curb Vandalism in City Schools," *Chicago Tribune*, July 30, 1961, A14; Charles A. Sach to Los Angeles Board of Education, April 10, 1962, box 2037, folder 1; Report of Correspondence: Phillips B. Freer to Phillip G. Bardos, president, Board of Education, April 11, 1974, box 1459, folder 1; Superintendent of Schools to LA Board of Education, Committee of the Whole, May 22, 1975, box 1459, folder 1, LAUSD.

49. Superintendent of Schools to LA Board of Education, via Business Operations Committee, June 30, 1975, box 1459, folder 1, LAUSD.

50. Superintendent of Schools to Mrs. Willard Murray and Mrs. Hilda Nigro, May 7, 1971, box 2037, folder 2, LAUSD.

51. The restitution program had been developed during the 1950s. "Proposed Amendment to Los Angeles Municipal Code," June 22, 1954, box 2036, folder 3; Association of Elementary School Administrators, June 24, 1954, box 2036, folder 2; "Transcript of Recording of the Subcommittee of the Vandalism Committee Meeting," July 21, 1954, box 2036, folder 2, LAUSD. In other cities, too, restitution rarely yielded more than 10 percent of total damages. Jeri J. Goldman, "Restitution for Damages to Public School Property," *Journal of Law & Education* 11, no. 2 (April 1982): 147–70. On restitution and recovery, see Superintendent of Schools to Mrs. Willard Murray and Mrs. Hilda Nigro, May 7, 1971, box 2037, folder 2, LAUSD; "Vandalism and Violence."

52. R. W. Jarrett to Mr. M. J. Seelbach, May 12, 1970, box 2037, folder 2, LAUSD.

53. Superintendent of Schools to LA Board of Education, via Business Operations Committee, June 30, 1975, box 1459, folder 1, LAUSD; Gayle Olson-Raymer, "The Role of the Federal Government in Juvenile Delinquency Prevention: Historical and Contemporary Perspectives," *Journal of Criminal Law & Criminology* 74, no. 2 (1983): 578–79.

54. Superintendent of Schools to LA Board of Education, April 22, 1971, box 2037, folder 1; Board of Education minutes, regular meeting, August 26, 1965, box 1459, folder 1; Superintendent of Schools to LA Board of Education, via Auxiliary Services Committee, Communication No. 1, September 2, 1965, box 1459, folder 1; Personnel Committee to LA Board of Education, February 6, 1975, box 1459, folder 1; Loren Miner to Dr. Julian Nava, December 17, 1970, box 2037, folder 2, LAUSD; Sar Levitan, "The Emergency Employment Act: An Interim Assessment," *Monthly Labor Review* 95, no. 6 (June 1972): 1–11.

55. William J. Johnston, superintendent, to John A. Simpson, April 16, 1974, box 1459, folder 1, LAUSD.

56. Felker-Kantor, *Policing Los Angeles*, 100; Alexander Liazos, "School, Alienation, and Delinquency," *Crime and Delinquency* 24, no. 3 (July 1978): 365; Anderson, "Vandalism in Unified School Districts," 18; Superintendent of Schools to LA Board of Education, via Committee of the Whole, February 20, 1975, box 1459, folder 1, LAUSD.

57. Clifford H. Allen, *School Insurance Administration* (New York: Macmillan, 1965), 37–38. For the district's earlier criticisms of private insurance, see "Transcription of Recording of Committee on Vandalism," July 8, 1954, collection 1923, box 2036, folder 3; Business Division to the Insurance Committee, April 27, 1953, box 2036, folder 1, LAUSD.

58. "School Arson and Insurance," *Long Beach (CA) Independent Press-Telegram*, April 20, 1969, 54; "Arson High and Getting Worse," *Los Angeles Sentinel*, March 18, 1971, A8; Superintendent of Schools to Mrs. Willard Murray and Mrs. Hilda Nigro, May 7, 1971, box 2037, folder 2; Superintendent of Schools to Los Angeles Board of Education, March 11, 1971, box 2037, folder 2, LAUSD.

59. Arthur Alan Deming, "School Fires and Fire Recovery Procedures" (PhD diss., University of Southern California, 1977), 134–36.

60. Deming, "School Fires," 136–37.

61. Alan T. Sohn, "An Analysis of School and Classroom Discipline Practices and Their Relationship to School Property Loss" (PhD diss., Temple University, 1983), 16; Casserly, Bass, and Garrett, *School Vandalism*, 7.

62. "Schools in South Find Desegregation Brings an Increase in Insurance Rates," *New York Times*, August 10, 1970, 21.

63. L. F. Edwards, "Insurance Costs: Up and Almost Away," *Nation's Schools* 85, no. 2 (February 1970): 52.

64. Bench Ansfield, "The Crisis of Insurance and the Insuring of the Crisis: Riot Reinsurance and Redlining in the Aftermath of the 1960s Uprisings," *Journal of American History* 107, no. 4 (March 2021): 899–921.

65. It is not coincidental that crime syndicates often hired high school students as torches. Jack Tanzman, "Insurance: A School District's Constant Concern," *School Management* 17, no. 4 (1973): 22–25; Earni Young, "Economy Blamed for 37 Percent Increase in Arson Toll in Ohio," *Marysville (OH) Journal-Tribune*, August 11, 1975, 9; *The Antiarson Act of 1979: Hearings before the Subcommittee on Intergovernmental Relations of the Committee of Governmental Affairs*, US Senate, 96th Cong., 1st sess., 162 (1979).

66. Dylan Gottlieb, "Hoboken Is Burning: Yuppies, Arson, and Displacement in the Postindustrial City," *Journal of American History* 106, no. 2 (September 2019): 390–416.

67. Edwards, "Insurance Costs," 51–55.

68. Roger Guiles, "Don't Get Burned When Buying Fire Insurance," *Nation's Schools* 93, no. 3 (1974): 36–38.

69. Steve Lawrence, "Suspected Arson Boosts School Insurance Rate," *Progress Bulletin* (Pomona, CA), June 7, 1970, 13; Pauline Lee to Los Angeles Board of Education, March 15, 1971, box 2037, folder 1, LAUSD.

70. Deming, "School Fires," 58–59.

71. Deming, "School Fires," 69, 90, 96–97, 159.

72. Labelle, "Cost: $1 Billion."

73. For insights into the financial straits of Long Island school districts, see Michael Glass, *Cracked Foundations: Debt and Inequality in Postwar Suburbia* (Philadelphia: University of Pennsylvania Press, forthcoming). For specific examples of insurance costs, see Dennis Reilly, "Coping with Vandalism in Family, School, and Community," *Theoretical Perspectives on School Crime* 1 (1978): 1132–62; "Alleged Arsonist Strikes Again at Levittown School," *Levittown (NY) Tribune*, July 24, 1974, 1; "Fire Ruins School Kitchen," *Levittown Tribune*, February 17, 1977, 1; Michael Knight, "Vandalism Puzzles Suburbs," *New York Times*, April 22, 1976, 35; Frances Cerra, "School Insurance: A Growing Burden," *New York Times*, July 3, 1977, section 21, 1; Ellen Mitcheli, "Schools Fight Back against Vandalism," *New York Times*, June 17, 1979, 12.

74. James Barron, "School Insurance at a Premium," *New York Times*, November 20, 1977, 21.

75. Francis X. Clines, "Insurance Crisis Plagues Schools," *New York Times*, February 14, 1971, section BQ, 89.

76. "Self-Insurance for Schools," *New York Times*, November 20, 1977, section LI, 12.

77. Mitcheli, "Schools Fight Back."

78. Mitcheli, "Schools Fight Back."

79. "Nassau School Study Cites Vandalism Cost," *New York Times*, April 13, 1981, B2. These numbers may understate the extent of the problem. Districts often underreported fire damage to avoid premium hikes. One administrator described a "culture of silence"

around the issue. *Phenomenon of Juvenile Firestarters: Hearing before the Subcommittee on Juvenile Justice of the Committee on the Judiciary*, US Senate, 99th Cong., 1st sess., 11 (April 23, 1985).

80. Mitcheli, "Schools Fight Back." For more recent examples of the problem, see Julie Blair, "Liability Insurance's Skyrocketing Costs Confound Districts," *Education Week*, February 6, 2002, 1.

81. Indeed, anecdotal evidence suggests that existing records may actually underreport the prevalence of vandalism in suburban areas. Edwards, "Insurance Costs," 52–53; Knight, "Vandalism Puzzles Suburbs."

82. David Loth, *Crime in the Suburbs* (New York: William Morrow, 1967), 98, 103.

83. Willem Van Vliet, "Vandalism: An Assessment and Agenda," in *Vandalism: Behavior and Motivations*, ed. Claude Lévy-Leboyer (New York: Elsevier Science, 1984), 20; Clarence Tygart, "Public School Vandalism: Some Revised Strain Theory Perspectives," *Urban Education* 22, no. 2 (July 1987): 154–71; Harold Goldmeier, "Vandalism: The Effects of Unmanageable Confrontation," *Adolescence* 9, no. 33 (Spring 1974): 50; Alexander Liazos, "School, Alienation, and Delinquency," *Crime and Delinquency* 24, no. 3 (July 1978): 366. Although admittedly imprecise, studies during the 1970s attributed only 9 percent of vandalism cases to racial antagonism. Stephen K. Baily, "Disruption in Urban Public Secondary Schools ca. 1970," 1970, series 29, box 4170, folder 3, NEA.

84. New surveys found that almost half of students claimed to have vandalized schools, which seemed to weaken psychopathy as a primary cause of vandalism. Indeed, longitudinal studies found that vandalism was one of the few offenses initially recorded at referral that had no relation at all to later "sociopathic personality traits." Joseph L. Venturini, "A Survey on Causes of School Vandalism," *High School Journal* 66, no. 1 (October/November 1982): 7–9; Stanley Cohen, "Campaigning against Vandalism," in *Vandalism*, ed. Colin Ward (London: Architectural Press, 1973), 233–40; Lévy-Leboyer, introduction to Lévy-Leboyer, *Vandalism*, 5.

85. Anderson, "Vandalism in Unified School Districts," 4.

86. Casserly, Bass, and Garrett, *School Vandalism*, 4.

87. J. Sélosse, "Vandalism: Speech Acts," in Lévy-Leboyer, *Vandalism*, 42–43.

88. Colin Ward, introduction to Ward, *Vandalism*, 17; Colin Ward, "Notes on the Future of Vandalism," in Ward, *Vandalism*, 283; Sol Cohen, "Sociological Approaches to Vandalism," in Lévy-Leboyer, *Vandalism*, 54–55.

89. Jeffrey D. Fisher and Reuben M. Baron, "An Equity-Based Model of Vandalism," *Population and Environment* 5, no. 3 (Fall 1982): 182–200.

90. Sélosse, "Vandalism," 42–43.

91. Lévy-Leboyer, introduction, 8–9; Clarence Tygart, "Public School Vandalism: Some Revised Strain Theory Perspectives," *Urban Education* 22, no. 2 (July 1987): 154–71; Sélosse, "Vandalism," 41.

92. Van Vliet, "Vandalism," 20; "Vandalism and Violence," 3; Michael Stern, "Vandals' Toll Measured in Dollars and Drabness," *New York Times*, July 14, 1969, 37.

93. V. M. Weinmayer, "Vandalism by Design: A Critique," *Landscape Architecture* 59 (1969): 286.

94. "Positive Approaches to Classroom Discipline," 1981, series 15, box 1658, folder 1, NEA; Amy F. Ogata, *Designing the Creative Child; Playthings and Places in Midcentury America* (Minneapolis: University of Minnesota Press, 2013), chap. 4; *Educational Change and Architectural Consequences* (New York: Educational Facilities Laboratories, 1968). See also James Rothenberg, "The Open Classroom Reconsidered," *Elementary School Journal* 90, no. 1 (September 1989): 68–86; and Larry Cuban, "The Open Classroom: Were Schools without Walls Just Another Fad?," *Education Next* 4, no. 2 (Spring 2004): 68–71.

95. Van Vliet, "Vandalism," 27.

96. Lévy-Leboyer, introduction, *Vandalism*, 8.

97. Examples of the policymakers' position can be found in Casserly, Bass, and Garrett, *School Vandalism*; and Allan M. Hoffmann, *Schools, Violence, and Society* (Westport, CT: Praeger, 1996). Typical of the academic position is the work of Stanley Cohen and Colin Ward, especially in Ward, *Vandalism*. See also E. E. Juillerat Jr., "Fires and Vandals: How to Make Them Both Unwelcome in Your Schools," *American School Board Journal* 159, no. 7 (January 1972): 23–24; Center for Juvenile Delinquency Prevention, *Vandalism: A Study of School Vandalism* (San Marcos: Southwest Texas State University, 1979).

98. Oscar Newman, *Defensible Space: Crime Prevention through Urban Design* (New York: Collier Books, 1973).

99. *School Security Handbook: Get a Handle on a Vandal* (Sacramento: California Department of Justice, 1981); Center for Juvenile Delinquency Prevention, *Vandalism*; David Wiesenthal, *Psychological Aspects of Vandalism* (Toronto: York University, 1990); Anderson, "Vandalism in Unified School Districts"; Denis Wood, "In Defense of Indefensible Space," in *Environmental Criminology*, ed. Paul J. Brantingham and Patricia Brantingham (London: Sage, 1981), 77.

100. Ward, introduction, 14. See also Zeisel, *Stopping School Property Damage*, 49; and Don H. Richardson, "Combating Vandalism in the Schools," *NASSP Bulletin* 60, no. 40 (May 1976): 61.

101. William J. Reese, "*Reefer Madness* and *A Clockwork Orange*," in *Learning from the Past: What History Teaches Us about School Reform*, ed. Diane Ravitch and Maris A. Vinovskis (Baltimore: Johns Hopkins University Press, 1995), 365.

102. April Zweig and Michael H. Ducey, *A Preparadigmatic Field: A Review of Research on School Vandalism* (Hackensack, NJ: NewGate Resource Center, 1978); Arnold P. Goldstein, *The Psychology of Vandalism* (New York: Plenum, 1996), 50; Ward, introduction, 13.

103. As late as the mid-1980s, no major organization was tracking the issue systematically. Goldstein, *Psychology of Vandalism*, 4. For an early history of longitudinal research in education, see Ethan Hutt, "'Seeing like a State' in the Post-war Era: The Coleman Report, Longitudinal Datasets, and the Measurement of Human Capital," *History of Education Quarterly* 57, no. 4 (2017): 615–25.

104. On security associations, see Daniel L. Duke and Vernon F. Jones, "Two Decades of Discipline—Assessing the Development of an Educational Specialization," *Journal of Research and Development in Education* 17, no. 4 (1984): 27–28. For other sources of research on vandalism, see Anderson, "Vandalism in Unified School Districts," 20; Peter D. Blauvelt, "The Ultimate Test," *Security Management* 35, no. 9 (September 1991): 89–93; Goldstein, *Psychology of Vandalism*, 4; Casserly, Bass, and Garrett, *School Vandalism*, 11; Sohn, "School and Classroom Discipline Practices," 9–10; Hilton H. Murphy, "Vandals, Arsonists, Bombs, Dogs" (paper presentation, American Association of School Administrators 105th Annual Convention, San Francisco, March 19, 1973); Birch Bayh, *Our Nation's Schools—a Report Card: "A" in School Violence and Vandalism* (Washington, DC: US Government Printing Office, 1976), 6; Shirley Neill, *Violence and Vandalism* (Arlington, VA: National School Public Relations Association, 1975), 8–9; "Vandalism and Violence."

105. Following large cities, states began to require reports of vandalism beginning in the mid-1970s. Deming, "School Fires," 4. See also William Sadler, "Vandalism in Our Schools: A Study concerning Children Who Destroy Property and What to Do about It," *Education* 108, no. 4 (1988); 556–60; "Vandalism and Violence"; Casserly, Bass, and Garrett, *School Vandalism*, 4; Charles B. Stalford, "Historical Perspectives on Disruption and Violence in Schools" (paper presentation, Annual Meeting of the American Educational Research Association, New York, April 4–8, 1977).

106. *Vandalism: Study of Selected Great Cities and Maryland Counties* (Baltimore: Baltimore City Schools, 1970).

107. The *Safe School Study* coincided with the reauthorization of the Omnibus Crime Control and Safe Streets Act. See Robert J. Rubel, "Analysis and Critique of HEW's *Safe School Study Report to the Congress*," *Crime & Delinquency* 24, no. 3 (July 1978): 257–65; Casserly, Bass, and Garrett, *School Vandalism*, 2; and *Anti-arson Act of 1979*, 46.

108. Bayh, *Our Nation's Schools*, 11–12.

109. Bayh, *Our Nation's Schools*, 6.

110. Bayh, *Our Nation's Schools*, 3.

111. Bayh, *Our Nation's Schools*, 5; Goldman, "Restitution for Damages," 147.

112. Bayh, *Our Nation's Schools*, 5, 7.

113. Stalford, "Historical Perspectives," 8.

114. See *Violent Schools, Safe Schools: The Safe School Study Report to Congress* (Washington, DC: National Institute of Education, 1977); Casserly, Bass, and Garrett, *School Vandalism*, 11; Sohn, "School and Classroom Discipline Practices," 9–10; Stalford, "Historical Perspectives," 10; Duke and Jones, "Two Decades of Discipline," 27–28; Reese, "*Reefer Madness*," 359.

115. Deming, "School Fires," 3; "Vandalism and Violence"; Bayh, *Our Nation's Schools*, 38.

116. Owen B. Kiernan, "School Violence and Vandalism," statement to Subcommittee to Investigate Juvenile Delinquency (Washington, DC: National Association of Secondary School Principals, April 16, 1975), 8–9.

117. For examples, see Neill, *Violence and Vandalism*, 47; Casserly, Bass, and Garrett, *School Vandalism*, 39; Reilly, "Coping with Vandalism," 1150; Superintendent of Schools to LA Board of Education, December 1, 1975, box 2037, folder 4, LAUSD.

118. On the history of vandalism in Baltimore, see "Public Asked to Help Curb Vandalism," *Baltimore Sun*, October 2, 1961, 36; Adam Clymer, "Vandals Do More Damage," *Baltimore Sun*, March 8, 1963, 5; Gerald W. Clarke, "Vandalism Data on Schools Aired," *Baltimore Sun*, December 6, 1963, 44; Stephen A. Bennett, "Vandalism Causes Schools Record $260,280 Damage," *Baltimore Sun*, June 7, 1968, C8; "BCPSS Budget Request," 1966, BRG31-14-Box 13, Baltimore City Archives (hereafter BCA). On the origins of Schaefer's initiative, see "News from the Baltimore Campaign against Vandalism," Spring 1982, William Donald Schaefer Papers (hereafter Schaefer Papers), box 472; "School Based Project to Combat School Vandalism," Schaefer Papers, box 315, BCA.

119. Memorandum, October 14, 1982, Schaefer Papers, box 859, BCA.

120. Joan Burrier Bereska to William Donald Schaefer, March 30, 1982, Schaefer Papers, box 315, BCA; Jacques Kelly, "James 'Jimmy' Kaplanges," *Baltimore Sun*, July 14, 2015, https://www.baltimoresun.com/obituaries/bs-md-ob-james-kaplanges-20150714-story.html. There were several chemical companies nationwide that carved out an anti-graffiti niche; see Diane White, "Graffiti by the Girls," *Boston Globe*, August 31, 1972, 37.

121. William Donald Schaefer to Mrs. Helen Grigal, March 29, 1982, Schaefer Papers, box 472; "Vandalism Script," n.d., Schaefer Papers, box 845, BCA.

122. "Suggested Techniques for the Public Agencies Subcommittee," n.d., Schaefer Papers, box 472; "Baltimore Campaign against Vandalism," n.d., Schaefer Papers, box 315, BCA.

123. Memorandum, November 19, 1981, Schaefer Papers, box 859; Michael A. Fletcher, "Anti-vandalism Project in City Schools Fails," n.d., Schaefer Papers, box 667, BCA.

124. Fletcher, "Anti-vandalism Project."

125. Peter D. Blauvelt, "Understanding Vandalism," 1977, Schaefer Papers, box 472; memorandum, October 19, 1984, Schaefer Papers, box 472; memorandum, n.d., Schaefer Papers, box 315, BCA.

126. William Donald Schaefer to Joel L. Wallerstrom, June 30, 1981, Schaefer Papers, box 315; "Vandalism and Restitution: Board Policy Reporting Procedures," May 1, 1981,

BCPS-220.05, Schaefer Papers, box 315, BCA. On the rise of law enforcement in schools nationally, see "Vandalism and Violence"; "Code of Student Rights and Responsibilities," series 22, box 1672, folder 19, NEA; Owen B. Kiernan, "School Violence and Vandalism," statement to Subcommittee to Investigate Juvenile Delinquency, 1975, series 29, box 1746, folder 7, NEA.

127. On the debatable effectiveness of target hardening, see Lévy-Leboyer, introduction, 5.

128. Gail Armstrong and Mary Wilson, "Delinquency and Some Aspects of Housing," in Ward, *Vandalism*, 64-84; V. M. Weinmayer, "Vandalism by Design: A Critique," *Landscape Architecture* 59 (1969): 286; Deming, "School Fires," 23.

VANDALISM AS SELF-FASHIONING

1. Jack Katz, *Seductions of Crime: Moral and Sensual Attractions in Doing Evil* (New York: Basic Books, 1988), 3–4, 10, 311.

2. Stanley Cohen, *Escape Attempts: The Theory and Practice of Resistance to Everyday Life* (New York: Routledge, 1992), 31.

3. Cohen, *Escape Attempts*, 31, 41, 114, 171.

4. See John Willinsky, ed., *The Educational Legacy of Romanticism* (Waterloo, ON: Wilfrid Laurier University Press, 2006).

5. Jean-Paul Sartre, *Being and Nothingness* (New York: Washington Square Press, 1993), 43.

6. Georges Bataille offers similar thoughts on negation and nonsense in *On Nietzsche*, trans. Bruce Boone (New York: Paragon House, 1992), xxix–xxx. For applications of this argument in educational theory, see Ian McPherson, "Kierkegaard as an Educational Thinker: Communication through and across Ways of Being," *Journal of Philosophy of Education* 35, no. 2 (2002): 157–74; Peter Roberts, "Happiness, Despair and Education," *Studies in Philosophy and Education* 32, no. 5 (2013): 463–75; Sean Steel, "On the Need for Dionysian Education in Schools Today," *Educational Theory* 64, no. 2 (2014): 123–41; and James Stillwaggon, "'A Fantasy of Untouchable Fullness': Melancholia and Resistance to Educational Transformation," *Educational Theory* 67, no. 1 (February 2017): 51–66.

7. This ambiguity derives from Romantic juxtapositions of good and evil in "natural" experience, present in the poetry of William Blake and others. See Peter A. Schock, "The Marriage of Heaven and Hell: Blake's Myth of Satan and Its Cultural Matrix," *ELH* 60, no. 2 (Summer 1993): 441–70.

8. For example, see Allan Bloom, trans., *The Republic of Plato* (New York: Basic Books, 1968), book 1, line 351.

9. David Sussman, "For Badness' Sake," *Journal of Philosophy* 106, no. 11 (November 2009): 617–18. A similar phenomenological approach appears in David McPherson, *Virtue and Meaning: A Neo-Aristotelian Perspective* (New York: Cambridge University Press, 2020), chap. 1.

10. Agnes Callard, "Unruliness," *Angry Rainbow Mermaids* (blog), August 11, 2018, http://angryrainbowmermaids.blogspot.com/2018/08/unruliness.html.

11. W. Van Vliet, "Vandalism: An Assessment and an Agenda," in *Vandalism: Behaviour and Motivations*, ed. Claude Lévy-Leboyer (New York: Elsevier Science, 1984), 27.

12. On the lifeworlds of children, see Mary Knapp and Herbert Knapp, *One Potato, Two Potato: The Folklore of American Children* (New York: W. W. Norton, 1976); Emily Claire Bruce, "Reading Agency: The Making of Modern German Childhoods in the Age of Revolutions" (PhD diss., University of Minnesota, 2015); Iona Opie and Peter Opie, *The Lore and Language of Schoolchildren* (Oxford: Clarendon, 1960); Iona Opie and Peter Opie, *Children's Games in Street and Playground* (New York: Oxford University Press, 1984);

David Nasaw, *Children of the City: At Work and Play* (New York: Anchor Books, 2012); Howard Chudacoff, *Children at Play: An American History* (New York: New York University Press, 2007); Brian Sutton-Smith, *The Ambiguity of Play* (Cambridge, MA: Harvard University Press, 1997); and Lawrence A. Hirschfield, "Why Don't Anthropologists Like Children?," *American Anthropologist* 104, no. 2 (June 2002): 611–27.

13. The concept of "limit experiences" derives from the earlier work of Karl Jaspers.

14. Madeleine Grumet, "The Theory of the Subject in Contemporary Curriculum Thought," in Willinsky, *Educational Legacy*, 194–95, 199.

5. BOOKS AND BOREDOM

1. John D. Eastwood, Alexandra Frischen, Mark J. Fenske, and Daniel Smilek, "The Unengaged Mind: Defining Boredom in Terms of Attention," *Perspectives on Psychological Science* 7, no. 5 (September 2012): 482–95; Mark Bauerlein, "Boredom in Class," *Education Next*, September 20, 2013, http://educationnext.org/boredom-in-class; Amber M. Northern and Michael J. Petrilli, "What Teens Want from Their Schools," *Educational Gadfly Weekly*, June 27, 2017, https://edexcellence.net/articles/what-teens-want-from-their-schools; Zachary Jason, "Bored Out of Their Minds," *Harvard Ed. Magazine*, no. 156 (Winter 2017): 18–25; Christopher Taibbi, "Giftedness and Classroom Boredom: Maybe It's Not All Bad," *Grappling with Giftedness* (blog), *Psychology Today*, March 11, 2013, https://www.psychologytoday.com/blog/gifted-ed-guru/201303/giftedness-and-classroom-boredom-maybe-its-not-all-bad.

2. Elizabeth S. Goodstein, "Between Affect and History: The Rhetoric of Modern Boredom," in *Boredom Studies Reader: Frameworks and Perspectives*, ed. Michael E. Gardiner and Julian Jason Haladyn (New York: Routledge, 2017), 23–25.

3. Teresa Belton and Esther Priyadharshini, "Boredom and Schooling: A Cross-Disciplinary Exploration," *Cambridge Journal of Education* 37, no. 4 (December 2007): 579–95.

4. See Noah Sobe, "Attention and Boredom in the 19th-Century American School: The 'Drudgery' of Learning and Teaching and the Common School Reform Movement," in *Aufmerksamkeit Zur Geschichte, Theorie und Empirie eines pädagogischen Phänomens*, ed. Sabine Reh, Kathrin Berdelmann, and Jörg Dinkelaker (Wiesbaden, Germany: Springer, 2015), 55–70; and Noah Sobe, "Concentration and Civilization: Producing the Attentive Child in the Age of Enlightenment," *Pedagogica Historica* 46, nos. 1–2 (February–April 2010): 149–60.

5. Tyson E. Lewis and Daniel Friedrich, "Educational States of Suspension," *Educational Philosophy and Theory* 48, no. 3 (2016): 238.

6. Peter Toohey, *Boredom: A Lively History* (New Haven, CT: Yale University Press, 2011), 82–85; John Burnet, *Aristotle on Education* (Cambridge: Cambridge University Press, 1967), 8–9.

7. Jean-Jacques Rousseau, *Emile, or On Education*, trans. Allan Bloom (New York: Basic Books, 1979), 123; A. S. Neill, *Summerhill: A Radical Approach to Childrearing* (New York: Hart, 1960), 31.

8. Olivia N. Saracho and Bernard Spodek, "Children's Play and Early Childhood Education: Insights from History and Theory," *Journal of Education* 177, no. 3 (1995): 129–48.

9. Michael Gardiner and Julian Jason Haladyn, "Monotonous Splendour: An Introduction to Boredom Studies," in Gardiner and Haladyn, *Boredom Studies Reader*, 8–10.

10. Lars Svendsen, *A Philosophy of Boredom* (Bath, UK: Reaktion Books, 2005), 17, 22.

11. Quoted in Goodstein, "Between Affect and History," 32. See also Kevin Hood Gary, "Boredom, Contemplation, and Liberation," *Philosophy of Education* (2013): 427–35.

12. Jan-Erik Mansikka, "Can Boredom Educate Us? Tracing a Mood in Heidegger's Fundamental Ontology from an Educational Point of View," *Studies in Philosophy and Education* 28, no. 3 (2009): 265–66.

13. Gary, "Boredom, Contemplation, and Liberation."

14. Sean Steel, "On the Need for Dionysian Education in Schools Today," *Educational Theory* 64, no. 2 (2014): 123, 140.

15. Lewis and Friedrich, "Educational States of Suspension," 237, 239–40.

16. Joris Vlieghe, "Experiencing Im-potentiality: Bollnow and Agamben on the Educational Meaning of School Practices," *Studies in Philosophy and Education* 32, no. 2 (2013): 190, 193, 199–201.

17. Alistair Miller, "The Promise of *Bildung*—or, 'A World of One's Own,'" *Journal of Philosophy of Education* 55, no. 2 (2021): 336 (Humboldt quoted in Miller, 334). For historical discussions of *Bildung* in American schools, see Jesse Raber, *Progressivism's Aesthetic Education: The Bildungsroman and the American School, 1890–1920* (New York: Palgrave Macmillan, 2018), 3–6; Johann Neem, *Democracy's Schools: The Rise of Public Education in America* (Baltimore: Johns Hopkins University Press, 2017), chap. 1; and Joseph Kett, *The Pursuit of Knowledge under Difficulties: From Self-Improvement to Adult Education in America, 1750–1990* (Stanford, CA: Stanford University Press, 1994).

18. Barbara Dalle Pezze and Carlo Salzani, "The Delicate Monster," in *Essays on Boredom and Modernity*, ed. Barbara Dalle Pezze and Carlo Salzani (Amsterdam: Rodopi, 2009), 5–33; Carol Z. Stearns and Peter N. Stearns, eds., *Emotion and Social Change: Toward a New Psychohistory* (New York: Holmes and Meier, 1988).

19. Svendsen, *Philosophy of Boredom*, 33–34; Dalle Pezze and Salzani, "Delicate Monster," 12–14; Edward Peters, "Notes toward an Archaeology of Boredom," *Social Research* 42, no. 3 (Autumn 1975): 493–511; Lucien Febvre, "Sensibility and History: How to Reconstitute the Emotional Life of the Past," in *A New Kind of History: From the Writings of Febvre* (New York: Harper and Row, 1973), 12–26.

20. Daniel Wickberg, "What Is the History of Sensibilities? On Cultural Histories, Old and New," *American Historical Review* 112, no. 3 (June 2007): 661–84.

21. Svendsen, *Philosophy of Boredom*, 41; Toohey, *Boredom*, 88; Belton and Priyadharshini, "Boredom and Schooling," 580–81.

22. Toohey, *Boredom*, 88, 146.

23. Judith Plotz, "The Perpetual Messiah: Romanticism, Childhood, and the Paradoxes of Human Development," in *Regulated Children/Liberated Children: Education in Psychohistorical Perspective*, ed. Barbara Finkelstein (New York: Psychohistory Press, 1979), 63–95.

24. Philippe Ariès, *Centuries of Childhood: A Social History of Family Life*, trans. Robert Baldick (New York: Vintage Books, 1962), 333–34.

25. See Michel Foucault, *Discipline and Punish: The Birth of the Prison*, trans. Alan Sheridan (New York: Pantheon, 1977).

26. Colin Greer, *The Great School Legend: A Revisionist Interpretation of American Public Education* (New York: Basic Books, 1972), 152.

27. For trenchant criticism of Ariès, see Nicholas Orme, *Medieval Children* (New Haven, CT: Yale University Press, 2001), 4–10. For responses to the "revisionist" school of educational history, see Diane Ravitch, *The Revisionists Revised: A Critique of the Radical Attack on the Schools* (New York: Basic Books, 1977); and Maris Vinovskis, *The Origins of Public High Schools: The Beverly High School Controversy* (Madison: University of Wisconsin Press, 1985).

28. Sobe, "Attention and Boredom."

29. David Hogan, "The Market Revolution and Disciplinary Power: Joseph Lancaster and the Psychology of the Early Classroom System," *History of Education Quarterly* 29, no. 3 (Autumn 1989): 381–417.

30. Carolyn Eastman, *A Nation of Speechifiers: Making an American Public after the Revolution* (Chicago: University of Chicago Press, 2010), chap. 1.

31. Emma Willard, *Abridged History of the United States* (New York: A. S. Barnes, 1849), American Antiquarian Society, Worcester, MA (hereafter AAS); Lyman Cobb, *Cobb's New*

Sequel to the Juvenile Readers, or Fourth Reading Book (Cincinnati: B. Davenport, 1847), AAS; Egbert Guernsey, *History of the United States of America* (New York: Cady and Burgess, 1848), AAS; Sabina Cecil, *Little Sophia, or The Picture-Book* (Philadelphia: E. R. Parker, 1819), AAS; William G. Webster, *A Sequel to Webster's Elementary Spelling-Book* (New York: George F. Cooledge and Brother, 1846), AAS.

32. Lady of Charleston, *Little Dora, or The Four Seasons* (Philadelphia: George S. Appleton, 1850), AAS.

33. Oliver Welch, *The American Arithmetic* (Exeter, NH: Nathaniel Boardman, 1814–18), AAS; Clifton Johnson, *Old-Time Schools and Schoolbooks* (New York: Macmillan, 1904), 159.

34. Andrew Fiss, "Textbook Burial and Student Culture before and after the Civil War, 1853–1880," *History of Education Quarterly* 57, no. 2 (May 2017): 221–46.

35. Patricia Crain, *Reading Children: Literacy, Property, and the Dilemmas of Childhood in Nineteenth-Century America* (Philadelphia: University of Pennsylvania Press, 2016), 127. See also M. O. Grenby, *The Child Reader, 1700–1840* (New York: Cambridge University Press, 2011), 279; Jane H. Hunter, "Inscribing the Self in the Heart of the Family: Diaries and Girlhood in Late-Victorian America," *American Quarterly* 44, no. 1 (March 1992): 51–81; Emily Claire Bruce, "Reading Agency: The Making of Modern German Childhoods in the Age of Revolutions" (PhD diss., University of Minnesota, 2015).

36. The books reviewed in this chapter represent a diverse set of subjects, age levels, and languages, including titles in German, Spanish, and French, and inscriptions from Sabbath schools, infant schools, elementary schools, and high schools. In keeping with educational trends of the period, they skew heavily toward the Northern states, with fewer than 5 percent printed or inscribed below the Mason-Dixon Line. In cases where identification is possible, they seem to have been owned by predominantly white, English-speaking families.

37. Crain, *Reading Children*, 110, 126.

38. Grenby, *Child Reader*, 29.

39. Karen Sánchez-Eppler, "In the Archives of Childhood," in *The Children's Table: Childhood Studies and the Humanities*, ed. Anna Mae Duane (Athens: University of Georgia Press, 2013), 213–37.

40. H. J. Jackson, *Marginalia: Readers Writing in Books* (New Haven, CT: Yale University Press, 2001), 90; Grenby, *Child Reader*, 28–29.

41. Lucy Hiller Lambert Cleveland, *Annette Warington, or Sequel to "The Black Velvet Bracelet"* (Boston: Benjamin H. Greene, 1832), AAS; Lindley Murray, *English Exercises* (Concord, NH: Isaac Hill, 1818), AAS.

42. Kevin J. Hayes, *Folklore and Book Culture* (Knoxville: University of Tennessee Press, 1997), 90, 96–98.

43. *Farrand's Course of Latin Studies* (Philadelphia: John Adams, 1805), AAS.

44. Cornelia Tuthill, *The Boy of Spirit: A Story for the Young* (Boston: Crosby and Nichols, 1863), AAS; John Todd, *Shaking Out the Reef, and Other "Gems"* (Boston: Henry Hoyt, 1863), AAS; *The Adventures of Little Tiny & the White Mouse* (New York: T. W. Strong, 1860–66), AAS.

45. Emma Willard, *Ancient Geography* (Hartford: Oliver D. Cooke, 1831), AAS.

46. Virginia W. Johnson, *The Kettle's Birth-Day Party* (Boston: Nichols and Noyes, 1869), AAS. See also Johnson, *Old-Time Schools and Schoolbooks*, 156–57.

47. *Scott's New Lessons in Reading and Speaking* (Philadelphia: A. Walker, 1816), AAS.

48. Johnson, *Old-Time Schools and Schoolbooks*, 157.

49. Harriet Myrtle, *Adventure of a Kite* (New York: Sheldon, 1856), AAS; *The Standard Third Reader for Public and Private Schools* (Boston: Sampson Phillips, 1857), AAS; John

Lauris Blake, *First Book in Astronomy: Adapted to the Use of Common Schools* (Boston: Lincoln and Edmunds, 1831), AAS.

50. A. N. Girault, *Vie de George Washington: Pris de l'anglais, et dédié a la jeunesse américaine* (Philadelphia: Peck and Bliss, 1856), AAS.

51. Blake, *First Book in Astronomy*.

52. Crain, *Reading Children*, 123; Grenby, *Child Reader*, 271; Neem, *Democracy's Schools*, 50; Kett, *Pursuit of Knowledge*, 16, 80–83.

53. Enoch Pond, *Murray's System of English Grammar* (Worcester: Peirce and Williams, 1830); *Childhood's Toys and Pasttimes* ([United States?], ca. 1840), AAS; *Standard Third Reader*.

54. Anna Letitia Barbault, *Lessons for Children* (Boston: Wells and Lilly, 1818), AAS.

55. Jane Marcet, *Conversations on Natural Philosophy: In Which the Elements of That Science Are Familiarly Explained* (Boston: Gould, Kendall and Lincoln, 1836), AAS.

56. Daniel Wise, *Fretful Lillia, or The Girl Who Was Compared to a Stingnettle* (Chicago: John R. Walsh, 1863), AAS.

57. Mary Trimmer, *A Natural History of the Most Remarkable Quadrupeds, Birds, Fishes, Serpents, Reptiles, and Insects* (Boston: Hilliard, Gray, Little, and Wilkins, 1832), AAS.

58. William G. Webster, *A Sequel to Webster's Elementary Spelling-Book* (New York: George F. Cooledge and Brother, 1846), AAS.

59. *Fables of Aesop and Others* (Philadelphia: R. Aitken, 1802), AAS.

60. G. P. Quackenbos, *Illustrated School History of the United States* (New York: D. Appleton, 1857), AAS.

61. Quackenbos, *Illustrated School History*; Nathaniel Holmes Morison, *A School Manual, Prepared for the Use of His Pupils* (Baltimore: William K. Boyle, 1867), AAS.

62. For more on marginalia and self-formation, see E. Jennifer Monaghan, *Learning to Read and Write in Colonial America* (Amherst: University of Massachusetts Press, 2005), 75–77, 377–78.

63. Cartographic knowledge of one's country was seen as a spur to patriotism and constituted a significant portion of the nineteenth-century curriculum. Susan Schulten, "Map Drawing, Graphic Literacy, and Pedagogy in the Early Republic," *History of Education Quarterly* 57, no. 2 (May 2017): 185–220; Jackson, *Marginalia*, 21.

64. Richard Phillips, *An Easy Grammar of Natural and Experimental Philosophy: For the Use of Schools* (Philadelphia: Kimber and Conrad, 1811), AAS.

65. Benjamin H. Coe, *Easy Lessons in Landscape Drawing, with Sketches of Animals and Rustic Figures, and Directions for Using the Lead Pencil: Designed for Schools* (Hartford, CT: Robins and Folger, 1840), AAS.

66. Emma Willard, *Ancient Geography: As Connected with Chronology, and Preparatory to the Study of Ancient History* (Hartford, CT: Oliver D. Cooke, 1831), AAS.

67. Peter Bullions, *A Practical Grammar of the English Language: With Analysis of Sentences* (New York: Sheldon, 1868), AAS.

68. *The Child's Botany* (Boston: S. G. Goodrich, 1829), AAS.

69. Alfred Crowquill, *Patty and her Pitcher* (New York: McLoughlin Brothers, 1874), AAS.

70. *The New England Primer, or An Easy and Pleasant Guide to the Art of Reading: To Which Is Added the Catechism* (Haverhill, MA: Horatio G. Allen, 1813), AAS.

71. *The Story Book: For Good Little Girls* (New York: Kiggins and Kellogg, 1849), AAS; *The Youth's Director, or A Series of Miscellaneous Thoughts & Reflections on Conversation & Actions* (St. Albans, VT: printed for the author, 1811), AAS.

72. *The Good Boy's Soliloquy* (New York: Samuel Wood and Sons, 1819), AAS.

73. Crain, *Reading Children*, 128.

74. C. F. l'Homond, *Epitome historiae sacrae: Ad usum tyronum linguae Latinae* (Philadelphia: Delaplaine and Hellings, 1810), AAS.

75. Warren Colburn, *First Lessons in Arithmetic* (Boston: Cummings and Hilliard, 1822), AAS.

76. Charles A. Goodrich, *A History of the United States of America* (Boston: Jenks, Palmer, 1851), AAS.

77. Gardiner and Haladyn, "Monotonous Splendor," 7.

78. Grenby, *Child Reader*, 282.

79. Grenby, *Child Reader*, 271, 283.

6. DESKS AND NOSTALGIA

1. John Dewey, *The School and Society* (Chicago: University of Chicago Press, 1900), 31–32.

2. Henry Barnard, *Practical Illustrations of the Principles of School Architecture* (Hartford, CT: Case, Tiffany, 1851), 13.

3. Larry Cuban, *How Teachers Taught: Constancy and Change in American Classrooms, 1890–1980* (New York: Longman, 1984), 7–8, 18; Alexandra Parker, "Students, Stay in Your Seats," National Museum of American History, July 1, 2013, http://americanhistory.si.edu/blog/2013/07/students-stay-in-your-seats-improving-19th-century-school-desks.html.

4. Martha Nussbaum, *Political Emotions: Why Love Matters for Justice* (Cambridge, MA: Belknap Press of Harvard University Press, 2013), 10–11.

5. Jonathan Zimmerman, *Small Wonder: The Little Red Schoolhouse in History and Memory* (New Haven, CT: Yale University Press, 2015), 125–26. For examples of this sort of hagiography, see Daniel Wolff, *How Lincoln Learned to Read: Twelve Great Americans and the Educations That Made Them* (New York: Bloomsbury, 2010).

6. "Smith Visits School of Boyhood Days; Finds Initials He Carved in His Old Desk," *New York Times*, March 3, 1924, 19.

7. Eric Avila, *Popular Culture in the Age of White Flight: Fear and Fantasy in Suburban Los Angeles* (Berkeley: University of California Press, 2004), chap. 4; Richard Francaviglia, "History after Disney: The Significance of 'Imagineered' Historical Places," *Public Historian* 17, no. 4 (Autumn 1995): 69–74; Walt Disney Hometown Museum, accessed August 18, 2022, https://www.waltdisneymuseum.org/.

8. "Unraveling the Mystery of the Old Wooden Desk Carved with 'JFK,'" CBS News, February 3, 2016, https://www.cbsnews.com/news/desk-carved-with-jfk-unraveling-the-mystery/.

9. S. J. Woolf, "Mr. Ford Shows His Museum," *New York Times*, January 12, 1936, SM1.

10. "Ford Reopens Childhood School at Dearborn; Sits among Pupils and Carves Initials in Desk," *New York Times*, September 16, 1929, 6.

11. Leonard Dinnerstein, *Antisemitism in America* (New York: Oxford University Press, 1994), chaps. 4–5; Steven Watts, *The Magic Kingdom: Walt Disney and the American Way of Life* (Columbia: University of Missouri Press, 2001), chap. 1; Avila, *Age of White Flight*, 125, 135-137.

12. Stephanie Koontz, *The Way We Never Were: American Families and the Nostalgia Trap* (New York: Basic Books, 2000); Sam Fallon, "The Rise of the Pedantic Professor," *Chronicle of Higher Education*, March 1, 2019, https://www.chronicle.com/article/The-Rise-of-the-Pedantic/245808.

13. Helmut Illbruck, *Nostalgia: Origins and Ends of an Unenlightened Disease* (Evanston, IL: Northwestern University Press, 2012), 19; Michael Löwy and Robert Sayre, *Romanticism against the Tide of Modernity* (Durham, NC: Duke University Press, 2001), 22–24, 70; Seth Cotlar, "The Challenges of Writing the History of Nostalgia Set in the Age

of Democratic Revolutions," Age of Revolutions, September 10, 2018, https://ageofrevolutions.com/2018/09/10/the-challenges-of-writing-a-history-of-nostalgia-set-in-the-age-of-democratic-revolutions/.

14. Martin McCallum, "Towards a Politics of Nostalgia: Nostalgic Memory and Community in Later Rousseau" (PhD diss., McGill University, 2016), 1, 5; Rita Koganzon, *Liberal States, Authoritarian Families: Childhood and Education in Early Modern Thought* (New York: Oxford University Press, 2021), 188.

15. Mark Lilla, *The Shipwrecked Mind: On Political Reaction* (New York: New York Review of Books, 2016); T. J. Jackson Lears, *No Place of Grace: Antimodernism and the Transformation of American Culture, 1880–1920* (New York: Pantheon Books, 1981); Corey Robin, *The Reactionary Mind: Conservatism from Edmund Burke to Sarah Palin* (New York: Oxford University Press, 2011); Gary S. Cross, *Consumed Nostalgia: Memory in the Age of Fast Capitalism* (New York: Columbia University Press, 2015); Illbruck, *Nostalgia*, 22–25, 137.

16. These categories are outlined in Svetlana Boym, *The Future of Nostalgia* (New York: Basic Books, 2001). For a psychological rehabilitation of nostalgia, see Constantine Sedkides, Tim Wildschut, Jamie Arndt, and Clay Routledge, "Nostalgia: Past, Present, and Future," *Current Directions in Psychological Science* 17, no. 5 (October 2008): 304–7.

17. Christopher Lasch, *The True and Only Heaven: Progress and Its Critics* (New York: Norton, 1991). As a self-proclaimed populist—a defender of the nuclear family, community welfare, and small-scale production—Lasch recognized that critics might construe his own positions as reactionary nostalgia, and it was to some degree to inoculate himself that he took up the topic. This is particularly true in regard to Lasch's opposition to second-wave feminism. See, for instance, Ellen Willis, "Backlash," review of *Women and the Common Life: Love, Marriage, and Feminism,* by Christopher Lasch, ed. Elisabeth Lasch-Quinn, *Los Angeles Times,* January 12, 1997, http://articles.latimes.com/1997-01-12/books/bk-17738_1_common-life.

18. Lasch, *True and Only Heaven*, 82. For a similar argument about progress and nostalgia, see Bernard Williams, *Shame and Necessity* (Berkeley: University of California Press, 1993), 9–10.

19. Lasch, *True and Only Heaven*, 117–18.

20. See also Robert Nisbet, *The Quest for Community* (New York: Oxford University Press, 1969); and Leroy S. Rouner, ed., *On Community* (Notre Dame, IN: University of Notre Dame Press, 1991).

21. Michael Sandel, "The Procedural Republic and the Unencumbered Self," *Political Theory* 12, no. 1 (February 1984): 81–96; Charles Taylor, *Ethics of Authenticity* (Cambridge, MA: Harvard University Press, 1992), 32–33, 44.

22. Paul Theobald and Dale T. Snauwert, "The Educational Philosophy of Wendell Berry," *ERIC Viewpoints* (1990): 3; Alasdair MacIntyre, *After Virtue: A Study in Moral Theory* (Notre Dame, IN: Notre Dame University Press, 2007), 204–5, 214–18; Noel Perrin, *First Person Rural: Essays of a Sometimes Farmer* (Boston: David R. Godine, 1978); Anthony Esolen, *Nostalgia: Going Home in a Homeless World* (Washington, DC: Regnery Gateway, 2018).

23. Nussbaum, *Political Emotions*, 211.

24. For critiques of unearned emotions, see Eamonn Callan, "Beyond Sentimental Civic Education," *American Journal of Education* 102, no. 2 (February 1994): 190–221; and Matthew D. Wright, *A Vindication of Politics: On the Common Good and Human Flourishing* (Lawrence: University Press of Kansas, 2019), 127–36.

25. G. Morgan Knight Jr., "Initial-Scarred School Desks Repaired by N.Y.A. Workers," *Evening Star* (Washington, DC), February 10, 1941, B7; Clifton Johnson, *The Country School in New England* (New York: D. Appleton, 1893), 51.

26. Zimmerman, *Small Wonder*, 27.

27. Hilary Green, *Educational Reconstruction: African American Schools in the Urban South, 1865–1890* (New York: Fordham University Press, 2016), 15.

28. Ellen M. Raynor and Emma L. Petitclerc, *History of the Town of Cheshire, Berkshire County, Massachusetts* (Holyoke, MA: Clark W. Bryan, 1885), 152. See also "The Old House," *The Devil's Lake (ND) World*, November 7, 1913, 4; "County Gleanings," *Penn's Grove (NJ) Record*, September 1, 1905, 3.

29. "Passing of the Old School Desks—Bethalto People Buying Up Desks They Carved On for Forty-Five Years," *Alton (IL) Evening Telegraph*, July 17, 1913, 3; "St. Gabriel Alumni Bid School Goodbye," *New York Times*, June 30, 1909, 4; "200 Bid Spiritedly for Collyer Items," *New York Times*, June 11, 1947, 54; "The Old School Desks," *San Francisco Chronicle*, February 2, 1913, 32.

30. "Old School House Saved," *Kansas City (MO) Journal*, July 13, 1898, 7.

31. "Bandits and Rats Rack Haverstraw," *New York Times*, April 7, 1922, 26; "Haverstraw Pupils to Study in Theater," *New York Times*, June 10, 1935, 19; "Farley's Initials on Old School Desk Cited in Row on Transfer of Stony Point Classes," *New York Times*, January 25, 1937, 21. For similar forms of resistance, see Campbell F. Scribner, *The Fight for Local Control: Schools, Suburbs, and American Democracy* (Ithaca, NY: Cornell University Press, 2016), chaps. 2–3.

32. "Desk from the Hope School," National Museum of African American History and Culture, accessed November 20, 2022, https://nmaahc.si.edu/object/nmaahc_2010.22.8; "Making a Way Out of No Way," National Museum of African American History and Culture, accessed November 20, 2022, https://nmaahc.si.edu/explore/exhibitions/making-way-out-no-way.

33. Brown v. Board of Education, 347 U.S. 483 (1954).

34. Vanessa Siddle Walker, *Their Highest Potential: An African American School Community in the Segregated South* (Chapel Hill: University of North Carolina Press, 1996); Thomas Sowell, "The Education of Minority Children," Hoover Institution, 2001, https://www.hoover.org/sites/default/files/uploads/documents/0817928928_79.pdf; David Cecelski, *Along Freedom Road: Hyde County, North Carolina and the Fate of Black Schools in the South*, introduction, chap. 1; Kimberly C. Ransom, "There Are Children Here: Examining Black Childhood in Rosenwald Schools of Pickens County, Alabama (1940–1969)" (PhD diss., University of Michigan, 2020); John Dittmer, oral history interview with Julia Matilda Burns, Library of Congress, March 13, 2013, https://www.loc.gov/item/2015669172/.

35. Adolph L. Reed Jr., *W.E.B. DuBois and American Political Thought: Fabianism and the Color Line* (New York: Oxford University Press, 1997), 159–60. See also Vincent Lloyd, *Black Natural Law* (New York: Oxford University Press, 2016), 118.

36. On competition in struggling urban communities, see David Imbroscio, "Urban Policy as Meritocracy: A Critique," *Journal of Urban Affairs* 38, no. 1 (2015): 79–104. On recent defenses of local schools, see Eve Ewing, *Ghosts in the Schoolyard: Racism and School Closings on Chicago's South Side* (Chicago: University of Chicago Press, 2018); Alasdair MacIntyre, *Ethics in the Conflicts of Modernity* (New York: Cambridge University Press, 2016), 203; Pauline Lipman, "The Landscape of Education 'Reform' in Chicago: Neoliberalism Meets a Grassroots Movement," *Education Policy Analysis Archives* 25, no. 54 (June 2017): 1–26; Kristen L. Buras, *Charter Schools, Race, and Urban Space: Where the Market Meets Grassroots Resistance* (New York: Routledge, 2015); Terrance Green, "'We Felt They Took the Heart Out of the Community': Examining a Community-Based Response to Urban School Closure," *Education Policy Analysis Archives* 25, no. 21 (March 2017): 1–30, https://epaa.asu.edu/ojs/article/view/2549.

37. Paul Theobald, *Teaching the Commons: Place, Pride, and the Renewal of Community* (Boulder, CO: Westview, 1997), 119–21.

38. Dariusz Gafijczuk, "Dwelling Within: The Inhabited Ruins of History," *History and Theory* 52, no. 2 (May 2013): 150.

39. Bonnie Honig, *Public Things: Democracy in Disrepair* (New York: Fordham University Press, 2017), 16.

40. Elizabeth Hansot, "Civic Friendship: An Aristotelian Perspective," in *Reconstructing the Common Good in Education: Coping with Intractable American Dilemmas*, ed. Larry Cuban and Dorothy Shipps (Palo Alto, CA: Stanford University Press, 2000), 173–85; Michael Berkman and Eric Plutzer, *Ten Thousand Democracies: Politics and Public Opinion in America's School Districts* (Washington, DC: Georgetown University Press, 2005); Anthony S. Bryk and Barbara L. Schneider, *Social Trust: A Moral Resource for School Improvement* (Washington, DC: US Department of Education, Office of Educational Research and Improvement, Educational Resources Information Center, 1996); Robert Asen, *Democracy, Deliberation, and Education* (University Park: Pennsylvania State University Press, 2015).

41. Fred Davis, *Yearning for Yesterday: A Sociology of Nostalgia* (New York: Free Press, 1979), 31; Martin R. West, "Why Do Americans Rate Their Local Public Schools So Favorably?," Brookings Institution, October 23, 2014, https://www.brookings.edu/research/why-do-americans-rate-their-local-public-schools-so-favorably/; Johann N. Neem, "The Founding Fathers Made Our Schools Public. We Should Keep Them That Way," *Washington Post*, August 20, 2017, https://www.washingtonpost.com/news/made-by-history/wp/2017/08/20/early-america-had-school-choice-the-founders-rejected-it.

7. WALLS AND THE TABOO

1. J. D. Salinger, *The Catcher in the Rye* (New York: Little, Brown, and Company, 1951), 201–4.

2. For an older example of panic, see *The Twenty-Third Annual Report of the State Board of Health* (New Haven: Connecticut State Board of Health, 1901), 28.

3. The etymologist Allen Walker Read made the first study of bathroom graffiti in 1933. "Inasmuch as the material has no inhibition as to vulgarity and obscenity," he wrote, "it throws light upon one aspect of the American people." The work was unpublishable under obscenity statutes at the time and did not appear in the United States for over forty years. Allen Walker Read, *Classic American Graffiti* (Waukesha, WI: Maledicta, 1977), 17.

4. For examples related to vandalism and latrinalia in particular, see Eugene D'Aquili, "The Influence of Jung on the Work of Claude Lévi-Strauss," *Journal of the History of the Behavioral Sciences* 11, no. 1 (1975): 84; Elizabeth Wales and Barbara Brewer, "Graffiti in the 1970s," *Journal of Social Psychology* 99, no. 1 (1976): 115–23; Edith Kramer, *Art as Therapy with Children* (New York: Schocken Books, 1971), 4–6. For general overviews of structuralism and its antecedents, see Jean Piaget, *Structuralism* (London: Routledge, 1968); Howard Gardner, *The Quest for Mind: Piaget, Lévi-Strauss, and the Structuralist Movement* (New York: Alfred A. Knopf, 1973); and Hunter Heyck, *Age of System: Understanding the Development of Modern Social Science* (Baltimore: Johns Hopkins University Press, 2015).

5. Alain Sayag and Annick Lionel-Marie, *Brassaï: The Monograph* (New York: Little, Brown, 2000), 292.

6. Brassaï, *Conversations with Picasso* (Chicago: University of Chicago Press, 1999), 273–74; Georges-Henri Luquet, "Sur les caractéres des figures humaines dans l'art paléolithique," *L'Anthropologie* 21 (1910): 409–23. As we will see in the subsequent chapter on broken windows, poststructuralists were interested in Paleolithic art as well, though for

slightly different reasons. See Yue Zhuo, "Alongside the Animals: Bataille's 'Lascaux Project,'" *Yale French Studies*, no. 127 (2015): 22–23.

7. Alan Dundes, "Here I Sit: A Study of American Latrinalia" (paper presentation, California Folklore Society conference, Berkeley, CA, 1966), 101; Abel L. Ernest and Barbara E. Buckley, *The Handwriting on the Wall* (Westport, CT: Greenwood, 1977), 2–3, 19, 27–28.

8. Mary Knapp and Herbert Knapp, *One Potato, Two Potato: The Folklore of American Children* (New York: W. W. Norton, 1976), 62, 85; Martha Wolfenstein, *Children's Humor* (Glencoe, IL: Free Press, 1954), xx–xxiii; Sandra McCosh, *Children's Humor: A Joke for Every Occasion* (New York: Grenada, 1979), xx; Robert Reisner, *Graffiti: Two Thousand Years of Wall Writing* (Chicago: Cowles, 1971), 148, 159, 163, 202; Nick Haslam, *Psychology in the Bathroom* (New York: Palgrave Macmillan, 2012), 128–29. For further studies of bathroom graffiti, see Terrance L. Stocker, Linda W. Dutcher, Stephen M. Hargrove, and Edwin A. Cook, "Social Analysis of Graffiti," *Journal of American Folklore* 85, no. 338 (October–December 1972): 356–66; D. D. Brewer and M. L. Miller, "Bombing and Burning: The Social Organization and Values of Hip Hop Graffiti Writers and Implications for Policy," *Deviant Behaviour* 11, no. 4 (October–December 1990): 345–69; Peter O. Peretti, Richard Carter, and Betty McClinton, "Graffiti and Adolescent Personality," *Adolescence* 12, no. 45 (Spring 1977): 31–42; Henry Solomon and Howard Yager, "Authoritarianism and Graffiti," *Journal of Social Psychology* 97 (October 1975): 149–50; Bill Adler, *Graffiti* (New York: Pyramid Books, 1972).

9. George Gonos and Nicholas Poushinsky, "Anonymous Expression: A Structural View of Graffiti," *Journal of American Folklore* 89, no. 351 (January 1976): 40–42; Wales and Brewer, "Graffiti in the 1970s," 127.

10. Haslam, *Psychology in the Bathroom*, 127, 132–33; Gonos and Poushinsky, "Anonymous Expression"; Adrian Birney, "Crack Puns: Text and Context in an Item of Latrinalia," *Western Folklore* 32, no. 2 (April 1973): 139–40.

11. Alfred C. Kinsey, *Sexual Behavior in the Human Female* (Philadelphia: W. B. Saunders, 1953), 673–75; Wales and Brewer, "Graffiti in the 1970s," 115–16; E. E. Landy and J. M. Steele, "Graffiti as a Function of Building Utilization," *Perception and Motor Skills* 25, no. 3 (December 1967): 711–12.

12. Peretti, Carter, and McClinton, "Graffiti and Adolescent Personality," 32; Adam Trahan, "Research and Theory on Latrinalia," in *The Routledge Handbook of Graffiti and Street Art*, ed. Jeffrey Ian Ross (New York: Routledge, 2016), 99; Wales and Brewer, "Graffiti in the 1970s," 115–23; J. H. Farr and C. Gordon, "A Partial Replication of Kinsey's Graffiti Study," *Journal of Sex Research* 11 (1975): 158–62; Diane White, "Graffiti by the Girls," *Boston Globe*, August 31, 1972, 37; Susanna Shaw, *Women in the John: A Collection of Graffiti from Women's Bathrooms* (San Francisco: Carolyn Bean Associates, 1978).

13. For similar critiques in adjacent fields, see Peter Harle, "Folklore and Structuralism," *Folklore Forum* 30, no. 1–2 (1999): 14.

14. Eli Zaretsky, *Political Freud* (New York: Columbia University Press, 2015), 164–65; Daniel K. Cho, "Thanatos and Civilization: Lacan, Marcuse, and the Death Drive," in *Marcuse's Challenge to Education*, ed. Douglas Kellner (Lanham, MA: Rowman and Littlefield, 2009), 59–78. For an example focused on student graffiti, see Frank J. D'Angelo, "Fools' Names and Fools' Faces Are Always Seen in Public Places: A Study of Graffiti," *Journal of Popular Culture* 10, no. 1 (Summer 1976): 108.

15. Herbert Marcuse, *Eros and Civilization: A Philosophical Inquiry into Freud* (Boston: Beacon, 1955), 36; Herbert Marcuse, "Repressive Tolerance," in *A Critique of Pure Tolerance*, ed. Robert Paul Wolff, Barrington Moore Jr., and Herbert Marcuse (Boston: Beacon, 1969), 96. Some scholars have associated rising vulgarity with the shift to a consumption-based economy and a broader cultural shift from continence to indulgence.

See Melissa Mohr, *Holy Sh*t: A Brief History of Swearing* (New York: Oxford University Press, 2013), 227.

16. Marcuse, *Eros and Civilization*, xxi, xxv.

17. Herbert Kohl, *Golden Boy as Anthony Cool* (New York: Dial, 1972), 25; Reisner, *Graffiti*, 159, 163.

18. Lisa Gelfand, *Sustainable School Architecture* (Hoboken, NJ: John Wiley and Sons, 2010), 61, 209.

19. For other examples, see Lizbet Simmons, "The Docile Body in School Space," in *Schools under Surveillance: Cultures of Control in Public Education*, ed. Rodolfo D. Torres and Torin Monahan (New Brunswick, NJ: Rutgers University Press, 2010), 65; Lynn Smith, "Worst Part of School? Bathrooms," *Los Angeles Times*, November 9, 1994, E1; Thomas-Lester Avis, "Cleanliness Shortchanged in Schools; Vandalism Outstrips Ability to Stock Soap," *Washington Post*, May 11, 2001, B3; Jonathan E. Briggs, "Restroom Project Proves a Source of Pride," *Los Angeles Times*, May 10, 2000, B2; "Camera in School Bathroom Curbs Vandalism but Sets Off Debate," *New York Times*, March 25, 1992, A21.

20. Aaron Kupchik and Nicole L. Bracy, "To Protect, Serve, and Mentor? Police Officers in Public Schools," in Torres and Monahan, *Schools under Surveillance*, 28; Simmons, "Docile Body," 65.

21. Lisa K. Waldner and Betty A. Dobratz, "Graffiti as a Form of Contentious Politics," *Sociology Compass* 7, no. 5 (2013): 377–89; Kohl, *Golden Boy*, 48–49.

22. James C. Scott, *Domination and the Arts of Resistance* (New Haven, CT: Yale University Press, 1990), 123–24, 127. See also Brian Sutton-Smith, *The Ambiguity of Play* (Cambridge, MA: Harvard University Press, 1997), 117–18; Stephen Duncomb, "Let's All Be Alienated Together: Zines and the Making of Underground Community," in *Generations of Youth: Youth Cultures and History in Twentieth-Century America*, ed. Joe Austin and Michael Nevin Willard (New York: New York University Press, 1998), 427–52.

23. Jennifer R. Wolgemuth, Mirka Koro-Ljungberg, and Timothy Barko, "(In Defense of) Pedagogies of Obscenity," *Power and Education* 12, no. 1 (2020): 23–28; Jennifer C. Ingrey, "The Public School Washroom as Heterotopia: Gendered Spatiality and Subjectification" (PhD diss., University of Western Ontario, 2013); Kathryn LaFever, "Foucault's Heterotopia and Pedagogical Space," *Didactiques* 2, no. 1 (2013): 70–80; Annegret Staiger, "School Walls as Battle Grounds: Technologies of Power, Space, and Identity," *Pedagogica Historica* 41, no. 4/5 (2005): 555–69; Cameron McAuliffe, "Young People and the Spatial Politics of Graffiti Writing," *Identities and Subjectivities* 4 (2016): 451–73.

24. Michel Foucault, "Of Other Spaces," in *Facing Value: Radical Perspectives from the Arts*, ed. Maaike Lauwaert and Francien van Westrenen (Amsterdam: Valiz, Den Haag, Stroom, 2017), 165–67. School bathrooms make a brief appearance in Foucault's earlier work, where he describes authorities at the École Militaire installing "half-doors" to monitor students in the stalls. Michel Foucault, *Discipline and Punish: The Birth of the Prison*, trans. Alan Sheridan (New York: Pantheon, 1977), 173.

25. Henri Lefebvre, *The Production of Space* (Malden, MA: Blackwell, 1984), 188; Edward W. Soja, *Thirdspace: Journeys to Los Angeles and Other Real-and-Imagined Places* (Cambridge: Blackwell, 1996); Willem van Vliet, "Exploring the Fourth Environment: An Examination of the Home Range of City and Suburban Teenagers," *Environment and Behavior* 15, no. 5 (September 1983): 567–88.

26. Jack Katz, *Seductions of Crime: Moral and Sensual Attractions in Doing Evil* (New York: Basic Books, 1988), 76.

27. Erik Erikson, *Young Man Luther: A Study in Psychoanalysis and History* (New York: W. W. Norton, 1962), 15; Dorothy Ross, "Freud and the Vicissitudes of Modernism in the United States, 1940–1980," in *After Freud Left: A Century of Psychoanalysis in America*, ed. John Burnham (Chicago: University of Chicago Press, 2012), 175–76.

28. See Erik Erikson, *Childhood and Society* (New York: W. W. Norton, 1963); and Erik Erikson, *Identity: Youth and Crisis* (New York: W. W. Norton, 1968). For applications of Erikson's thought, see Stanley Cohen, *Escape Attempts: The Theory and Practice of Resistance* (New York: Routledge, 1992), 156.

29. Erich Fromm, *Escape from Freedom* (New York: Holt, Rinehart, and Winston, 1976), 258.

30. Erich Fromm, *The Anatomy of Human Destructiveness* (Greenwich, CT: Fawcett, 1975), 69–71. The cultivation of selfhood precipitated a sharp exchange between Marcuse and Fromm in *Dissent*. Fromm argued that gratification and lack of inhibition meant that the individual was never alone with himself and had no need of self-awareness. Hedonism was not sufficient, and indeed could be easily co-opted by the capitalist machine. See Erich Fromm, "The Human Implications of Instinctivistic 'Radicalism,'" *Dissent*, Fall 1955, 346. See also Neil McLaughlin, "The Fromm-Marcuse Debate and the Future of Critical Theory," in *The Palgrave Handbook of Critical Theory*, ed. Michael J. Thompson (New York: Palgrave Macmillan, 2017), 481–500. Marcuse, too, noted the need for privacy in preserving the instincts, worrying that "oversocialization" in mass society could misdirect natural libidinal pleasures. Herbert Marcuse, "Aggressiveness in Advanced Industrial Society," Marxists Internet Archive, 1967, https://www.marxists.org/reference/archive/marcuse/works/aggressiveness.htm.

31. Hannah Arendt, "The Crisis in Education," in *Between Past and Future: Eight Exercises in Political Thought* (New York: Viking, 1968), 186, 188.

32. Aaron Schutz, "Is Political Education an Oxymoron? Hannah Arendt's Resistance to Public Spaces in Schools," *Philosophy of Education* (2001): 325.

33. Hannah Arendt, *The Human Condition* (Chicago: University of Chicago Press, 2018), 69.

34. Arendt, "Crisis in Education," 174–75; Arendt, *Human Condition*, 247.

35. Arendt, "Crisis in Education," 181.

36. Arendt, *Human Condition*, 71.

37. On Arendt and anonymity, see Patchen Markell, "Anonymous Glory," *European Journal of Political Theory* 16, no. 1 (2015): 77–99.

38. Schutz, "Political Education," 330.

39. Gert Biesta, *Beyond Learning: Democratic Education for a Human Future* (Boulder, CO: Paradigm, 2006), 85, 107.

40. Biesta, *Beyond Learning*, 74, 93–95.

41. Neil Dhingra, "Student Free Speech and Schools as Public Spaces," *Educational Theory* 69, no. 6 (November 2019): 659, 662–63.

42. Kupchik and Bracy, "Protect, Serve, and Mentor?," 28.

43. Michael Bonnet, "Education and Selfhood: A Phenomenological Investigation," *Journal of the Philosophy of Education* 43, no 3 (2009): 363–64.

44. Paul Goodman, *Compulsory Mis-education* (New York: Horizon, 1964), 83.

45. Goodman, *Compulsory Mis-education*, 85–86, 89, 91.

46. Goodman, *Compulsory Mis-education*, 96.

47. Miriam Forman-Brunell, *Girlhood in America: An Encyclopedia* (Santa Barbara, CA: ABC-CLIO, 2001), 430.

48. White, "Graffiti by the Girls." See also Bridget Read, "Students Suspended after Posting Bathroom Note about a Rapist," The Cut, October 16, 2019, https://www.thecut.com/2019/10/students-suspended-for-posting-bathroom-notes-about-a-rapist.html; and Jocelyn Amevuvor, "Communities in the Stalls: A Study of Latrinalia Linguistic Landscapes," *Critical Inquiry in Language Studies* 16, no. 2 (2019): 90–106.

49. Salinger, *Catcher in the Rye*, 201.

50. Max van Manen and Bas Levering, *Childhood Secrets: Intimacy, Privacy, and the Self Reconsidered* (New York: Teachers College Press, 1996), 90–91; Willem van Vliet,

"Vandalism: An Assessment and Agenda," in *Vandalism: Behaviour and Motivations*, ed. Claude Lévy-Leboyer (New York: Elsevier Science, 1984), 27; Wolgemuth, Koro-Ljungberg, and Barko, "Pedagogies of Obscenity."

51. Nicole Bishop, "Trust Is Not Enough: Classroom Self-Disclosure and the Loss of Private Lives," *Journal of the Philosophy of Education* 30, no. 3 (1996): 437. See also van Manen and Levering, *Childhood Secrets*, 150–51; Bonnet, "Education and Selfhood," 359.

8. WINDOWS AND EUPHORIA

1. Michael D. Casserly, Scott A. Bass, and John R. Garrett, *School Vandalism: Strategies for Prevention* (Lexington, MA: Lexington Books, 1980), 15; Birch Bayh, *Our Nation's Schools—a Report Card: "A" in School Violence and Vandalism* (Washington, DC: US Government Printing Office, 1976), 25–29; William Sadler, "Vandalism in Our Schools: A Study concerning Children Who Destroy Property and What to Do about It," *Education* 108, no. 4 (1988): 556–60.

2. Hiram, "A Plan for Establishing Schools, &c," quoted in Benjamin Justice, ed., *The Founding Fathers, Education, and the "Great Contest": The American Philosophical Society Prize of 1797* (New York: Palgrave MacMillan, 2013), 240; William George Bruce, *School Architecture: A Handy Manual* (Milwaukee: American School Board Journal, 1910), 33.

3. Daniel Freund, *American Sunshine: Diseases of Darkness and the Quest for Natural Light* (Chicago: University of Chicago Press, 2012), 30–32, 84–88.

4. Amy F. Ogata, *Designing the Creative Child: Playthings and Places in Midcentury America* (Minneapolis: University of Minnesota Press, 2013), 128.

5. For instance, see William Leach, *Land of Desire: Merchants, Power, and the Rise of a New American Culture* (New York: Vintage, 1993), 62–63.

6. Rich Church, "School Vandalism (in the Olden Days)," Town of Nelson, New Hampshire, accessed October 10, 2022, http://townofnelson.com/school-vandalism-in-the-olden-days.

7. John M. Martin, *Juvenile Vandalism: A Study of Its Nature and Prevention* (Springfield, IL: Thomas Books, 1961), 103. See also V. L. Allen, "Toward an Understanding of the Hedonic Component of Vandalism," in *Vandalism: Behaviour and Motivations*, ed. Claude Lévy-Leboyer (New York: Elsevier Science, 1984), 78.

8. "Vandalism and Violence: Innovative Strategies Reduce Cost to Schools," 1971, series 40, box 4207, folder 1, National Education Association Archives, George Washington University, Washington, DC. One study found that almost half of adolescents admitted to defacing or destroying property, but that most did not understand their behavior as criminal or malicious; most saw it as a game or a means of retaliation against particular individuals at school. Casserly, Bass, and Garrett, *School Vandalism*, 16; Martha M. Eliot, "What Is Vandalism?," *Federal Probation* 18, no. 1 (March 1954): 4; Dorothy Barclay, "Destructiveness in Children," *New York Times*, March 7, 1954, section SM, 56.

9. Mihai Spariosu, *Dionysus Reborn: Play and the Aesthetic Dimension in Modern Philosophical and Scientific Discourse* (Ithaca, NY: Cornell University Press, 1989), 167–68.

10. Jerome Bruner, *Play—Its Role in Development and Evolution* (New York: Basic Books, 1976), 20. For other examples, see Jean Piaget, *The Origins of Intelligence in Children* (New York: W. W. Norton, 1963); Lev S. Vygotsky, "Play and Its Role in the Mental Development of the Child," *Soviet Psychology* 5 (1967): 6–18; Eleanor Duckworth, *The Having of Wonderful Ideas, and Other Essays on Teaching and Learning* (New York: Teachers College Press, 2006); Jack Katz, *Seductions of Crime: Moral and Sensual Attractions in Doing Evil* (New York: Basic Books, 1988), 53.

11. Katz, *Seductions of Crime*, 67; J. Sélosse, "Vandalism: Speech Acts," in *Vandalism: Behaviour and Motivations*, ed. Claude Lévy-Leboyer (New York: Elsevier Science, 1984),

44; Mihaly Csikszentmihalyi and Reed Larson, "Intrinsic Rewards in School Crime," *Crime & Delinquency* 24, no. 3 (July 1978): 322–35.

12. Johan Huizinga, *Homo Ludens: A Study of the Play-Element in Culture* (London: Routledge, 1998), 4; Spariosu, *Dionysus Reborn*, 189–90, 195–96. See also Karl Groos, *The Play of Man* (New York: D. Appleton, 1913), 400–406.

13. Jeremy Bentham, *Theory of Legislation* (London: Kegan Paul, Trench, Trubner, 1908), 106.

14. Huizinga, *Homo Ludens*, 4–6.

15. Barbara Weber, "Childhood, Philosophy, and Play: Friedrich Schiller," *Journal of Philosophy of Education* 45, no. 2 (May 2011): 236. See also Jean-Jacques Rousseau, *Emile, or On Education*, trans. Allan Bloom (New York: Basic Books, 1979); Immanuel Kant, "Lectures on Pedagogy," in *Anthropology, History, and Education*, trans. Mary Gregor (New York: Cambridge University Press, 2007), 447; and Hannah Ginsborg, "Lawfulness without Law: Kant on the Free Play of Imagination and Understanding," *Philosophical Topics* 25, no. 1 (Spring 1997): 37–81.

16. Quoted in Weber, "Childhood, Philosophy, and Play," 242–44. See also Judith Plotz, "The Perpetual Messiah: Romanticism, Childhood, and the Paradoxes of Human Development," in *Regulated Children/Liberated Children: Education in Psychohistorical Perspective*, ed. Barbara Finkelstein (New York: Psychohistory Press, 1979), 66; Brian O'Connor, "Play, Idleness, and the Problem of Necessity in Schiller and Marcuse," *British Journal for the History of Philosophy* 22, no. 6 (2014): 1098–99; Joe Moshenska, *Iconoclasm as Child's Play* (Stanford, CA: Stanford University Press, 2019), 8–10.

17. Quoted in Carol Leslie Rosenberg, "Towards an Aesthetic Education: An Interpretation of Rousseau, Schiller, and Kierkegaard" (PhD diss., Harvard University, 1985), 66.

18. Friedrich Schiller, *On the Aesthetic Education of Man* (Hoboken, NJ: Bibliobytes, 1999), 23.

19. Friedrich Nietzsche, *The Birth of Tragedy*, trans. Douglas Smith (New York: Oxford University Press, 2000), 22. For a historical overview of Dionysian ecstasy, see Barbara Ehrenreich, *Dancing in the Street: A History of Collective Joy* (New York: Metropolitan Books, 2007).

20. Nietzsche, *Birth of Tragedy*, 229.

21. Sharon Hunter, "Agency and Sovereignty: Georges Bataille's Anti-humanist Conception of Child," *Journal of Philosophy of Education* 54, no. 5 (October 2020): 7, 11–13.

22. Michel Foucault, "A Preface to Transgression," in *Language, Counter-memory, Practice: Selected Essays and Interviews*, trans. Donald F. Bouchard and Sherry Simon (Ithaca, NY: Cornell University Press, 1977); Chris Jenks, *Childhood*, 2nd ed. (New York: Routledge, 2005), 138–40.

23. Alexander Irwin, *Saints of the Impossible: Bataille, Weil, and the Politics of the Sacred* (Minneapolis: University of Minnesota Press, 2002), 9–10; Georges Bataille, *On Nietzsche*, trans. Bruce Boone (New York: Paragon House, 1992), xx.

24. Nietzsche, *Birth of Tragedy*, 3, 8; Brian Sutton-Smith, *The Ambiguity of Play* (Cambridge, MA: Harvard University Press, 1997), 151–152; Øksnes, "We Sneak Off to Play What We Want!," in *The Philosophy of Play*, ed. Emily Ryall (New York: Taylor and Francis, 2013), 142.

25. Friedrich Nietzsche, *Philosophy in the Tragic Age of the Greeks*, trans. Marianne Cowan (Washington, DC: Regnery, 1962), 62. These quotes are cited in Sutton-Smith, *Ambiguity of Play*, 112–13.

26. David Rathbone, "Nietzsche's Doctrine of 'Kinderland,'" *New Nietzsche Studies* 8, no. 3/4 (Winter 2011/Spring 2012): 56; Bataille, *On Nietzsche*, xxix–xxx, 17.

27. Avi Mintz, "The Disciplined Schooling of the Free Spirit: Theory in Nietzsche's Middle Period," *Philosophy of Education* (2004): 163; Hunter, "Agency and Sovereignty," 10.

28. Csikszentmihalyi and Larson, "Intrinsic Rewards," 323–24.

29. Csikszentmihalyi and Larson, "Intrinsic Rewards," 323, 328–29.

30. Sean Steel, "On the High School Education of a Pithecanthropus Erectus," *High School Journal* 98, no. 1 (Fall 2014): 12.

31. Steel, "High School Education," 16. See also Laura Piersol, "Our Hearts Leap Up: Awakening Wonder within the Classroom," in *Wonder-full Education: The Centrality of Wonder in Teaching and Learning across the Curriculum*, ed. Kieren Egan, Annabella Cant, and Gillian Judson (New York: Routledge, 2014), 3–21.

32. Steel, "High School Education," 11–12, 16; Sean Steel, "On the Need for Dionysian Education in Schools Today," *Educational Theory* 64, no. 2 (2014): 128.

33. Anders Schinkel, "Education as Mediation between Child and World: The Role of Wonder," *Studies in Philosophy and Education* 39 (2020): 479–92; Anders Schinkel, "The Educational Importance of Deep Wonder," *Journal of Philosophy of Education* 51, no. 2 (May 2017): 541, 545.

34. Schinkel, "Deep Wonder," 538–39; Schinkel, "Education as Mediation," 488.

35. Allen, "Hedonic Component of Vandalism," 77–89; Jamin Carson, "The Sublime and Education," *Journal of Aesthetic Education* 40, no. 1 (Spring 2006): 79–93; Teju Cole, "The History of Photography Is a History of Shattered Glass," *New York Times Magazine*, November 15, 2017, https://www.nytimes.com/2017/11/15/magazine/the-history-of-photography-is-a-history-of-shattered-glass.html.

36. Schiller, *Aesthetic Education of Man*, part 4 (letter 27), 52.

37. Vernon L. Allen and David B. Greenberger, "An Aesthetic Theory of Vandalism," *Crime and Delinquency* 24, no. 3 (July 1978): 310–11; Walter Ong, "Agonistic Structures in Academia: Past to Present," *Daedalus* 103, no. 4 (Fall 1974): 233.

38. For further discussion, see Steven A. Stolz, "Nietzsche on Aesthetics, Educators, and Education," *Studies in the Philosophy of Education* 36 (2017): 683–95; Mintz, "Disciplined Schooling."

39. Erich Fromm, *The Anatomy of Human Destructiveness* (New York: Holt, Rinehart, and Winston, 1973), 7–8, 274–75. See also Bruner, *Play*, 57; Clifford Geertz, "Deep Play: Notes on the Balinese Cockfight," *Daedalus* 134, no. 4 (2005): 72; A. H. Maslow, *Toward a Psychology of Being* (New York: D. Van Nostrand, 1968), 212.

40. For examples, see Walter Reckless, *The Crime Problem* (New York: Appleton-Century-Crofts, 1967), 14–15; Travis Hirschi, *Causes of Delinquency (Berkeley: University of California Press, 1969), chap 1. Examples from schools, specifically, include* Hyman S. Lippman, "Vandalism as an Outlet for Aggression," *Federal Probation* 18, no. 1 (March 1954): 5–6; Arnold P. Goldstein, *The Psychology of Vandalism* (New York: Plenum, 1996), 27; Donald J. Shoemaker, *Juvenile Delinquency* (New York: Rowman and Littlefield, 2009), 116.

41. Albert K. Cohen, *Delinquent Boys: The Culture of the Gang* (Glencoe, IL: Free Press, 1955), 59-61. Also significant is the work of the psychologist Fritz Redl. See Barclay, "Destructiveness in Children"; Fritz Redl and David Wineman, *Controls from Within: Techniques for the Treatment of the Aggressive Child* (New York: Free Press, 1952); and Fritz Redl and David Wineman, *Children Who Hate: The Disorganization and Breakdown of Behavior Controls* (New York: Free Press, 1960).

42. Philip G. Zimbardo, "The Human Choice: Individuation, Reason, and Order versus Deindividuation, Impulse, and Chaos," *Nebraska Symposium on Motivation* (1969): 290; Philip G. Zimbardo, *A Social-Psychological Analysis of Vandalism: Making Sense of Senseless Violence* (Springfield, VA: National Technical Information Service, 1971), 9.

43. Zimbardo, "Human Choice," 251–52.

44. Zimbardo, "Human Choice," 240, 243, 246–47.

45. Zimbardo, *Social-Psychological Analysis*, 6.

46. Zimbardo, *Social-Psychological Analysis*, 6, 11–12; Philip G. Zimbardo, "Vandalism: An Act in Search of a Cause," *Bell Telephone Magazine*, July/August 1972, 15, Stanford Digital Repository, https://purl.stanford.edu/zh121vf2570.

47. George L. Kelling and James Q. Wilson, "Broken Windows: The Police and Neighborhood Safety," *Atlantic*, March 1982, https://www.theatlantic.com/magazine/archive/1982/03/broken-windows/304465/. For some of the genealogy from Zimbardo to Kelling and Wilson, see Bench Ansfield, "The Broken Windows of the Bronx," *American Quarterly* 72, no. 1 (March 2020): 103–27; and Sam Collings-Wells, "From Black Power to Broken Windows: Liberal Philanthropy and the Carceral State," *Journal of Urban History* 48, no. 4 (2022): 739–59, https://journals.sagepub.com/doi/full/10.1177/0096144220956617.

48. Kelling and Wilson, "Broken Windows."

49. Jason Blakely, *We Built Reality: How Social Science Infiltrated Culture, Politics, and Power* (New York: Oxford University Press, 2020), 90–99; Bernard H. Harcourt, *Illusion of Order: The False Promise of Broken Windows Policing* (Cambridge, MA: Harvard University Press, 2001), 6.

50. For early examples, see Rousseau, *Emile*, book 2; Frédéric Bastiat, *What Is Seen and What Is Not Seen, or Political Economy in One Lesson*, trans. W. B. Hodgson (London: W. H. Smith, 1859), 7; Martha Heineman Pieper and William Joseph Pieper, *Smart Love: The Compassionate Alternative to Discipline That Will Make You a Better Parent and Your Child a Better Person* (Boston: Harvard Common Press, 1999), 308.

51. Alexander Miller, "Vandalism and the Architect," in *Vandalism*, ed. Colin Ward (London: Architectural Press, 1973), 114; Casserly, Bass, and Garrett, *School Vandalism*, 37; "Vandalism and Violence"; Shirley Neill, *Violence and Vandalism* (Arlington, VA: National School Public Relations Association, 1975), 8–9; Michael B. Katz, *Class, Bureaucracy, and Schools: The Illusion of Educational Change in America* (New York: Praeger, 1975), xvi.

52. "Vandals Redesign Schools," *New York Times*, November 20, 1959, 30.

53. Syd Salt and L. J. Karmel, "The Windowless School," *The Clearinghouse* 42, no. 3 (1967): 176–78.

54. Quoted in Colin Ward, "Notes on the Future of Vandalism," in Ward, *Vandalism*, 311.

55. Similar arguments appear in Howard Chudacoff, *Children at Play: An American History* (New York: New York University Press, 2007), 1–2; Øksnes, "We Sneak Off," 141–42; and Scott G. Eberle, "The Elements of Play: Toward a Philosophy and Definition of Play," *Journal of Play* 6, no. 2 (Winter 2014): 214–33.

56. Spariosu, *Dionysus Reborn*, 186.

57. Erik Erikson, "Play and Actuality," in *Play and Actuality: A Symposium*, ed. Maria W. Piers (New York: Norton, 1972), 131–33.

58. Erikson, "Play and Actuality," 158–59, 166–67. Schiller makes a similar point, writing that in play, the individual "artificially retraces his childhood in his maturity, forms for himself a state of Nature in his ideas, which is not indeed given him by experience but is the necessary result of his rationality, [and] borrows in this ideal state an ideal aim which he never knew in his actual state of Nature." Quoted in Rosenberg, "Towards an Aesthetic Education," 59.

VANDALISM AND THE HISTORICAL SUBLIME

1. Edmund Burke, *A Philosophical Enquiry into the Origin of Our Ideas of the Sublime and Beautiful* (New York: Columbia University Press, 1958). For a wider history, see Philip Shaw, *The Sublime* (New York: Routledge, 2017).

2. Later writers would dispute the necessity of fear. On Henry David Thoreau's depiction in "Ktaadn," for example, see Richard J. Schneider, *Civilizing Thoreau: Human Ecology and the Emerging Social Sciences in the Major Works* (Rochester, NY: Camden House, 2016), 121–23.

3. Burke, *Sublime and Beautiful*, 57.

4. See Louis A. Sass, "Madness and the Ineffable: Hegel, Kierkegaard, and Lacan," *Philosophy, Psychiatry & Psychology* 16, no. 4 (December 2019): 319–24.

5. Quoted in Hayden White, *The Content of the Form: Narrative Discourse and Historical Representation* (Baltimore: Johns Hopkins University Press, 1987), 68–71.

6. White, *Content of the Form*, 74; Anne Rigney, *Imperfect Histories: The Elusive Past and the Legacy of Romantic Historicism* (Ithaca, NY: Cornell University Press, 2001); Vybarr Cregan-Reid, "Forgetting the Past and the Future: Macaulay, Carlyle, and the 'Shoreless Chaos' of History," in *Discovering Gilgamesh: Geology, Narrative, and the Historical Sublime in Victorian Culture* (Manchester, UK: Manchester University Press, 2013). Trans- or superhistorical appeals also appear in Friedrich Nietzsche, *On the Advantage and Disadvantage of History for Life*, trans. Peter Preuss (Indianapolis: Hacket, 1980).

7. Frank Ankersmit, "Hayden White's Appeal to Historians," *History and Theory* 37, no. 2 (May 1998): 188–89.

8. White, *Content of the Form*, 66; Peter Novick, *That Noble Dream: The "Objectivity Question" and the American Historical Profession* (New York: Cambridge University Press, 1988).

9. White, *Content of the Form*, 71.

10. White, *Content of the Form*, 60–61. There have long been debates about whether the sort of historical pessimism and nihilism outlined here are radical and emancipatory or profoundly conservative. See also Neil Clark, "The Greatest of Ghost Stories," *American Conservative*, October 28, 2016, https://www.theamericanconservative.com/articles/the-greatest-of-ghost-stories/.

11. Charles A. Beard, "Written History as an Act of Faith," *American Historical Review* 39, no. 2 (January 1934): 225–26, 228.

12. Quoted in Willem Otterspeer, *Reading Huizinga* (Amsterdam: Amsterdam University Press, 2010), 136–37.

13. Fernand Braudel, "History and the Social Sciences: The Longue Durée," *Braudel Center Review* 32, no. 2 (2009): 181, 185.

14. Patrick H. Hutton, "The History of Mentalities: The New Map of Cultural History," *History and Theory* 20, no. 3 (October 1981): 237–59; Donald R. Kelley, *Frontiers of History: Historical Inquiry in the Twentieth Century* (New Haven, CT: Yale University Press, 2006). The examples are drawn from Robert Darnton, *The Great Cat Massacre, and Other Episodes in French Cultural History* (New York: Basic Books, 2009); Natalie Zemon Davis, *The Return of Martin Guerre* (Cambridge, MA: Harvard University Press, 1983); and Carlo Ginzburg, *The Cheese and the Worms: The Cosmos of a Sixteenth-Century Miller* (New York: Penguin Books, 1982).

15. For examples, see George A. Reisch, "Chaos, History, and Narrative," *History and Theory* 30, no. 1 (February 1991): 1–20; Daniel Wickberg, "What Is the History of Sensibilities?," *American Historical Review* 112, no. 3 (June 2007): 668–69; and George G. Iggers, "Rationality and History," in *Developments in Modern Historiography*, ed. Henry Kozicki (New York: St. Martin's, 1993), 30.

16. In addition to White, see Frank Ankersmit, *Sublime Historical Experience* (Stanford, CA: Stanford University Press, 2005); and Reinhart Koselle, *Sediments of Time: On Possible Histories* (Stanford, CA: Stanford University Press, 2018).

17. Hayden White, *Metahistory: The Historical Imagination in Nineteenth-Century Europe* (Baltimore: Johns Hopkins University Press, 1973), introduction; Ankersmit, *Sublime Historical Experience*, 4; Mary Fulbrook, *Historical Theory* (New York: Routledge, 2002), 63–72; Dominick LaCapra, *History, Literature, and Critical Theory* (Ithaca, NY: Cornell University Press, 2013), 149.

18. Hannah H. Kim, "Camus and Sartre on the Absurd," *Philosopher's Imprint* 21, no. 32 (December 2021): 2.

19. John Updike, "Notes and Comment," *New Yorker*, December 9, 1967, 51.

20. "It is one thing to make an idea clear," wrote Edmund Burke, "and another to make it *affecting* to the imagination." Burke, *Sublime and Beautiful*, 101; Hayden White, "The Aim of Interpretation Is to Create Perplexity in the Face of the Real," *History and Theory* 48, no. 1 (February 2009): 74.

21. Until the mid-nineteenth century, many viewers sought sublimity by gazing at physical artifacts, the "prodigies," "curiosities," and "wonders" kept in private collections. David Wilson, the curator of the Museum of Jurassic Technology, a modern collection of curiosities, writes that such experiences can still "reintegrate people to wonder." Marcia Tucker, the director of New York's New Museum, agrees. When one looks at curiosities, she says, "everything initially just seems self-evidently what it is. There's this fine line, though, between knowing you're experiencing something and sensing that something is wrong. There's this slight slippage. . ." As Lawrence Weschler writes, one "continually finds himself shimmering between wondering *at* (the marvels of nature) and wondering *whether* (any of this could possibly be true). And it's that very shimmer, the capacity for such delicious confusion . . . that may constitute the most blessedly wonderful thing about being human." Wilson and Tucker quoted in Lawrence Weschler, *Mr. Wilson's Cabinet of Wonder* (New York: Vintage Books, 1995), both on 39; Weschler's quote on 60.

22. Lionel Gossman, "Anecdote and History," *History and Theory* 42, no. 2 (May 2003): 161, 163–64; Christopher Bram, *The Art of History: Unlocking the Past in Fiction and Nonfiction* (Minneapolis: Graywolf, 2016), 35–56.

23. Gossman, "Anecdote and History," 162; White, *Content of the Form*, 7.

24. "Burns School for Love," *New York Times*, December 19, 1913, 1.

25. "Girl Teacher Tells of School Bombing," *New York Times*, February 28, 1928, 9; "Reed Attacks Story of Bombed Teacher," *New York Times*, March 2, 1928, 5.

26. "Miss Denton Was Buried," *Hopkinsville Kentuckian*, December 12, 1916, 1; "Hounds Put Crime Shadow on Woman," *Lexington (KY) Herald*, September 16, 1909, 2; "Daughter Accuses Mother of Burning Down Pleasanton School," *Evening News* (San Jose, CA), March 1, 1912, 8; "From Far and Near," *Cook County (IL) Herald*, March 5, 1909, 10.

27. "Feud Renewed with Arson," *Washington Post*, July 25, 1908, 9.

28. Untitled article, *Donaldsville (LA) Chief*, January 18, 1873, 1.

29. "Eight Glen Cove Firemen Accused of Arson," *New York Times*, September 11, 1929, 1.

30. "Four Boys Fire School, Hoping to Go to Florida without Being Missed, to Speculate in Land," *New York Times*, January 6, 1926, 3.

31. J. Drummond Bone, "A Sense of Endings: Some Romantic and Postmodern Comparisons," in *Romanticism and Postmodernism*, ed. Edward Larrissy (New York: Cambridge University Press, 1999), 75.

32. Ankersmit, for example, argues that history comes into being in moments of loss or estrangement—when a recognition of change breaks the past off from the present—but that historical imagination initiates a countervailing moment of love or reclamation through historical imagination. Ankersmit, *Sublime Historical Experience*, 9; Herman Paul, *Key Issues in Historical Theory*, 23–24.

33. Friedrich Nietzsche, "On the Uses and Disadvantages of History for Life," in *Untimely Meditations*, trans. R. J. Hollingdale (New York: Cambridge University Press, 1997), 57–123; Sigmund Freud, *The Uncanny* (New York: Penguin Books, 2003); LaCapra, *History, Literature, Critical Theory*, 149.

34. Michelle Faubert, "John Ferriar's Psychology, James Hogg's *Justified Sinner*, and the Gay Science of Horror Writing," in Larrissy, *Romanticism and Postmodernism*, 84–85, 93.

35. A contemporary, stylized version of this phenomenon can be found in Scott Carrier's radio reporting. For instance, see "The Test," in "The Job That Takes over Your

Life," *This American Life*, September 27, 1996, https://www.thisamericanlife.org/37/the-job-that-takes-over-your-life/act-one.

36. Michael Lesy, *Wisconsin Death Trip* (New York: Pantheon Books, 1973); Peter Manseau, *Melancholy Accidents: Three Centuries of Stray Bullets and Bad Luck* (Brooklyn: Melville House, 2016). Michel Foucault offers a brief panorama of madness in eighteenth-century France in *Language, Madness, and Desire: On Literature*, trans. Robert Bononno (Minneapolis: University of Minnesota Press, 2015), 14. For criticisms of Lesy's work in particular, see A. D. Coleman, "Michael Lesy (I): *Wisconsin Death Trip*," in *Light Readings: A Photography Critic's Writings, 1968–1978* (New York: Oxford University Press, 1979): 150–52.

37. Peter Silver, *Our Savage Neighbors: How Indian War Transformed Early America* (New York: W. W. Norton, 2008), 62, 83, 265–80.

38. Paul E. Johnson and Sean Wilentz, *The Kingdom of Matthias: A Story of Sex and Salvation in Nineteenth-Century America* (New York: Oxford University Press, 2012).

39. See Justin E. H. Smith, *Irrationality: A History of the Dark Side of Reason* (Princeton, NJ: Princeton University Press, 2019), 4; and Wolfgang J. Mommsen, "Social Conditioning and Social Relevance of Historical Judgments," *History and Theory* 17, no. 4 (1978): 26–27. For a dissenting view on the importance of the accidental and counterfactual, see Edward Carr, *What Is History?* (New York: Alfred A. Knopf, 1962).

9. SHARDS

1. David Maraniss, *Barack Obama: The Story* (New York: Simon and Schuster, 2012), xiii–xiv.

2. Untitled article, *Clarksburg (WV) Telegram*, November 30, 1894, 1.

3. Margaret Reist, "Brewster: I Never Meant to Burn Down LPS Offices," *Lincoln (NE) Journal Star*, May 30, 2012, https://journalstar.com/news/local/education/brewster-i-never-meant-to-burn-down-lps-offices/article_bb083b04-9f6e-54a0-a9dd-1ba3ed26068d.html.

4. "Stones Speak for Pupils," *New York Times*, August 22, 1946, 16.

5. "Third Attempt to Burn Building," *Lincoln (NE) Star*, November 26, 1920, 1.

6. "Murder Charge Given Priority to Case Here," *Santa Ana (CA) Register*, August 18, 1923, 3; "History of Sakura Gakuen," accessed August 19, 2022, https://sakuragakuen.org/about-us/history-of-sakura-gakuen/; "Sets Fires, Loss $5,000,000," *New York Times*, August 18, 1923, 4.

7. Katie Kull, "Black Student Admits to Writing Racist Graffiti in Parkway Central Bathrooms," *St. Louis Post-Dispatch*, September 29, 2021, https://www.stltoday.com/news/local/education/black-student-admits-to-writing-racist-graffiti-in-parkway-central-bathrooms/article_7b5f7146-aeac-5f50-badb-00e7226907a9.html.

8. Jeff Maysh, "Hysteria High: How Demons Destroyed a Florida School," Medium, October 29, 2019, https://medium.com/@jeffmaysh/hysteria-high-how-demons-destroyed-the-miami-aerospace-academy-jeff-maysh-5a31b4770f29.

9. Untitled article, *Pennsylvania Gazette*, June 5, 1766, 1.

10. *Schools: Occupancy Fire Record* (Boston: National Fire Protection Association, 1965), 4.

11. Lindsay Lowe, "School Year Ends Early at Texas High School after Senior Prank Goes Too Far," *Today*, May 20, 2022, https://www.today.com/parents/parents/school-year-ends-early-texas-school-senior-prank-goes-far-rcna29797.

12. Herbert Kohl, *Golden Boy as Anthony Cool* (New York: Dial, 1972), 12.

13. "Girl Vandal Caught; Daubed Police Cars," *New York Times*, November 8, 1936, 12.

14. Anna Borgman, "Racist, Antisemitic Graffiti Appear at 2 Howard Schools," *Washington Post*, January 22, 1997, B6.

15. "A School Blown Up by Dynamite," *New York Times*, March 27, 1883, 1.

16. "Boy Tries to Burn School," *New York Times*, May 9, 1917, 7.

17. Jeffrey S. Solochek, "TikTok's 'Devious Licks' Are Trashing School Restrooms: Pasco Cracks Down," *Tampa Bay Times*, September 15, 2021, https://www.tampabay.com/news/education/2021/09/15/tiktoks-devious-licks-are-trashing-school-restrooms-pasco-cracks-down/.

18. "Trailed by Bloodhounds," *New York Times*, September 16, 1913, 1.

19. Teresa Watanabe, "Mothers Deny Vandalism Role," *Los Angeles Times*, January 14, 2014, AA1.

20. [Lorraine M. Radtke], "Student Violence and Vandalism: Turning Back the Tide," Lorraine M. Radtke Papers, Mss. 64, University of Wisconsin–Milwaukee Archives.

21. "2 Boys Wreck School Buses in North Carolina," *New York Times*, February 26, 1995, 19.

EPILOGUE

1. "Student's 'Unfair Punishment' Sparks Changes for School Discipline," WSB-TV Atlanta, May 11, 2015, https://www.wsbtv.com/news/local/students-unfair-punishment-sparks-changes-school-d/53873930/; Halle Sembritzki, "Teen Arrested for Vandalizing Tulare County School Bathroom as Part of TikTok Trend, Deputies Say," YourCentralValley.com, September 17, 2021, https://www.yourcentralvalley.com/news/local-news/teen-arrested-for-vandalizing-tulare-county-school-bathroom-as-part-of-tiktok-trend-deputies-say/.

2. As Michel de Montaigne wrote, "There is no one who, if he listens to himself, does not discover in himself a pattern all his own, a ruling pattern, which struggles against education." Michel de Montaigne, "On Repentance," in *Essays*, trans. Charles Cotton (Auckland, NZ: Floating Press, 2009), 1373.

Bibliographic Essay

Vandalism does not always leave centralized or detailed records. Even institutional responses to the phenomenon can be surprisingly diffuse. Costs could be suppressed by officials afraid of bad publicity, absorbed into nonitemized operating expenses, or spread across various arms of school administration, insurance companies, and law enforcement agencies, all of which kept (or failed to keep) separate records. For the convenience of scholars who may choose to pursue similar topics, this note outlines the most helpful archival sources in this book, as well as other potential sources for future research.

Most of the primary sources for this project came from digital newspaper articles. The online archives of the *New York Times*, the *Baltimore Sun*, and the *Washington Post*; the "Chronicling America" collection (from the Library of Congress); "America's Historic Newspapers" (from Readex); and for-profit services such as Newspapers.com all provided access to helpful stories of arson, bombing, and wrecking. There were hundreds of articles that I could not include, and doubtless thousands more that appeared in newspapers outside the available databases. A quick search should give a sense of the nature and scope of the problem, as well as the timeless quality that this book tries to communicate.

The first centralized efforts to track school destruction came after the Civil War, when vigilante violence against African American schools attracted the attention of the US government. Two sources were particularly helpful. A congressional investigation into the Ku Klux Klan—*The Report of the Joint Select Committee to Inquire into the Condition of Affairs in the Late Insurrectionary States* (1872)—is available in thirteen volumes through the University of Pennsylvania library system and at the Internet Archive (Archive.org). The records of the Freedmen's Bureau's educational division are available on microfilm at the National Archives and Records Administration, in College Park, Maryland, and digitally through FamilySearch (https://www.familysearch.org). As noted in chapter 1, these sources were not always systematic in their documentation of destruction, but they remain a rich repository of information for future historians.

Scholars interested in property destruction during the twentieth century would do well to review the disciplinary and budgetary records of particular school districts, particularly in urban areas. A helpful place to start is *Vandalism: Study of Selected Great Cities and Maryland Counties* (Baltimore: Baltimore City Schools, 1970), which features data from various cities around the country. This book has focused on Los Angeles and Baltimore, in particular, because of specific incidents that occurred in those cities, but also because of the convenient organization of their archival records. The records of the Los Angeles Unified School District are available through the UCLA archives, and feature school board minutes, correspondence, and budget adjustments specific to the district's security section. The papers of Mayor William Schaefer, who led a prominent antivandalism campaign, are available at the Baltimore City Archives, as are some records related to the Baltimore City Schools.

Although there is plenty of published material from congressional committees devoted to juvenile delinquency prevention, there are even more documents (only partially referenced here) in the Estes Kefauver papers, at the University of Tennessee, Knoxville; and the Birch Bayh papers, at Indiana University Bloomington. Finally, the Wisconsin Historical Society has materials for almost any aspect of US history. Relevant to this topic are television scripts featuring teenage vandals; state legislators' research into the causes of vandalism, available in the Horace Wilkie papers; and photographic negatives of high school destruction (not pictured in this book) from the *Capital Times*.

For researchers interested in physical evidence of populist violence and childish misbehavior, I would recommend the collections of the Smithsonian museums in Washington, DC, particularly the National Museum of American History and the National Museum of African American History and Culture. Anyone doing work on schoolbooks from the eighteenth or nineteenth century would profit immensely from the extensive and well-catalogued holdings of the American Antiquarian Society, whose staff is immensely cheerful and helpful with nonexperts.

Index

Addams, Jane, 66
adolescence, 45, 58–59, 68, 74–75, 104, 132–34, 135–36
aesthetics. *See* beauty
African Americans, 20–21, 124–26, 68, 157–58, 162; attacks on, 9–11, 22–35, 95; and discriminatory punishment, 78–86, 89, 95; and resistance, 6–7, 41–42, 76–77, 80–82
Aichhorn, August, 71
Alvord, J. W., 27
anecdotes: as evidence, 3, 152–53
anti-Catholicism, 7, 20, 38, 40
antisemitism, 20, 74–75, 159
architecture, 10, 13–14, 91, 138–39; and fire prevention, 50, 52, 54
Arendt, Hannah, 100, 130, 134–35
Aristotle, 104
arson, 15–17, 37–40, 55, 62–63, 125, 144, 152–53, 155–57, 160; and African-American schools, 24–26, 29, 31–34, 79–83, 90, 95; causes of, 4, 46–48, 71, 77, 100; and insurance, 86–88; rates of, 56
art therapy, 71
Asian Americans, 40, 156

Barnard, Henry, 17–18
"barring out," 14–15
Bataille, Georges, 99n6, 101, 141, 144
Bath school bombing, 39, 43–44
bathrooms, 4, 8, 60, 81, 100, 129–37, 157, 159–60
Bayh, Birch, 93
beautification, 2, 59, 94
beauty, 18, 91, 106–8, 140–43, 147, 149–51
behaviorism, 109
Bentham, Jeremy, 139
Berry, Wendell, 100, 123
Bettelheim, Bruno, 71–73
Bildung, 100, 104–6, 109, 118
Blair, Francis, Jr., 33–35
bomb threats, 41, 135–36
bombs, 9, 39, 43–44, 47, 60, 74, 80, 152, 159
books: destruction of, 15, 70, 110; and marginalia, 104, 111–18

boredom, 13, 60, 65, 70, 75, 113, 116–18; history of, 106–9; theories of, 99, 100, 103–6, 110–11
Braudel, Fernand, 151
"broken windows theory," 145–46
Brown v. Board of Education, 79, 125
Bruner, Jerome, 139
Burke, Edmund, 149–50, 152
Burrowes, Thomas H., 18
"busing" (desegregation), 80–81

Camus, Albert, 145, 151
Catcher in the Rye, 129–30
Catholic schools, 7, 20, 38, 40, 55, 120
charter schools, 160
cherry bombs, 60
child labor, 38, 45, 59–60
Child Safety Act, 66
children: criminalization of, 5, 10, 63–64, 83; as historical actors, 8, 101; mentalities of, 3–4, 6–8, 97–99, 111–18, 123–24, 132–37; as political actors, 10, 15–16, 45, 66, 163
Children's Bureau, 60, 74
children's court, 60, 62–64, 84
civil rights, 10, 21, 26, 32, 42, 61, 77–83, 85
"civil violence," 83
Clark, Joe, 76
Cohen, Albert, 67
Cohen, Stanley, 98
common schools, 17–19
Communism, 38, 61, 72, 74
communitarianism, 67, 123, 127
compulsory attendance, 9–10, 38, 43–45, 59–60
Congressional hearings, 30–35, 60–61, 86, 92–93
conservatism, 39, 84–85, 100, 119–21, 123
constructivism, 139
"control theory," 143–45
corporal punishment, 14, 19, 42, 46, 85
counterculture, 7, 67–68
criminology, 38, 64–69, 74–75
critical theory, 6–8, 91, 97, 100, 108, 130–32

temporary classrooms, 80
textbooks, 15, 109–10
Thrasher, Frederic, 64–68
TikTok challenge, 159–60

urban schools, 2, 10, 40–41, 45, 55, 63–66, 138;
and communities, 67, 127; and insurance,
53, 87; and police, 82–86; public perceptions
of, 76, 78, 160, 162; and racial unrest, 21,
26, 80–82, 87; and systemic reform, 55–56,
92–94; and "target hardening," 132, 146

"vandalism accounts," 61, 94
vigilantism, 7, 9, 16, 21, 29–30, 45; ethics of,
11–13

wantonness, 3, 5, 68, 74, 89–90, 99, 140–41,
144–45, 149, 164

White, Hayden, 150–51, 153
white supremacy. *See* racism
window-breaking, 1–2, 15, 20–21, 41, 45, 67,
76, 79, 81–82, 94, 156–57; and aesthetics,
143; cost of, 87, 93; causes of, 71, 80, 101,
139–40, 143–47; and neglect, 13, 145–46;
prohibitions on, 19, 139
Wittels, Fritz, 71
wonder, 142–43
working class, 6–7, 21, 38, 45–46, 67–68, 72
Works Progress Administration, 59
World War I, 45, 47
World War II, 59–60

youth culture, 9, 45, 60, 67–68, 104–6, 130–31,
135–36

Zimbardo, Philip, 143–45